SELLING BEYOND

eBay

SELLING BEYOND

eBay

Foolproof Ways to Reach More Customers and

Make Big Money on Rival Online Marketplaces

Greg Holden

AMACOM

American Management Association

New York • Atlanta • Brussels • Chicago • Mexico City • San Francisco
Shanghai • Tokyo • Toronto • Washington, D.C.

Special discounts on bulk quantities of AMACOM books are available to corporations, professional associations, and other organizations. For details, contact Special Sales Department, AMACOM, a division of American Management Association, 1601 Broadway, New York, NY 10019.
Tel.: 212-903-8316. Fax: 212-903-8083.
Web site: www.amacombooks.org

This publication is designed to provide accurate and authoritative information in regard to the subject matter covered. It is sold with the understanding that the publisher is not engaged in rendering legal, accounting, or other professional service. If legal advice or other expert assistance is required, the services of a competent professional person should be sought.

Library of Congress Cataloging-in-Publication Data

Holden, Greg.
  Selling beyond eBay : foolproof ways to reach more customers and make big money on rival online marketplaces / Greg Holden.
    p.   cm.
  Includes bibliographical references and index.
  ISBN-10: 0-8144-7349-0
  ISBN-13: 978-0-8144-7349-8
  1. Internet marketing.   2. Internet auctions.   3. Selling.   I. Title.
HF5415.1265.H654   2006
658.8'7—dc22

                                                    2005036479

Printing number

10   9   8   7   6   5   4   3   2

Contents

SELLING BEYOND

eBay

PART **I**

Preparing a Multichannel Sales Effort

Should You Sell Beyond eBay?

Why move beyond eBay? It's a natural question to ask, even if you have picked up this book because you are thinking of trying different online auction marketplaces. After all, eBay is a comfortable and well-established commercial website. In fact, it's one of the world's most popular marketplaces. If you wish to put your products before the greatest number of "eyeballs," you stand a very good chance of doing so on eBay.

However, now that it's been around for a full decade, eBay's rate of growth is slowing down. Don't misunderstand me: the heft of a giant is still impressive even if that giant is no longer growing like a weed. It is mind-boggling that eBay has an estimated 150 million members worldwide. According to an MSNBC report, an estimated $80,000 worth of transactions take place on the site every minute, every day.[1]

No matter what its size, every company knows the inherent dangers of sitting on its laurels. And there are more and more contenders nipping at the heels of eBay. The number of websites that let you buy and sell, create an online storefront, or post classified advertisements is growing steadily.

Therefore, if you focus solely on eBay for your online auction sales, you might be selling yourself short. Some auction sites are less expensive and more user-friendly than eBay. Plus, you can reach dedicated collectors through a wide variety of niche auction sites. And you can increase your profit margin by moving some—if not all—of your sales from eBay to other venues. Consider the computer and accessories wholesaler Exel-i, Inc. This company used to sell 100 percent of its merchandise on eBay under several user IDs, including LaptopBroker.com. When eBay raised its fees for Gallery photos, Buy It Now sales, and eBay Stores, the company decided to save as much as $55,000 per month simply by not using Gallery photos and Buy It Now fixed prices. Then, the company began to move its merchandise away from eBay. Now, eBay accounts for only 30 percent of Exel-i's sales. The rest comes from sales on the company's website, Amazon.com, other online venues, and direct sales to business customers. It's to your advantage to look beyond eBay to save money and find new customers. And this book will show you how to do it.

Online Auctions Are Growing

For many years, eBay really could claim to be the only viable game in town. Hopeful challengers rose up, only to slink away in defeat. In just the last year or two, however, several other auction sites have begun to gain traction. Their success can be traced to factors such as eBay's fee increases and to more individuals around the world acquiring access to the Internet. Sites such as Alibaba and TaoBao in China and iOffer, Bidville, uBid, and IronPlanet in the United States are attracting more and more customers, thereby enabling these sites to diversify.

Who Will Benefit from This Book

This book is for several different types of sellers, all of whom are ready to expand their horizons beyond eBay. They don't necessarily feel compelled to leave eBay altogether; they simply want to look for new options and new customers:

- The first group can be described as *The Dissatisfied*. These sellers have established themselves on eBay; they have a steady supply of merchandise to sell; and they make sales every week. But they are tired of watching the number of potential buyers dwindle. As a result, the number of bids on their items is going down. And their sell-through rates (the number of items they put up for sale compared with the number that are actually sold) are becoming increasingly dismal. In other words, they are hitting the wall in terms of profits and sales.

- The second group is *The Disgruntled*. They are beginning to feel that eBay is taking lessons from the federal government in how to undercut their profits. They love the feeling they get when they sell lots of merchandise at a good price, but then crash into despair when they get a bill from eBay. They growl every time they estimate their profits, only to realize that eBay's fees have cut into them severely.

- The last group is *The Discoverers*. They are in business to stay and want to fish off all sides of the pier. They realize that a successful online business doesn't depend on a single service provider like eBay for success and want to keep their options open. They want to sell directly to the public through as many "front doors" as possible, whether these are websites or brick-and-mortar stores.

Whether you are angry with eBay or just looking for more sales, if you are reading this book, you are ready to move beyond the friendly confines of eBay and explore new ways to connect with customers and build your business.

This Book Is for Sellers

Selling Beyond eBay moves beyond the basics of shopping and buying on auction sites and doesn't get bogged down with topics like comparison shopping. Written with ambitious sellers in mind, this book:

- Describes popular auction options other than eBay and how to get started with them
- Explores ways to balance your eBay sales with sales on other marketplaces
- Shows you how to maintain your security and privacy even as you increase your visibility around the Web
- Provides you with a general overview of the auction scene outside of eBay
- Suggests ways to market your sales and your business through your own website

Indeed, you can get just as much profit selling on your own or through other auction venues as you can on eBay. You can also combine a sales presence on eBay with sales on your website or other marketplaces to significantly boost your income.

What You Need to Get Started

Assuming that you have already done some selling and buying on eBay and other e-commerce sites, you already have access to a computer with an Internet connection. You already have some merchandise to sell and a camera for photographing it.

Beyond these tangible items, is there anything you need to move to other auction sites and find success? I think the answer is yes; you need something you can't buy at the computer store. Yet, it's something that all successful entrepreneurs have—you need the right frame of mind. You need vision, foresight, confidence, and a willingness to try new things. Here are some tangible steps for achieving these qualities:

Come Up with a Plan

Any time you want to embark on a new venture, whether it's making a commitment to sell on eBay on a full-time basis or on a regular part-time basis, it helps to have at least a general notion of where you want to go. You don't necessarily have to write down exactly what you're going to do and how everything is going to happen: "I'm going to sign up with that new auction site by May 15; I'm going to open my e-commerce website by June 15; I'm going to have sales of $3,000 per month by Sept. 15."

You *can*, of course, write up this sort of business plan. Businesspeople do it all the time, in consultation with business planners. I know of one eBay PowerSeller who has created her own business plan. But you and I both know that the vast majority of sellers on eBay or other auction sites didn't start out with a plan. They started small as they became accustomed to the idea of selling, tried different types of merchandise, and gradually realized that they could turn their sales efforts into a full-time business activity. Although you don't have to go to such lengths, you should at least consider—and even better, write down—your goals for moving beyond eBay:

- Your main goal should be to find new customers and increase your profits, rather than simply wanting to "get back" at eBay for one reason or another. Because eBay still sets the standards, you won't win if that's your only goal.

- You want to develop a more professional business presence than eBay can provide through its About Me page feature. In other words, you want to create a website with a shopping cart and payment system so customers can make purchases from you directly—and you don't want to pay another monthly hosting fee to eBay for its relatively new Pro Stores feature.

- You want to sell in multiple locations at the same time, and use your various business sites to draw attention to each other.

Most sellers don't have a well-formulated plan when they start selling online. They simply want to clean out their closets or make some "fun money" to supplement their regular income. What turns occasional sellers into committed, full-time business-people is the fact that, as a result of their online sales activities, they had a realization and a desire. That's just what you need to come up with, too. I'm talking about:

- The *realization* that you can sell items to other individuals via the Internet. Not only that, but you need the confidence that you can complete transactions on a consistent basis so that the more you sell, the more you'll make.

- The *desire* to have a consistent source of income, if not a full-time business of your own.

Of course, you also need a source of merchandise, the time to prepare sales descriptions and manage your e-mail, and a system for packing and shipping. But I'm assuming you have those already because you've been selling on eBay. (In case you haven't, I refer you to *eBay Business the Smart Way, 2nd Edition* by Joseph T. Sinclair.)

A Sales Niche

It's good to have at least a general idea of what you want to sell when you start looking for auction marketplaces beyond eBay. That's because what you sell can have a bearing on the auction site you choose. If you sell collectible coins, you should look for a website like Teletrade Auctions (http://www.teletrade.com), which specializes in online coin auctions. You might also want to have sources of merchandise that you can transfer from one site to another.

When you have a sales niche, you have a target audience in mind. The goal then becomes to have an existing list of customers as well. This set of customers, some of whom are inclined to revisit your store repeatedly, is essential if you are planning to move from one website to another. It's a perfect opportunity to contact your previous customers with an announcement about your new location—which, incidentally, also serves to remind them that you are still in business and they should take another look at your current line of merchandise.

 Tip: Describe your customers. Try to have a sense of who your ideal customers are, what kinds of merchandise they are looking for, and where they hang out on the Internet. It might be useful to condense a description of your ideal or target customer to a single sentence. If you are able to identify your target market clearly, you'll have an easier time deciding which auction sites you want to join.

Finding your niche, ideally, means more than just knowing what you want to sell and being able to describe your typical or ideal customer. It also means you like what you do and have enthusiasm for it. Getting started with any auction marketplace, whether it's eBay or not, requires effort. Essential tasks like choosing a user ID, opening an online store, or determining how to work with the new auction site's sales listing system take some extra work, which will go more smoothly if you are enthusiastic about what you do.

Be Open-Minded, Be Adventurous

Each beginning seller on the Internet is at the same place: with zero sales and zero feedback comments (*feedback* is the system used on eBay and other auction sites in which buyers and sellers leave comments for one another to describe whether a transaction went well or not). Everyone starts out small, in other words. You build up your sales gradually, until, after a period of weeks or months, you are selling steadily and your main challenge is increasing your level of productivity.

When you move to auction sites beyond eBay, you are making a leap. You may not achieve success instantly. You may have to try different sites and different types of merchandise before you can sell at a profit on a consistent basis.

- *Be patient with yourself and don't become discouraged.* Give yourself several weeks before you draw any conclusions.

- *Your various Web pages should work together.* Make sure your Web pages are pointing at one another, which improves your general level of visibility as well as your placement in Google search results.

- *Market your online sales effectively.* Buy keywords or Google AdWords to boost your sales.

- *Don't put all your eggs in one basket.* Try different sites to determine which ones work the best for you.

 Note: AdWords is a marketing system created by Google that enables anyone to market their products and services more effectively using the world's best-known search engine. You tell Google how much you are willing to pay for certain words that describe what you sell. For instance, if you sell athletic shoes, you might pay 50 cents per click for the words *sneaker* or *cross-trainer*. If someone searches for those words, an ad displaying a link to the website of your choice appears on the list of Google search results. The position of the ad and the frequency with which it appears depend on how much you pay for the term relative to others who have also paid, and on how many times visitors actually click on your ads.

The bestsellers on eBay and other auction sites succeed because they have a winning attitude. They may buy more than they need; they may have to absorb some losses from lines of merchandise that don't sell; they may run into debt occasionally. But they love to sell, and they put all of their energies into making their businesses work. A spirit of adventure and being open to new challenges is essential for moving beyond the familiar and more-or-less predictable world of eBay.

Online Auction Basics

This book touches on auction techniques and approaches that are common to eBay and all auction sites, such as the need to keep a good reputation by providing excellent customer service, the need to present yourself in a professional manner, and the need to find a steady stream of good merchandise to sell. But I won't bore you with details about the basics of buying and selling on eBay or other auction sites.

Rather, I assume that you're comfortable buying and selling on eBay already and that you aren't starting from scratch. I also assume that you have a foundation for your business, so that you will be really ready to move on to new auction sites. You don't need to be a PowerSeller or an eBay millionaire to move to another site. However, it helps if your feet have already gotten wet and you've developed some sort of routine and a level of competence on eBay. You don't jump out of an airplane with a parachute unless you have had some instruction and know your equipment. By the same token, you don't jump to these other auction sites without having at least tried eBay first and becoming familiar with the routine.

About the Author

Both eBay and the World Wide Web have been very, very good to me. But that doesn't mean I am employed by other auction sites or that I am paid to endorse them. My goal is to give you an unbiased, objective view of options you have available throughout the Web. I'll be the first to state that I am particularly enthusiastic about selling online. In fact, I recommend to friends and family who want to make some extra money or try a new career that they give serious thought to selling on the Web in general or on online auction sites in particular.

I have been writing about the Web and computers since 1995, and I've been a member of eBay since 1997. Over the years I've written eight books about either eBay or online auctions. I also sell at auctions myself, have my own websites, and help other companies to create websites.

I've been buying collectibles for many years, and lately, I've begun to sell a variety of things at auctions, including antiques given to me on consignment, shoes, and household goods. I've learned a lot from selling, including the knowledge that, if you take a chance and are willing to put in a lot of hard work, you can significantly enrich your life by selling to people online. Ideally, you can make new friends, spread goodwill, and provide yourself with a significant amount of extra income. Your success depends on how much effort and time you are willing to expend. That is the idea behind *Selling Beyond eBay:* by expanding your sales opportunities, you'll improve your business and boost your bottom line at the same time.

Make the Move!

If you're reading this book, you are already hungry for experiences beyond eBay. You share the classic desire of every entrepreneur to strike out on one's own and become self-sufficient. I urge you to venture outside the confines of the "big dog" in the auction marketplace and find the "pick of the litter"–a smaller, less expensive, and more personalized site that's just right for you.

You don't have to reinvent the wheel. Your experience on eBay will be very useful in expanding your business and boosting your level of success. You still have plenty of time to get in on the ground floor and find new markets for your products and services. If you have an established relationship with eBay, that's great–because eBay isn't going to go away anytime soon. But it isn't the only game in town, either. The new questions for you to consider are which site is the best for you and which sales option will help boost your bottom line. This book will help you move beyond eBay to sell smarter than ever before.

Note

1. David Faber, "Ten Things You Didn't Know About eBay," MSNBC, June 29, 2005, http://msnbc.msn.com/id/8391726.

CHAPTER **2**

Creating a Solid Foundation on eBay

Once you have identified your business focus, as well as the products you want to sell and the customers you want to reach, you can take the first step in enlarging your business beyond eBay. But paradoxically, that step involves working with eBay itself. You need to decide how eBay will fit in your business plans. For a few individuals who are fed up with eBay, the answer is already clear: not at all. Those readers will probably want to skip this chapter and move on to subsequent topics.

To my mind, completely writing off eBay is counterproductive. If you're an animal keeper and you're trying to examine some baby gorillas in a cage, you simply can't ignore the proverbial 500-pound gorilla lurking in the background. That's eBay. The site so thoroughly dominates the field of online auctions at this point that abandoning it altogether is unwise unless you already have a well-established business that can run independently. (And if that's the case, you probably don't need this book.) This chapter will suggest ways to use eBay to your advantage—to work with the site to establish a solid business foundation that you can transfer to other venues. Once you learn to run your business successfully on eBay, you can more easily do the same on other websites. And once you are clear about the problems associated with eBay, you can make your best effort to overcome them when you move to new sales venues.

The Problem with eBay

If you look at the statistics, it's hard to point out an obvious problem with the world's leading auction marketplace. At the time of this book's production, eBay is still one of the most popular sites on the Web. A survey conducted in June 2005 by AC-Neilsen reported that more than 724,000 Americans rely on eBay for their primary or secondary source of income.[1] What's the problem, then?

The problem is that it's not as easy to sell on eBay as it once was. I've interviewed dozens of PowerSellers (sellers who make anywhere from $1,000 to $25,000 per month on eBay in gross income and maintain a high level of customer satisfaction) in the past few years. Many of them are using eBay primarily as a customer acquisition tool for sales. They gain customers through eBay and then do everything they can to sell directly to those customers through their own websites so that they don't have to use eBay as an intermediary and pay eBay's fees. They're also moving to other auction venues such as Yahoo! and Amazon.com. Is it time for you to make the same move, too? If you are running into the situations, challenges, or problems described in the sections that follow, you should consider supplementing your eBay sales with new venues.

 Tip: You can read more about the survey of eBay entrepreneurs at http://www.auctionbytes.com/cab/abn/y05/m07/i25/s02.

Lack of Innovation

Things do change on eBay—but the changes aren't always designed to make it easier or less expensive to sell on the site. At times, eBay comes up with new options like ProStores, updates Turbo Lister or other software, or occasionally offers promotions that let you add a subtitle to your sales for free. However, you don't see changes such as the following ones:

- Promotions that will bring you more customers, such as new advertising campaigns.
- Reductions in eBay's fees.
- A way to access more than just the last ten days of completed auctions. Even if such access were available for a nominal fee, it would be of tremendous benefit to sellers who want to know a reasonable starting price for their merchandise or the best time to schedule a sale.

On the positive side, eBay has made its software platform (technically, this is known as its application programming interface, or API) available to third parties for a fee. This means you have the option of signing up with providers like Infopia (http://www.infopia.com), Marketworks (http://www.marketworks.com), Andale (http://www.andale.com), or Zoovy (http://www.zoovy.com) in order to search several months' worth of completed auctions or automate the process of listing items for sale. You can use eBay's own tools, like Turbo Lister, eBay Blackthorne, or Sales Assistant, but the first one is limited, and the second two carry a monthly fee. The bottom line is that things don't change very quickly on eBay.

Note: An article on AuctionBytes, a website that follows eBay and other auction venues, reported that several prominent eBay staff people left in 2005 to join other organizations. Jeffrey McManus, a former senior manager of eBay's platform evangelism team, moved to Yahoo!, which operates one of eBay's main competitors, Yahoo! Auctions. Louis Monier, who helped eBay develop its search capabilities, moved to the best-known search service on the Internet, Google. Both complained of a lack of innovation at eBay. (Read about their decisions to leave eBay at http://auctionbytes.com/cab/abn/y05/m07/i27/s02.)

Too Many Sellers, Not Enough Buyers

Over and over I hear the same complaints: "There are more sellers on eBay than buyers," or "eBay has to do more to attract buyers." It's true, even though eBay boasts about the number of its eBay Stores. (These virtual stores are websites that eBay allows its members to create where they put their items up for sale, either by seeking bidders for items they are auctioning off or by selling items at a fixed price.)

Note: According to the market analysis company Hoover's, eBay hosts an estimated 161,000 stores on its U.S. website alone, while hosting more than 250,000 stores around the world. (For more information, see http://www.hoovers.com/ebay/–ID__56307–/free-co-factsheet.xhtml.)

When you try to figure out what to sell on eBay, you run into competition. You find, typically, that there are already a dozen people who are selling what you are selling. Often, the competitors are far larger than you. Because they have the resources and experience to put lots of sales online, they can sell for less. The bottom line is that eBay is set up to attract sellers, not buyers.

Rising Seller's Fees on eBay

In early 2005, eBay's sellers were in an uproar when the auction site increased its monthly fee for running an eBay Store. The increase of $9.95 to $15.95 per month might not seem like a lot at first. And for well-established PowerSellers who complete dozens or even hundreds of transactions per month, the increase is barely noticeable. However, if you sell only one or two things through your eBay Store and make a profit of only $10 to $50 per month, the increase is significant.

Success on eBay depends on the simple, age-old principle of "buy low, sell high." Because sellers often spend many hours each week in finding merchandise, photographing it, listing it, and packing and shipping it, they need to make some money to make all this work worthwhile. Let's say that, like me, you try to make at least $9 or $10 on a typical auction sale. You find a nice pair of Nike Air Jordan shoes for $3. You list them for $12.99 (which sounds nicer and more inviting than $13), and one bidder buys them for that price. Does that mean you make $10 on the sale? Not necessarily. Here is an example of how eBay's current fees work:

- Insertion fee: $.35
- Gallery photo fee: $.35
- Four photos (if hosting through eBay's Picture Services, which charges $.15 per image after first one): $.45
- Final value fee: $.68

There may be other fees as well. If you list your item through an eBay Store, you have to pay a $15.95 hosting fee to eBay. If you underestimate the shipping cost—for instance, if you charge $9 for shipping and the cost actually turns out to be $9.30 (a blunder that has happened to me), you lose 30 more cents on the deal. Then, if your buyer uses the popular payment service owned by eBay, PayPal, you incur the fee PayPal charges you to receive the payment from a seller—add another 50 cents or so. Your $9.99 profit turns out to be $7.36. Suppose you spent an hour or more on all the tasks associated with completing this transaction: You're essentially working for less than $8 per hour. Is that a good rate? The point is that you want to minimize the fees that your seller subtracts from you, which over time, and over many sales, add up.

Lack of Security

With every group of sales you make, there always seem to be one or two people who don't respond right away. You have to wonder whether or not they are going to turn from slow responders to nonpaying bidders (NPBs). NPBs are the bane of every eBay seller. Pursuing them is time consuming and not always fruitful, plus eBay's Unpaid Item Process works agonizingly slowly. It's up to you to close the dispute once it's open so that you can relist your item—and during that period, the item isn't selling.

Other auction sites, such as uBid (http://www.ubid.com), prequalify everyone who registers to bid on the site. Shoppers must submit a credit card number at registration, which uBid uses to verify the member's identity.

At the same time, eBay continually encounters problems with security. Members receive e-mails encouraging them to give out their personal information for fraudulent reasons. Accounts are hijacked; fraudulent bids are placed; stolen credit card numbers are used to make purchases. Sellers who are depending on eBay for all or part of their income deserve to feel more secure when they put their hard-earned merchandise, time, and money on the line.

Lost in the Shuffle

In addition, eBay boasts that when you put an item up for sale, you make it available to tens of millions of potential customers. That's not necessarily a good thing. If there aren't any people in those tens of millions who actually want what you have to offer, you don't have any real advantage.

Not only that, but it's easy to get lost amid the millions. Selling on the Web is all about being found. You want your sales listing to be found out of the billions of other Web pages by people who are looking for exactly the item you have to offer. You increase the odds of this type of success by choosing an auction site, mall, or other venue that is frequented by as many shoppers as possible. You also dramatically increase the odds by making sure your sales descriptions are indexed by search engines like Google.

When you open a store on eBay, you are only one of millions. Although eBay indexes your eBay Store listings on search services like Google, sellers who have signed up with sites like iOffer find that they get higher placement in search results faster.

 Note: Getting a good placement on search results on Google and other services is a complex and hotly debated subject. Because Google's exact formula for determining which websites get listed at the top of a set of results is a secret, it's impossible for me to provide you with scientific reasons on how to get the best placement. However, it is widely known that the more links you make to a particular Web page, the greater that page's chances are of being listed near the top. It is to your advantage to make as many links as you can between different Web pages to improve your visibility on the search services.

Personal Help Is in Short Supply

One of the longest-running complaints about eBay is the lack of personal help—that is, the difficulty of finding people at eBay who will personally answer questions and walk you through procedures of one sort or another. This problem isn't as pronounced as it was in the past. You can click on LIVE HELP and type messages to eBay staff. But the system is plagued by the usual delays inherent in any live chat system. You have to wait several minutes for the help staff person to appear; you might get shuttled from one staff person to another; and you find that the process of typing and receiving messages is time consuming. This is what happened to me when I had a question about my own eBay Store (see Figure 2-1). My question was eventually answered, but it took about a half hour to do so. Members of other auction sites report that they have no problem getting in touch with their site's help staff.

Figure 2-1. It's easy to open an eBay Store, but hard to get quick personal help when you need it.

© Greg Holden.

Find the Right Auction Site for Your Sales Niche

When you are considering moving beyond eBay, you don't necessarily want to be thinking about what to sell or finding merchandise to sell. You should already have a supply of merchandise to sell, and know what your sales niche is. Why? When you have a clear knowledge of what you want to sell, you can make an informed decision about where to sell it. Many of the alternatives to eBay are specialty sites that appeal to a niche audience of collectors and enthusiasts. If you have already connected with that audience on eBay, you can move on and find higher bids for your merchandise by reaching exactly the people who want them. Table 2-1 presents some examples of the specialty auction sites you can check out.

Table 2-1. Niche auction sites.

Site	URL	Sales Niche	Advantages
WineBid.com	http://www.winebid.com	Wine	You consign wine to the site, which handles appraisals and shipping
PenBid.com	http://www.penbid.com	Antique pens, pencils, and books about them	Free listings; community discussion boards
LabX	http://www.labx.com	Lab equipment, medical equipment, analytical instruments	Attracts medical equipment buyers
Just Beads!	http://www.justbeads.com	Beads, jewelry, stones, beaded bags	No charge for relisting unsold items; free photo hosting; free e-mail account
Pottery Auction	http://www.potteryauction.com	Pottery	Live chat utility for discussing pottery with others; listing and relisting are free
Sedo	http://www.sedo.com/main.php3?lanquaqe=us	Domain names	Listing is free; sellers can neqotiate with buyers
IronPlanet	http://www.ironplanet.com	Heavy machinery, asphalt, trucks	Commissions of 6 to 8 percent are charged, but IronPlanet helps market merchandise and provides inspections for them

Get a Solid Business Foundation with eBay

It is true that eBay is a terrific place to start a new business. If you've never bought or sold before except at the occasional garage sale, you can use the site not only to get your feet wet in the business world but also to start off your business on a solid footing. Use eBay to your advantage by starting a store and creating a brand name, developing a list of customers whom you can contact for repeat sales, developing a solid feedback rating, creating an About Me page that you can use to promote your website, and opening an eBay Store that you can use in tandem with your other auction sales outlets.

Opening an eBay Store

You don't *need* to have an eBay Store open to move off of eBay. But a store is another part of having a firm foundation on eBay from which you can branch out. An eBay Store gives you a way to list a large quantity of merchandise in different categories. It also gives you another way to meet customers so you can drive them to your website or other auction venues where you sell items. Each time you list an item in your store, you can have ten similar items to which you can direct buyers. I know some sellers who list only a tenth of their merchandise in their eBay Stores to save money on eBay fees, while they list the rest of their merchandise on their websites. They are prohibited by eBay from making a direct link from one of their sales descriptions to an external website. However, if someone asks a question about an item or makes a purchase, that person is encouraged to visit the website for many more options. In other words, once you have assembled a list of steady customers on eBay, you do everything you can to drive them to your website.

Developing a Clientele

Although eBay doesn't have a built-in mechanism for encouraging buyers to return to the same seller over and over, it does encourage sellers to provide shipping discounts on multiple purchases. The site also encourages *cross-selling*—the practice of recommending other items to someone who is shopping for a single item. The "see more items from this seller" feature accomplishes this practice for many eBay merchants. However, many third-party vendors provide a more sophisticated version of this cross-selling feature. For example, Vendio (http://www.vendio.com) gives its clients the ability to present an animated slide show of their other items for sale in the body of each sales description.

If you don't want to subscribe to Vendio or another auction provider, you can still market yourself to existing eBay customers by using the techniques described in the following sections.

Upselling

If you have ever made a purchase on Amazon.com, the well-known online bookseller, or with another prominent online merchant, you've probably experienced *upselling.* When you make a purchase, you are encouraged to buy another, similar item. This process is upselling—as the virtual customer heads to the online checkout area, he or she is given a chance to buy something else.

Upselling that occurs as a shopper prepares to check out by making a purchase from an online catalog is a complex affair that may require special programming. But you can perform upselling yourself as an eBay seller. When you receive the standard end-of-auction message from eBay stating that a purchase has been made, you send out an invoice to your buyer. The invoice has a space at the bottom for a short e-mail message. You can add a message like the one shown in Figure 2-2. In case you can't read the message at the bottom of the image, here it is:

Before you send payment, take a look at my Allen Edmonds size 10M wingtip shoes in my eBay Store. I'll be happy to combine shipping on multiple purchases.

By upselling, you develop a one-to-one relationship with your customers. You get them used to hearing from you with special sales offers. You can maintain that relationship by sending them periodic e-mail announcements.

Using E-Mail Marketing

Once you have a list of satisfied customers, don't let them simply fall by the wayside and move on to other eBay sellers. Keep in touch with them and let them know that you still exist. Entice them with special promotions that you present only to them. Online shoppers love to feel that they are getting inside information or special deals that aren't available to other consumers. You can use such promotions to cultivate ongoing relationships with your customers and to build loyalty—loyalty that you can take with you when you move beyond eBay to a website or new auction marketplace.

Suburban Paper Products, a printer located near Indianapolis, Indiana, has accu-

Figure 2-2. Do your own upselling to develop repeat business with your eBay customers.

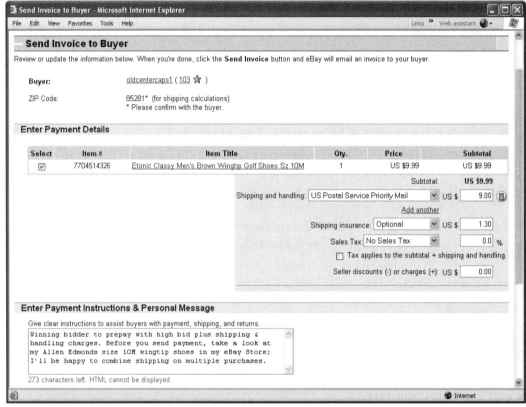

© Greg Holden.

mulated a database of twenty thousand online customers since the company began selling paper scraps and kits in 2001. Every month or so, company president Jeff McCullough sends out what he describes as an "e-mail blast" to those customers. The e-mail message contains colorful graphics and images that tell recipients in an instant what's being offered. An example is shown in Figure 2-3.

Create a Sales System

Nobody ever said selling on eBay or other websites was easy. When you are self-employed, you *really* learn what it means to work hard. You need to keep track of a dizzying array of activities such as finding merchandise, preparing items for sale, photographing merchandise, keeping up with your e-mail, processing payments, packing and shipping—and the list goes on.

Figure 2-3. Use e-mail to build loyalty among your existing eBay customer base.

© Jeff McCullough of Suburban Paper Products.

The way to thrive amid this apparent chaos is to come up with a system. Create a standard listing template that you can use for all your eBay sales as well as your sales on other auction sites. The template should contain standard boilerplate information about your preferred methods of payment and shipping, your returns policy, and your company. Prepare a regular schedule of activities that you can perform so you don't overlook anything. Table 2-2 shows an example.

It's difficult to limit your activities so that you have one or two days off, especially

Table 2-2. Sample sales schedule.

Day of Week	Activity	Comments
Sunday	Prepare items for auction; answer questions.	You can also schedule sales to start in advance if you don't want to work on Sunday.
Monday	Pack; send invoices.	If many of your sales end on Sunday, most of this day can be spent on packing and shipping.
Tuesday	Prepare sales descriptions; pack and ship.	This could be a day of rest, provided you don't have any packing to do.
Wednesday	Pack and ship; answer e-mail; obtain merchandise.	Packing and shipping can occur any day of the week, depending on when purchases are made.
Thursday	Obtain merchandise; prepare sales descriptions.	If you have a large number of sales that you want to start and end on the weekend, begin photographing and writing descriptions now.
Friday	Obtain merchandise; prepare sales listings; answer e-mail.	Thursday and Friday are good days to shop at garage sales or other venues.
Saturday	Prepare sales listings for Sunday.	If you attend garage sales and flea markets, most of your day may be taken up with shopping.

when you're just starting out on new auction sites. However, it's also important to balance your home life and your work activities so that you don't experience burnout. Being burned out doesn't just affect your personal life; it can also drain the enthusiasm you need for dealing with customers and suppliers in a positive, friendly way.

Build Up Your Feedback

Every new business needs credibility. One of the best ways to develop trust is to assemble a set of testimonials, or recommendations from satisfied customers. Through its feedback system, eBay gives you an easy way to gather testimonials. The feedback you accumulate on eBay can be cited on your website as evidence of how trustworthy you are. You can make statements such as the following:

- "eBay PowerSeller"
- "eBay Titanium PowerSeller" (obviously, this is much better, if it applies to you)
- "eBay seller for 8 years; feedback rating over 5,000"

You can even make a link to your feedback profile on eBay so that people can investigate the comments that have been left for you. Of course, before you refer prospective customers, you have to accumulate a good feedback rating by shipping quickly, being responsive to questions, and accepting returns. David T. Alexander prominently mentions his eBay sales and his thirty years of experience on his David T. Alexander Collectibles website (http://www.dtacollectibles.com, shown in Figure 2-4). He sells comics and magazines through two eBay Stores and his own website, and at trade shows around the United States.

Create an About Me Page

Credibility also results from the way you present yourself, whether online or in person. By giving you the space to create an About Me page, eBay gives you a helping

Figure 2-4. Your eBay feedback can help build trust in other sales venues such as a website.

© David Alexander.

hand with presenting yourself personally. This page gives you a place to talk about your qualifications as a seller. Be sure to mention any trade associations you belong to, any certifications you have, or anything that indicates your level of knowledge and experience in your chosen sales area. My own About Me page is shown in Figure 2-5. Here, I call attention to my experience as a collector and the fact that I've written a few books about eBay, which should make me a knowledgeable seller. Perhaps the best thing about an About Me page is the fact that eBay allows you to make links to other websites, such as your own e-commerce online store.

Figure 2-5. Create a free About Me page to build credibility and link to your website.

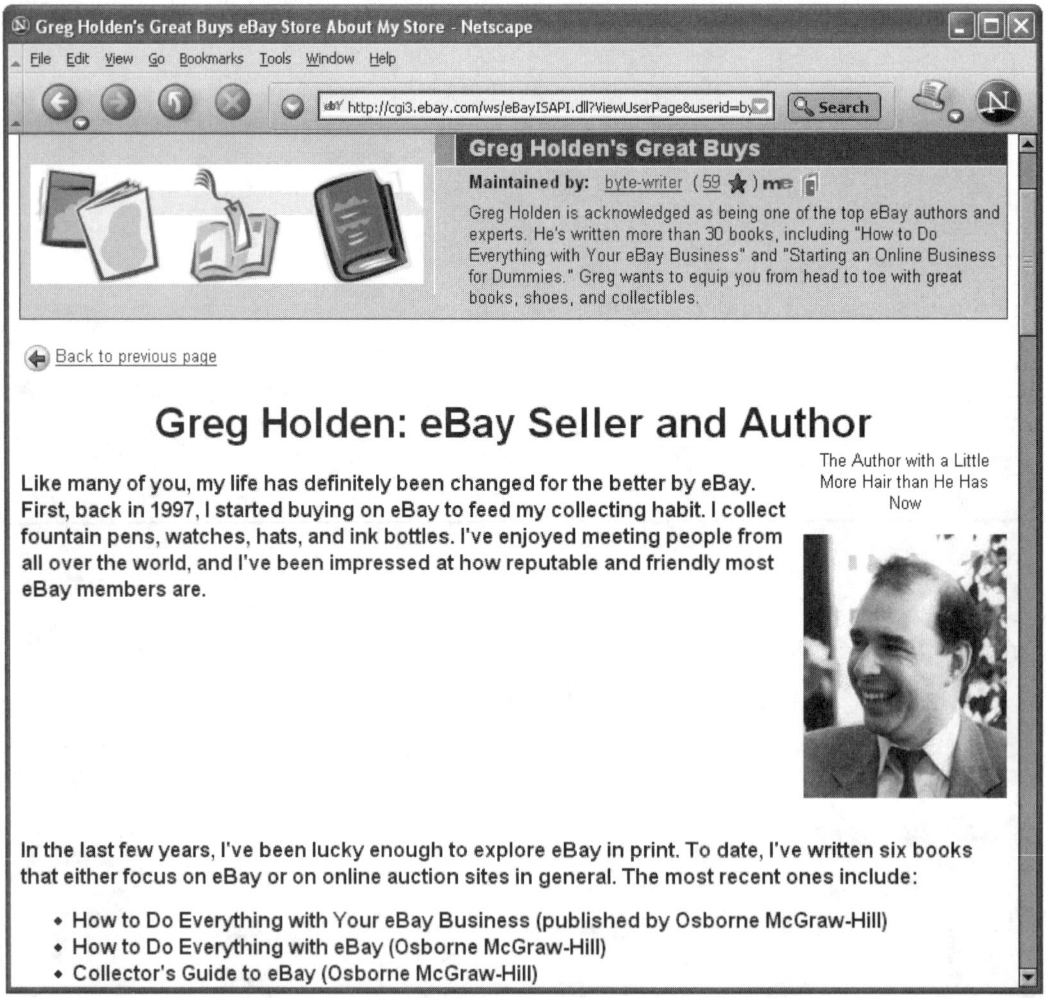

© Greg Holden.

Note: Books like *eBay the Smart Way* by Joseph T. Sinclair give you detailed instructions on how to create your own eBay About Me page—not simply to type a sentence or two about who you are and what you sell, but to provide detailed reasons why buyers should trust you, as well as links to your website and other sales venues.

Don't Abandon eBay

The message I'm trying to convey in this chapter is simple: Don't abandon eBay. The site gives you one of the best ways to get your business's name and your products before the eyes of millions of potential customers. A business presence on eBay serves as a firm foundation. However, don't depend on it for all of your online sales income, either.

Pitfalls of Selling Beyond eBay

Because eBay is the predominant auction marketplace, taking the lion's share of buyers and sellers, and because it has such a well-established system of sales and payments, you are bound to run into some challenges when choosing other sales venues. Being aware of the following challenges will make you a better seller:

- *Lack of Exposure.* eBay's big advantage is the sheer number of members who shop on it. The moment you move off eBay, your visibility goes down dramatically. You just don't find as many potential buyers, and bids, for what you have to sell.

- *Lack of Stability.* Many smaller auction sites come and go, and there is a danger that they can fold up completely and with little warning.

- *Lack of Frills and Perks.* Other auction sites don't have the bells and whistles to which eBay users might be accustomed. You might not get the opportunity to create a Web page that specifically describes you or your business, or a storefront, or discussion forums where you can get tips and share opinions with other members.

- *Lack of Integration with Payment Services.* Because eBay owns PayPal, it's easy to process payments and print shipping labels using that service. When you go outside eBay, you can still use PayPal but you have to find another service provider for printing shipping labels, printing postage, and so forth.

You can offset these problems, in part, by choosing specialty sites—sites whose members are passionate about what you have to offer because they are knowledgeable collectors, or simply because they love what you have. If you have fountain pens for sale, by all means sell on PenBid.com, for instance. Another thing you can do is to avoid putting all your eggs in one basket.

The Multichannel Approach

It's called *multichannel selling*—the use of multiple sites on the Internet from which you can sell your merchandise. This approach allows small retailers to benefit from the exposure that massive sites like Amazon and eBay offer, while also giving them the opportunity to do business more profitably on their own sites or on alternative auction sites.

The website Startup Journal reported an interesting story on Bolinger Antiques, which had been selling on eBay until the late 1990s. After eBay's fee increases, the owner moved to a site called Bidville (http://www.bidville.com), which he said has "a lot of potential." He estimates that he makes about 60 percent of his online sales through eBay, compared with about 40 percent through Bidville. Another very active eBay PowerSeller (who wished to remain anonymous) told me that having developed a strong customer base on eBay helped his company move to other marketplaces. He stated: "Because of the huge clientele base (multimillion customers) that we earned over the years on eBay, it was a lot easier for us to gain a foothold in the overstock marketplace."

Whether you are a small-time or big-time seller, you don't need to abandon eBay completely. As described in Chapter 7, you can expand your operations to sites where you can sell things you would never sell on eBay. The bottom line is that you should come up with a plan and know what you need to do to survive. You'll learn more about planning your own survival process in Chapter 3.

Note

1. "New Study Reveals 724,000 Americans Rely on eBay Sales for Income," July 21, 2005 (http://investor.ebay.com/ReleaseDetail.cfm?ReleaseID = 170073&FYear =).

CHAPTER **3**

Searching for Life Beyond eBay

When one creature dominates an environment, it can be difficult for others to survive, let alone thrive. A friend of mine has a small parrot called a conure that looks colorful and quite harmless. But after bringing the bird home, other pets started disappearing or turning up deceased. Now that the finches and parakeets are gone, the conure rules the roost alone.

Luckily for you and me, eBay doesn't look like it's about to rule the roost completely like our friend the parrot. Although it's without doubt the big dog in the field, plenty of others survive in the pack and are even thriving in their own virtual doghouses. You owe it to yourself to investigate these sites, many of which are described in subsequent chapters. An article on InternetRetailer.com reported that Rockbot tomgolf.com, which has racked up annual sales of $14 million and once used eBay as its exclusive sales outlet, is moving to other sales venues because of dwindling profit margins on eBay. The need to explore new options applies even if you're still making sales on eBay because it never hurts to look around for new opportunities, and you're likely to make a better decision if you're not in crisis mode and have time to think about the move that's best for you.

The same factors that drove you to sell on eBay in the first place can give you the impetus to look for more sales success beyond it. The key is to take a systematic approach. If you suddenly say, "I've had it with eBay!" and immediately close your store and end your sales, you're only going to hurt yourself. How are you going to make up the income you've lost while you open a new store? Expanding your business and taking it to new locations requires the same sort of planning that is required to start up a new business. Take the time to follow the planning steps described in this chapter and you'll make a reasoned decision that will be good for business.

Analyze Your Current eBay Sales

It doesn't take rocket science to figure out that sellers are beginning to consider moving away from eBay because their profit margins are dwindling. Their primary goal is to gain more profit for each item they sell. In general, they don't move away from eBay to find more potential customers: eBay's market pull is unmatched in the online auction industry, and its marketplace is one of the best-traveled on the World Wide Web. Sellers who move away from eBay will find fewer shoppers at other sites. However, by choosing the right sites, they might find more *paying* customers, and customers who will pay more for what they purchase.

Determine Your Minimum Profit Margin

How much profit can you expect from eBay? At what point does it make sense to move elsewhere? There isn't any single formula guaranteed to fit every conceivable Web store. You know from your own selling that some one-of-a-kind collectibles might sell for a 200 or 300 percent profit, or even higher. But for sustained sales, you need a smaller and more predictable profit. The key is to take the average profit you've been making on your merchandise, which has been enough to keep your business afloat, and make that your baseline profit. If you go below that for a month or two, it's probably time to start looking for other options.

Here's an example: Suppose you have ten laptop computers to sell on eBay. You obtained the machines for $500 each. You want to sell them for a 50 percent profit—at least $750, or a profit of $2,500 total. You put them up for sale with a starting price of $750. You find that only six of the laptops sell, and the final purchase prices range between $750 and $800. What's your profit margin? Add up the following:

- Purchase price: $5,000
- Total revenue from six sales: $4,800
- Listing fees: $4.80 x 10 = $48
- Gallery fees: $.35 x 10 = $3.50
- Final Value Fees: $165 total
- PayPal fees: $12

The discouraging thing is that you have lost $428.50 on this deal. Naturally, you have to relist the two computers that didn't sell. You might sell them eventually, but you have to pay the listing and gallery fees each time you do so. So your total profit is not going to be terribly high.

The truth is that profit margins have to be quite high on eBay (or on any online auction site) to compensate for the fact that sell-through is seldom, if ever, 100 percent. A more reasonable profit margin for the ten laptops listed in the previous example would be 100 percent, or $1,000. If six of the laptops sell for $1,000 to $1,100 and your exact total purchase price is, say, $6,180, then you are able to absorb the approximately $300 worth of fees you would incur (higher sales prices result in higher Final Value Fees) and you would end up with a profit of $880. You might be able to sell the four other laptops later on at a lower price or at another sales venue such as Overstock.com or uBid.

Even with a profit margin of $880 on this one sale, you would have to determine whether the profit margin is enough to cover your eBay Store fees, the fees you pay to any employees who help you with packing or shipping, and so on. That is why I can't tell you what your minimum profit margin should be; you need to determine how much you need to make each month in order to make selling on eBay worth your while. If you calculate that you need a minimum of $1,000 to cover your costs and give you a sufficient income, and your profit drops to $880 or less, for instance, it's time to look for other sales options.

Seller Leaves eBay, Boosts Profit Margin

Sell-through rates and profit margins are critical to success, and they played a key role in the movement of one wholesale computer supplier away from eBay. Exel-i, Inc., a company based in Gaithersburg, Maryland, once used eBay as its exclusive sales channel. When eBay increased its fees, Exel-i's sales and procurement manager John Wieber explained that it became clear to his company that some new approaches were needed that didn't depend so much on eBay. In addition to ceasing the use of Buy It Now sales and Gallery photos to save as much as $55,000 per month, Exel-i did the following:

- Upgraded its LaptopBroker website (http://www.laptopbroker.com), shown in Figure 3-1, a storefront set up and managed through ChannelAdvisor (http://www.channeladvisor.com)
- Experimented with putting 115 items up for sale on Amazon.com as a selected merchant
- Moved to putting more merchandise on other online sales channels

According to Wieber, "eBay sales are growing overall, but as a percentage of our business it is becoming less significant. Currently, eBay is about 30 percent of our business. We get about 10 percent of sales from our website, 8 percent from Amazon, and 10 percent from other online channels. Our main focus is on our wholesale business to corporate end users, other online sellers, and computer service companies."

Currently Exel-i has approximately seven hundred items for sale on Amazon.com. Wieber says he doesn't tailor merchandise to particular venues (selling prime items on eBay and excess inventory on other sites, for instance). "We sell similar items across all channels." As far as sell-through rates on eBay, he comments: "The days of 50 to 75 percent sell-through rates are long over. If we get to 50 percent we are thrilled. The average PowerSeller is probably at 33 percent."

Figure 3-1. The owner of this website upgraded it and made it more of an e-commerce venue to become less dependent on eBay.

© Ina and David Steiner of AuctionBytes.

Plan Your Business Expansion

When is it the right time to expand your eBay business to other locations? When your profit margin needs a boost—that's one answer. However, you'll increase your chances of success if the following conditions apply:

•   *Make sure you can sustain your existing business.* Don't move to another location if you're already struggling to make sales or achieve any kind of profit. It's best to expand or move when you have had steady sales—if not increasing profits—for the past several months. You'll be better able to absorb the costs and slow startup associated with a startup site if you are already making a profit on eBay.

• *Do some research on your new venue.* Before you choose a place to sell, read some recent news articles about it—as well as more specific information presented later in this book. If you were doing research at the time this is being written, for instance, you would learn that Overstock.com has been in business only a year, but that its auction clientele has been growing slowly—even though it's still only a fraction of eBay's customer base. You'd also learn that Amazon.com Auctions is dwindling in popularity and Amazon.com itself is playing it down in favor of its Marketplace listings.

• *Look at the market your new venue attracts.* Determine what kind of buyer you want to attract, and find a marketplace that attracts those shoppers. If you're looking for buyers for your heavy equipment, for example, you'll be better off selling on IronPlanet.com than on iOffer, for instance.

• *Get your financing lined up.* Will you need new computer equipment to sell in your new location? Will you need additional storage space? Determine where and how you'll obtain the financing to pay for it.

• *Make sure you have the help you need.* You will need a competent and efficient management team to help you get a new location up and running.

 Tip: This book's Appendix A, Online Auction Marketplaces, lists a variety of online sales venues to consider when you're expanding beyond eBay.

Get to Know the Basics

You don't have to be a business expert to expand to a new online business venue. You just need to know the basics. Many of them are things that sound like clichés but that still ring true: the customer is king; learn which of your products are profitable and which are not; keep your products moving; understand your customers' needs and wants. Most of this is common sense, but some of it is just learning the basics and putting them into practice. See Table 3-1.

Diversify Your Product Line

One effective way to expand your business is to expand your product line. Try to find products or services that are like the ones you sell already. Import or export products

Table 3-1. Retail terms.

Term	What It Means
Sell-Through	The number of items you sell compared with the number of items you put up for sale. As you probably know from your eBay sales, your sell-through rate can vary widely depending on the time of the year and the desirability of what you have to offer.
Compound Annual Growth Rate (CAGR)	This is a term usually used to describe the return on an investment compounded over time. In the case of auction sales, it can be useful to get the "big picture" about your business and track how much your sales income has gone up over the past year—if it has gone up at all. If CAGR is going up, you're in a better position to move beyond eBay than if it is stagnant or going down.
Lead Time	The time needed to complete one task before another can begin. Before you can put items up for sale, you need to photograph them and write descriptions, for instance. You need to allow yourself some lead time if you want your sales to begin on a specific day.
Loss Leader	A strategy that works for many businesses in which goods or services are sold at a price that will generate little or no profit in order to attract customers to other products the business is selling. You see this on eBay and other auction sites that sell "one-cent CDs" and other cut-rate items.
Repeats	A term I am making up to describe the number of times you have to list something before it sells. Often, you have to list an item two or three times before it attracts a successful bid.
Return on Investment (ROI)	The income a business generates as a result of its purchases and its sales of products and/or services.

that are like yours or that match your existing selection in some way. If you sell shoes, expand to shoe polish, shoelaces, and other shoe care accessories, for instance.

Keep Track of Fees, Costs, and Losses

I'm no accounting expert. I'm great at telling people to use slick home accounting tools like QuickBooks, Quicken, and Microsoft Money. But do I use such programs myself? You win the door prize if your answer is a resounding no. That doesn't mean I don't take meticulous care when it comes to tracking inventory and recording expenses and income. In fact, I take great satisfaction at writing down items, model numbers, and purchase prices when merchandise arrives. I take even greater pleasure at recording total sales income when a group of sales ends. I should use a database program like Access, but the truth is I mark it in a long, long Microsoft Word table I have set up for myself. See Table 3-2.

Table 3-2. Greg's sales record.

Item number	Arrived	Brand	Description	Purchase Price	Sales Price	Listing Fees (Est.)	Profit/ Loss
16-7	7/23	Earth Shoe	Mountain Loafer Mocs	$2.00	$12.99	$2.00	$8.99
16-8	7/24	Various	Three Calculus Textbooks	N/A	$9.99	$1.75	$8.24
17-5	7/30	Coach	Women's Station Bag, Brown Leather	$10.00	$19.99	$3.50	$6.49
18-2	8/1	Hudson Bay Company	Oversize Blanket	$10.00	$57.00	$5.48	$41.52
18-3	8/2	Kenneth Cole	Women's Pumps Size 5	$2.00	No Sale	$1.00	− $1.00

I also maintain a second record that tracks each group of auction sales as they end. See Table 3-3.

Table 3-3. Overall sales figures.

Date	Items Offered	Items Sold	Gross Sales Revenue	Original Purchase Price	Total eBay Fees	Profit
7/23 (Sat)	12	6	$96.23	$13.75	$9.96	$72.00
7/24 (Sun)	20	9	$218.00	$50.00	$27.00	$141.00
7/31 (Sun)	28	14	$330.48	$74.00	$25.00	$221.48

Whether you use a database, an accounting program, a word processing book, or an old-fashioned ledger book, the important thing is to keep the records somewhere. The value of such figures isn't always apparent until you've been compiling them for a while. Over time, you can look at your figures and see whether or not income is increasing, or whether your sales are flat. Being flat isn't necessarily a bad thing—unless your expenses are going up because you're hiring employees, taking out new advertisements, and so forth. If that's the case, you need to see some upward movement in your sales figures to simply break even.

 Caution: Don't grow your business too quickly. It is more important to manage the rate of growth in a way that can be controlled so that you can get a complete picture of the state of the market for your goods or services. You'll also have a good idea of whether there is a market that can sustain you for months or years to come.

Identify New Markets

Although eBay is the perfect venue for individuals who want to sell to other individuals, it leaves out a huge market—other businesses. If you want to conduct business-to-business (B2B) e-commerce, eBay may not be the best place. Business purchasers are accustomed to buying in high quantity. Rather than finding twelve buyers for your twelve laptop computers, for instance, you might be able to find a business buyer for all twelve items on uBid (described in Chapter 6) or Overstock.com (described in Chapter 13).

There is also the question of the *type* of buyer you are trying to reach. Typically, eBay buyers are looking for bargains. They want the lowest price they can possibly get for an item. Many of them go to eBay specifically to avoid having to pay full retail price for consumer goods. On sites like Amazon.com, you are more likely to reach a "retail buyer"—a customer who is used to paying full price (or almost full price) for merchandise, and who will give you more of a profit for what you have to sell.

Try placing a few free sales listings in venues like the popular Craigslist (http://www.craigslist.org), for instance, or in the online version of your local newspaper. If nothing else, it will let you know that you are able to sell your items on venues other than eBay.

Look Around, Test the Water

When John Wieber of Exel-i, Inc., which operates such eBay-based businesses as LaptopBroker.com, became disenchanted with eBay's increasing fees and decreasing profit margins, he began to upgrade his company's website. He also experimented by putting 115 computer-related items up for sale on Amazon.com as one of its elected merchants. When those items sold well, he gradually increased his inventory on Amazon.

Just as you probably tried out eBay by putting a selected number of items up for sale in the beginning, you can do the same with other outlets like uBids, iOffer, or Amazon. LaptopBroker.com operates a storefront through ChannelAdvisor.com. It also sells on Amazon. Even though its eBay feedback showed more than twenty-four thousand items sold in the past at the auction site, the company is currently offering only fourteen items for sale in its eBay Store.

Get the Scoop with Newsgroups

I know how difficult it is to actually stop and talk to people when you have many different types of work-related tasks to complete. It can be difficult to take the time to scan newsgroups that cover the auction scene, but the key word is *time*. Look on it as a business activity, much like gathering inventory to sell, taking photos, or paying the bills. The more time you spend talking to others who are in the same situation as you, the bigger your payoff will be.

Although eBay has a lively set of discussion boards, you never know whether or not the "pinks" (the eBay employees, whose messages are always highlighted in pink) are listening. To get an unbiased opinion about eBay from people who don't feel constrained to talk about it, check out the message boards that cover the auction industry as a whole.

One of the best discussion areas is run by a friend of mine, Ina Steiner. Ina operates AuctionBytes (http://www.auctionbytes.com), a website that observes eBay and all other auction sites. AuctionBytes has a well-moderated discussion area (http://www.auctionbytes.com/forum/phpBB/index.php, shown in Figure 3-2) where you can ask questions or "lurk" as you listen in on discussions by sellers who are exploring sites other than eBay.

InkFrog is a site run by a company that provides software tools for managing auctions on eBay. It has a set of forums, including a thread devoted to eBay and online auctions (http://community.inkfrog.com/index.php).

Plan Your Advertising Campaign

Being on eBay, you have a built-in level of exposure to millions of potential buyers. When you move away from eBay, you need to be proactive about advertising, whether you want to get the word out about a new storefront on a bigger marketplace or about

Figure 3-2. AuctionBytes provides forums for discussion eBay and other auction venues.

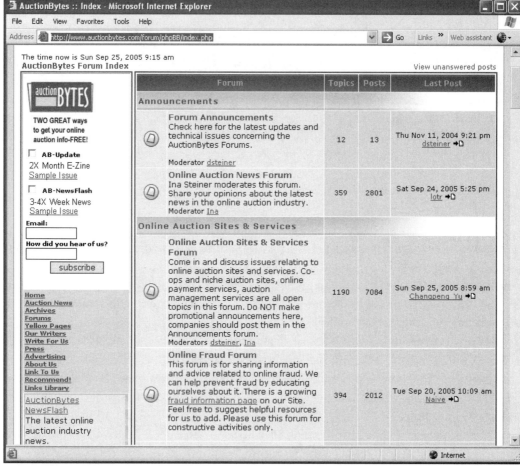

© John Wieber of Exel-I, Inc.

your website. Does your site work with Google AdWords to list your sales the way eBay Stores do? Does the site market itself well?

Advertising is just one of several things you can mention in a brief business and marketing plan you can draw up when you're shopping for new marketplaces. Even if you have a general idea of how you plan to operate, it can be helpful to write down the facts and figures on paper to keep everything straight. Be sure to record the following:

General Information

Description of Your Business: _____

Products and Services: _____

Market Analysis

Industry: _____

Major Trends: _____

Major Competitors in This Field: _____

Description of Your Customers

Age: _____

Sex: _____

Profession: _____

Financial Information

Resources

Cash Available for Expansion: _____

Investor/Partner Contribution: _____

Bank Loan: _____

Total: _____

Expenses

Monthly Fee Paid to Marketplace: _____

Other Listing Fees per Month (Est.): _____

Extra Purchasing Expenses: _____

Goals

Number of Transactions/Month: _____

In this chapter, you learned the importance of doing some planning and ensuring that you have a firm foundation on eBay before you move your sales operations to new venues. Although some successful sellers are able to abandon eBay entirely and set up shop in other, more affordable marketplaces, most sellers will be better off keeping eBay in the mix—that is, selling a limited number of items on eBay while directing as many customers as possible to their other sales. It's not just a matter of creating new websites and listing more items on other sites, either. Ideally, you'll be able to carry your reputation and your professionalism to those sites as well. Chapter 4 examines strategies for maintaining your business identity even as you take on new user IDs and open new storefronts.

PART II

Branching Out to New Auction Venues

C H A P T E R **4**

Carrying Your Experience and Reputation to New Venues

You've spent months—perhaps years—developing a good reputation on eBay. You've accumulated a good feedback rating; you may have qualified for PowerSeller status; you have glowing commendations from satisfied customers. You're ready to take your business to new venues. You want to open a zShop on Amazon; you're working on a Yahoo! Store; you're going to be upgrading your own website. The question is whether you will need to start from scratch with each of these new ventures. Do you have to build a new reputation on your new marketplace of choice?

Ideally, you should make every effort to leverage your reputation as a competent and trustworthy seller on eBay to expand your online sales. You don't have to start from ground zero when you are opening up a shop on Overstock.com, Amazon.com, Yahoo!, Bidville, or any of the other auction and sales marketplaces mentioned later in this book. In fact, you cannot attain prominent exposure on any of these market-places without having a good reputation to begin with. It's up to you to be a sales-person—in this case, a salesperson for yourself.

In this chapter, you'll learn some techniques for making a smooth transition from eBay to another auction venue. You'll learn how to play on your good reputation on eBay to build the same kind of reputation elsewhere. One good thing leads to another in the world of e-commerce as well as in the "real" world. You'll discover that your efforts to reach out and build a good reputation not only increase your level of customer satisfaction but also boost your bottom line.

Lose Your User ID, Maintain Your Identity

MC Electronics (http://www.mcelectronic.com, shown in Figure 4-1) is a seller of sports memorabilia and electronics located in Gillespie, Illinois. An eBay member since October 2000, owner Mark Carpani became a silver PowerSeller and eventually built up a feedback rating of 1,600 on eBay. (A feedback rating is a total based on the number of positive, neutral, and negative comments an eBay member receives from the people with whom he or she does business.) However, he now says he's "pretty much through" with eBay and doesn't plan to sell there any more. He's opened a storefront with the help of auction service provider Andale (http://www.andale.com; see Chapter 14 for more). He also has a business presence on Overstock.com, Bidville, and Yahoo! Mark says that having a good feedback rating and an About Me page gives you a base from which you can make a smooth and effective transition to other marketplaces.

Figure 4-1. This electronics seller abandoned eBay and is thriving on other websites, including his own.

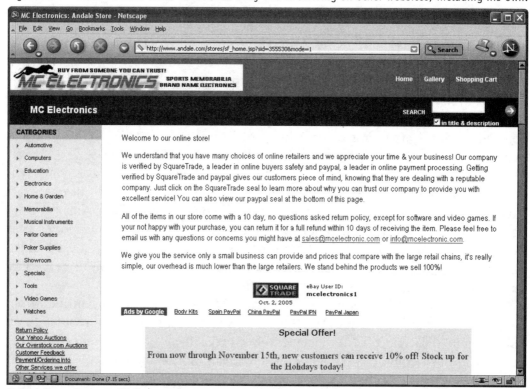

© Mark Carpani, owner, MC Electronics.

 Tip: Look closely at Figure 4-1. You'll notice that Mark has displayed a logo from Square Trade (http://www.squaretrade.com), an organization that certifies online businesses that provide a high level of

> customer service. He also provides his eBay user ID (mcelectronics1) and a statement about his money-back guarantee. Taken together, these items are bound to inspire trust in prospective buyers.

Mark offers new sellers the following advice:

We started on eBay selling collectibles and sports cards. These were small value items that helped us build our feedback on eBay. The best advice I could give anyone is to build your feedback to at least fifty to seventy-five positive comments from other eBay members on purchases by selling small value items that will not hurt you financially if they don't sell well before you go out and try to run with the big players. An eBay seller with one positive feedback can list the same item as another seller with a hundred positives and the seller with one positive will lose money on the sale every time. The feedback system is what makes eBay so popular; everyone who buys and sells on eBay will say the same thing. You have to take some time to build your business up; you can't just walk out of your house and start selling on eBay and turn a profit. It takes time.

Mark says he began building a good reputation with an About Me page on eBay. He took care to craft the kinds of statements about honesty and the importance of customer satisfaction that are guaranteed to build trust.

"We created an About Me page on eBay and tweaked and fiddled with it over the years to ensure our customers know up front that we are a legitimate business. We post our return policy so our customers can refer back to it if necessary and so they know up front what the terms are."

Once he developed a solid business on eBay, Mark was able to wind down his eBay business in reaction to eBay fees that seemed to rise dramatically every year. According to Mark, "The fees were taking up about 19 percent of our profit, and any businessperson will tell you that's too big of a chunk. This is when I started to post things on Overstock.com and Yahoo! as well as other auction sites. We then started our own storefront and pretty much left eBay in the dust. We are pretty much completely done with eBay, I think." The MC Electronics home page on Overstock.com and shown in Figure 4-2 includes the detailed statements about shipping, returns, and customer service that are quoted later in this chapter.

Blow Your Own Horn

You know all about your business, and so do your eBay shoppers, but don't depend on your new customers at Overstock.com or Yahoo! Auctions to know that or to find

Figure 4-2. Spread the word about your professionalism by creating home pages on multiple marketplaces.

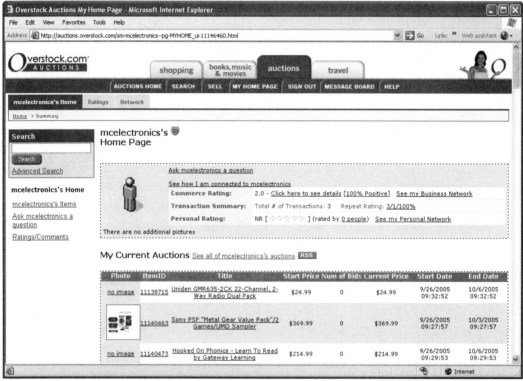

© Mark Carpani, owner, MC Electronics.

out all the good things about you. Be sure you tell people about yourself, why you like what you do, and not only that but why you're *good* at what you do, too. You might say something like:

> I've been selling electronics components for years. I started selling while I had a repair business in suburban Chicago. I used to end up with leftover components and started selling them at flea markets and through classified ads. To my surprise, I liked meeting other radio enthusiasts who turned out to be my customers. I try to carry the same sort of enthusiasm over to my auction business. If you ever have a question about one of my components or a problem, feel free to contact me. My goal is 100 percent customer satisfaction.

Remember that prospective customers are visiting your profile page precisely because they want to find out about you. You don't have to identify yourself by name if you don't want to. On the other hand, if you want to use your name, it will boost your page's personal appeal. Any personal background that relates to what you buy or sell will help to build interest. If you sell baby clothes, for instance, photos of your own children wearing the clothes will help portray you as an authority on the subject.

Cite Your Feedback Rating

Your feedback from eBay may not carry over to your auctions on another marketplace, but there's nothing wrong with citing exactly what your feedback is on eBay. Here is what MC Electronics says:

Since October 2000, our company has a 99.1 percent feedback rating, with over 1,600 satisfied customers on eBay! We value our customers and would like to thank them for their business. . . . We are verified through eBay, PayPal, Overstock.com, and SquareTrade. We are proud eBay Silver PowerSellers, so buy with confidence. . . . Our company uses modern technology but still practices old-fashioned business sense. We simply don't believe in the "make the sale and forget the customer" attitude that has taken over the industry.

Most sites will also allow you to make a hyperlink from your profile page to your feedback profile page on eBay. If you use iOffer's tool Mr. Grabber, as described later in this chapter, you can import your feedback comments from eBay to your home page on that site.

Inspire Trust

Simply creating a profile page on a marketplace site will boost trust among prospective customers. You can also boost trust by telling them how long you have been selling online, how many transactions you have completed, how many positive comments you have received, and so forth. Tell shoppers why they should trust you, and why you are better than the competition (presumably, you *are*, after all). Mark Carpani says this on his Overstock.com profile page:

Our products are 100 percent new or factory reconditioned. If there is an (R) behind the model, the item is factory reconditioned. All of our items have a full manufacturer's warranty and we stand behind our products 100 percent. Our customers will not get stuck with a used item that doesn't work. Check out our website to see what our customers have said about their experience with MC Electronics. All of our Sports Memorabilia is 100 percent authentic and comes with a COA when applicable. These items are manufactured by Steiner Sports, a leader in the sports memorabilia industry!

Testimonials from satisfied customers are another guaranteed way to build trust. Adding quotes from them will tell people that your customers have taken the time to thank you for your level of service.

Build Your Reputation on BizRate

You know about building a feedback rating on eBay. Wouldn't it be nice if there was a feedback system you could apply to your e-commerce website or to your storefronts on other sales venues? That's the idea behind BizRate, a shopping search engine that aggregates sales listings from a variety of websites. It enables shoppers to do comparison shopping, so when a search is conducted, the site returns a variety of sales listings with different prices.

BizRate also provides ratings for merchants based on the shopping experiences of more than 1.3 million active shoppers who have volunteered to provide reviews, and from stores that are designated *customer certified* because they allow shoppers to submit feedback while they are in the process of making purchases. You can list your own store in BizRate's database and invite your own shoppers to submit feedback. It's free to register, and you can find out more at http://www.bizrate.com/interstitial/btob.html.

Offer a Warranty

One of the best ways to get customers to trust you is to have a liberal return policy. If you make a statement on your website or in your profile page, you'll be sure to inspire trust. Consider a statement like the following:

All merchandise purchased from Greg's Great Buys carries a seven-day, money-back return policy. If for any reason you are dissatisfied with

> your item, you can send it back for a full refund (as long as you pay shipping). If we make a mistake in the description or in the shipping process, we will refund both the purchase price and shipping cost. We also offer a ninety-day warranty on all items. We are committed to your satisfaction and we thank you for your business.

Also pay attention to any manufacturers' warranties. If you sell merchandise that is under warranty, be sure to include the warranty information in the body of the sales description and invite customers to e-mail you if they have any questions.

Provide Lots of Shipping Details

As you already know, fast and careful shipping is critical to customer satisfaction. The moment a buyer hands over his or her money, that person is wondering when the item purchased will actually arrive. Although eBay has affiliations with United Parcel Service (UPS) and the U.S. Postal Service (USPS), other auction and sales venues do not. It's even more important, when selling outside of eBay, to assure customers that you will pack and ship their merchandise in a timely manner. Try listing the following shipping information on your site:

> We are committed to fast and careful shipping. Instant payments through PayPal will be processed within twenty-four hours of payment. Personal checks and money orders require seven days to clear. But your order will be shipped Priority Mail with free delivery confirmation. Other shipping options are available; please contact us at info@gregs shoestore.com for more information.

It might seem obvious to you, but telling people how you pack your items, what sort of shipping method you use, and how long it typically takes for delivery makes you look more organized and professional.

Relist Unsold eBay Auction Items

When you're making a transition to move to another auction site, one question you need to answer has to do with your merchandise. Are you going to sell exactly the same sorts of things you offer on eBay? Are you going to offer a different product line? One option for coming up with products to sell on eBay is to gather up those things that have not sold and relist them on other sites.

A logical place for relisting unsold items is iOffer, a site where sellers can make merchandise available either for a fixed price or on a best offer basis. A prospective buyer makes an offer, and the seller can either accept the offer or make a counteroffer. It makes sense to take merchandise that didn't sell for your original price on eBay and see what the market will bear for these items on iOffer or another website where bargaining and haggling is encouraged. (See Chapter 5 for more information on websites that encourage the fine art of bargaining.)

Grab Your Feedback and Sales with Mr. Grabber

Mr. Grabber is a sales tool that is made available to iOffer members. It enables you to import your feedback rating from the following auction sites:

- eBay (http://www.ebay.com)
- Yahoo! Auctions (http://auctions.yahoo.com)
- Bidville (http://www.bidville.com)
- Overstock.com (http://www.overstock.com)
- Sell.com (http://www.sell.com)

Besides bringing over feedback, you can also import items that have not sold. You can bring them over to iOffer with a few mouse clicks and put them up for sale again. Mr. Grabber is easy to use. Once you've registered for an account with iOffer, go to the Mr. Grabber home page (http://www.ioffer.com/mrgrabber) and click the link HERE in the heading Click Here to start using Mr. Grabber. Then follow these steps:

1. When the login page appears, enter your iOffer user ID or e-mail address and your password, and click LOGIN.

2. On the next page, you are asked to choose the site from which you want to import your data, and your username on that site. You can then choose whether to import your feedback rating, your unsold items, or both.

3. A page appears notifying you that "item duplication" will take several hours and when the process is completed, you'll find your items in your Pending Items area on iOffer.

4. When several hours have passed, check your Pending Items area. You can then activate which items you want to sell. Click the IMPORT-ITEMS FROM EBAY link (or Yahoo!, or Overstock.com, or another site, if you have imported listings from there).

If you want to put all the items up for sale on iOffer, you only have to click the BULK UPLOAD YOUR ITEMS link. But it's important to review the items that have been imported. In my case, no fewer than 123 active listings and unsold items were brought over from eBay's database, and I had to carefully select the ones to sell. Some were items that were already up for sale in my eBay Store, and I didn't want them to be sold elsewhere at the same time. At least two were items that were listed as "unsold" on eBay at one time but that were actually sold after relisting.

Note: There is no restriction on whether you can have an item for sale on eBay and iOffer at the same time. But if you have an item for auction on eBay and it sells on iOffer, you have to end the sale immediately on eBay, which might cause disgruntled bidders to leave you negative feedback. Conversely, if something sells on eBay, you then have to remember to terminate the sale on iOffer. You don't want to run the risk of selling one item twice. In my opinion, it's safer to sell something in one venue at a time.

5. Uncheck any items you don't want to sell immediately on iOffer from the list of your active listings and unsold items. (See Figure 4-3.)

6. When you're absolutely certain you've checked the items you want to bring over to iOffer and unchecked the rest, click the ACTIVATE CHECKED button at the bottom of the list.

After you have activated the listings you want to sell on iOffer, the list refreshes and all the items are checked once more. Notice at the top of the list that your iOffer user ID now carries your eBay or other feedback rating next to it.

In the blue shaded box at the upper right-hand corner of the screen, click MY IOFFER. Click CURRENT ITEMS in the left-hand column to view the sales you just carried over to iOffer. I was pleasantly surprised to find that my entire eBay description—including all the photos I had uploaded and the formatting I had used—were carried over to iOffer. (See Figure 4-4.)

Figure 4-3. Mr. Grabber imports feedback and sales listings from other sites to iOffer.

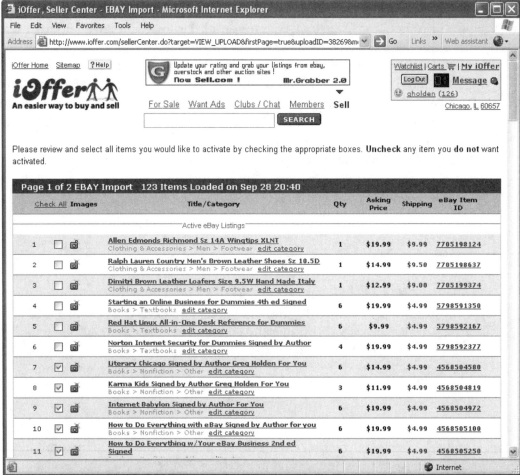

© Offer Inc.

 Note: Mr. Grabber gives you a convenient way to duplicate items you had for sale on other sites. But it doesn't actually make those items any more desirable. If your items failed to sell because they were run-of-the-mill and there was nothing attractive about them, there is a good chance iOffer's buyers will react the same way. (For more information about iOffer, see Chapter 5.)

Figure 4-4. When you carry sales over to iOffer, you get any formatting and photos you originally created.

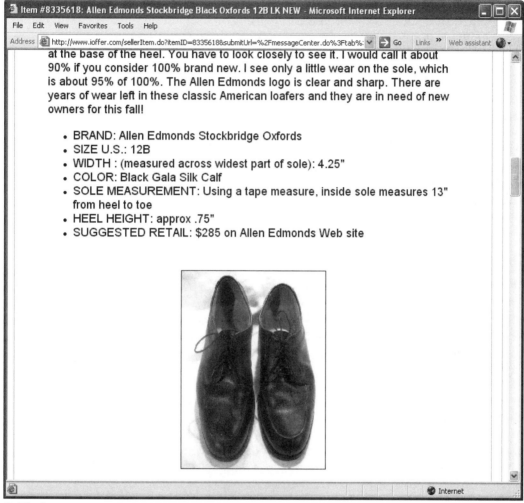

at the base of the heel. You have to look closely to see it. I would call it about 90% if you consider 100% brand new. I see only a little wear on the sole, which is about 95% of 100%. The Allen Edmonds logo is clear and sharp. There are years of wear left in these classic American loafers and they are in need of new owners for this fall!

- BRAND: Allen Edmonds Stockbridge Oxfords
- SIZE U.S.: 12B
- WIDTH : (measured across widest part of sole): 4.25"
- COLOR: Black Gala Silk Calf
- SOLE MEASUREMENT: Using a tape measure, inside sole measures 13" from heel to toe
- HEEL HEIGHT: approx .75"
- SUGGESTED RETAIL: $285 on Allen Edmonds Web site

© Offer Inc.

Clear Out Your Excess Inventory

When you're moving from eBay to other venues, how do you divide up your inventory? Having multiple sales venues gives you new options. You can target specific buyers via specialty sites like those described in Chapter 9. Or, if you have excess inventory that didn't sell originally on eBay, you can use sites like iOffer or Overstock .com as places to sell your leftovers at bargain prices. Some approaches are described in the sections that follow.

The Loss Leader Approach

Loss leaders are items that are put up for sale at bargain prices. The prices are so low, in fact, that you might not make any profit on them at all. You might take a loss on an individual sale. Why do this? You expand your customer base, build trust, and use the loss leader sales to drive customers to other, higher priced merchandise that brings you better profit margins.

The Main Destination Approach

Another way in which sellers integrate their eBay sales with sales on other sites is to use eBay primarily for customer acquisition. After all, eBay brings more potential shoppers than any of its competitors. These sellers maintain a limited presence on eBay and do everything they can to point shoppers to their websites or to other places where they sell.

The Get Out of "FeeBay" Approach

"FeeBay" is one of several nicknames given to eBay by those who object to its many sellers' fees. Their primary goal is to abandon the site altogether and make better profits by selling on lower priced venues, or by selling on their own websites and not having to pay any fees to a third party. In a few cases, sellers who are especially unhappy with eBay will simply close up shop and immediate devote all their energies to selling elsewhere. In most cases, sellers cut down gradually on their eBay sales over a period of months. Then, when they have a steady flow of business on other sites, they say good-bye to eBay.

The approach you choose is up to you. The important thing to remember is that you have options. In Chapter 5, you'll learn how to exercise one of those options and sell in a new yet old-fashioned way—by bargaining with your customers.

CHAPTER **5**

Accurately Valuing Your Merchandise

People often think of eBay and other auction sites as nothing more than big virtual garage sales. But at garage sales, haggling over merchandise is a time-honored tradition. On eBay, you can offer something at a best offer price, but this feature isn't widely used, as far as I can tell. Most other sites, like Yahoo! Auctions and Amazon .com auctions, give sellers the option to sell something at a fixed price or at auction. Those who miss the time-honored give-and-take that left both buyer and seller feeling that they "got something" for their negotiations are left with no options.

Unless they turn to a few auction sites that encourage their customers to strike an agreed-upon price for what they have to sell, that is. In this chapter, you'll learn the ins and outs of haggling and bargaining online with prospective buyers. Although the sites described in this chapter streamline the process of settling on a price for your merchandise, you have to be careful. When you haggle, you always have to keep your bottom line in mind, because it doesn't do any good to sell something at a loss or at a profit that doesn't cover the time and trouble you took to put the item up for sale in the first place.

The key is to start with an accurate price so that, when haggling occurs, you're still going to make a reasonable profit. Accordingly, this chapter examines how to research items before you sell them, so you know what they're worth in the marketplace. That way, you'll be able to keep in mind a minimum price that you don't go below. You'll also learn the pros and cons of the online marketplaces that turn haggling into a system, so you can sell more, keep your customers satisfied, and maintain your bottom line as well.

Researching the Value of What You Have to Sell

In order to bargain with your customers, you have to set boundaries. You have to establish a reasonable starting price, and you have to have at least a fairly good idea of what the item is worth in the marketplace so that you don't overhaggle and end up with a net loss in the deal. This section points you to some useful resources for determining the value of merchandise online. Antique and collectible price guides are good for specialized items, but for electronics and household goods, you can get up-to-date prices at these locations with just a few mouse clicks.

Comparing Prices with Froogle

Froogle (http://froogle.google.com) is the shopping search utility provided by the popular online search service Google. You enter the item you're looking for in the Froogle search box, and the service gives you a list of products that match your description, what stores were searched, and comparative prices. This is an extremely quick way to discover current prices for common household items that are new or relatively new, such as vacuum cleaners and stereo speakers. When using Froogle for price comparison, make sure that you're correctly matching the model, year, and condition of your item to the one you see listed in the search results.

I have to admit that, initially, I didn't think Froogle was a good place to research prices on antiques and collectibles. I considered eBay or Terapeak (see Chapter 14) to be good places to look up prices on eBay completed auctions, which at least indicate the value of an item at the time the sale was held. My mother gave me a Pepsi Cola thermometer to sell on consignment on eBay, and we had no idea what it was worth. Just for fun, I entered the terms "Pepsi Cola thermometer" in the Froogle search box and clicked the SEARCH FROOGLE button. To my surprise, I realized that Froogle also searches eBay Store contents, and those stores include auction offerings as well as fixed-price sales. Not only that, but Froogle returns other resources such as antique price guides that are related to the item in question. The results of my search included:

- Two Pepsi Cola thermometers currently offered for a $65 Buy It Now price in two separate eBay Stores
- A 1960s restaurant equipment supply catalog that includes a listing for these thermometers
- A collectible soda pop price guide book offered for sale for $20 on eBay
- A new book entitled *Advertising Thermometers* (there's a guidebook for everything, apparently!) offered on the Booksamillion.com website

While a search of eBay's completed auctions is a good idea when you're doing research, don't overlook Froogle for researching those unusual or one-of-a-kind collectibles you are preparing to sell, too.

Tip: Froogle descriptions are also a good source for specifications and product descriptions that can help you when you're writing sales listings on auction sites. Be careful not to cut and paste the descriptions word for word, because all content on the Internet is protected by copyright whether a copyright notice is present or not. However, you may find it useful to use some of the product data in your own descriptions, as long as you use your own words to prepare them.

Searching for Collectibles with Kovels.com

Kovels is the most trusted name for pricing antiques and collectibles, and fortunately for you, they have an excellent website (http://www.kovels.com). This site has all of the well-known antiques and collectible price guides written by Ralph and Terry Kovel and available for purchase, which might serve you well if you find yourself mostly pricing the same kind of item. There's a yellow pages of antiques, where you can search for appraisers, auctions, and conservators. Best of all, there's a price guide.

You have to register for a free account to get access to the prices listed on the website, but then you get to search an enormous database of specific items to match your price to their standard. The database is easy to use and broken down into a multitude of individual categories, which incidentally help you draft your listing in the terms with which collectors are familiar. If you mention in your listing that your price came from the Kovels' books or website, you will hear little argument from potential buyers about the item's worth.

Using the Kelley Blue Book

The sale of vehicles online is steadily becoming more of an everyday, routine event rather than a novelty. Sites like eBay Motors have well-developed systems for obtaining vehicle inspections and working out details with vehicle shipping services so buyers will be willing to place bids. Other sites let you sell your car online, too; wherever you sell, however, you have to set an accurate starting price or reserve bid for your sale. The price has to be accurate because prospective buyers have access to a wide variety of online utilities for determining the data of different vehicles.

The Kelley Blue Book is the most recognized name in assessing the value of used vehicles. The organization's website (http://www.kbb.com) reflects its expertise. The site is extremely user-friendly, comprehensive, and best of all, tailored to your local area. This is a site to use not just when you're researching prices for your items, but also when you're considering a purchase. Every make, model, and year is included in the database, and you can search for the trade-in price with a dealer, the suggested retail price, or the private party price, which will probably be your most common transaction. Bluebook also lets you add your car to its listings and reach additional buyers. All in all, this site is a premier resource.

Driving Home the Deal on Your Own Vehicle

Several websites other than eBay Motors focus solely on buying and selling motor vehicles. At CarsDirect (http://www.carsdirect.com), a vehicle listing costs a flat $25. Your ad stays online for up to thirty days or until the vehicle is sold. At AutoTrader.com (http://www.autotrader.com), you can sell your vehicle either on the AutoTrader web-site or on the printed version. Prices range from a flat $29 to $49 for each listing. At Cars.com, listings cost about the same: $25 to $50. All of the aforementioned sites include utilities for researching the value of your car, truck, motorcycle, or other vehicles, too.

Visit CARFAX (http://www.carfax.com) to order a vehicle history report you can include with your sales description. The report tells prospective buyers whether or not the car has been rebuilt, flooded, salvaged, stolen, or had other major problems.

When your vehicle is sold, you should prepare a bill of sale that conforms to your state's motor vehicle requirements. AutoTrader.com maintains a page full of links to state motor vehicle websites at http://www.autotrader.com/research/shared/article .jsp?article_id = 13236.

Researching Prices at BizRate

BizRate (http://www.bizrate.com) is a free comparison shopping site and seller rat-ings service. In Chapter 4, BizRate was listed as a resource for merchants who want to add their business descriptions to the site's database. But BizRate is known primar-ily as a site where shoppers (and sellers) can research prices of household and every-day merchandise.

 Note: BizRate is useful for shopping for new or almost-new consumer merchandise. When I attempted to research my antique Pepsi Cola ther-mometer, BizRate deleted the brand name "Pepsi" and turned the search terms into "cola thermometer." A handful of new Coca-Cola (not Pepsi Cola) thermometers were returned; they were all listed in one online store.

BizRate works much like Froogle: You enter what you are looking for, and it searches the inventories of other stores and presents you with an array of options. What makes BizRate worth using? For one thing, you receive more information from a search than with Froogle. Bizrate tells you the number of items available at a store, the price, and gives you a link to reviews rating the store's quality and speed. The following example is for a popular digital camera, the Sony Cyber-Shot DSC-P200:

- Price range: $299 to $430 at a whopping sixty-two different online stores
- Product rating: Five stars out of five; you can read the reviews on the BizRate site by clicking one of the stars included in the description
- 7.2 Megapixels
- Zoom: 3X Optical, 6X Digital

Not only that, but you can read more reviews on each of the online stores that carry the item in question; links to each store's description are included with BizRate's description.

Knowing how many examples of a particular item are already available online can be important when you're trying to set your own price, because you can set a higher price if items are unusual or uncommon. And knowing what a later model is selling for can help you estimate a reasonable price for an earlier model of the same item. Bizrate helps with online searches, and it will pick the best-rated or lowest-priced item price from among your search results for you.

Using Andale Price Finder

Andale (http://www.andale.com) will sell you software that will do everything for you that this book has just been showing you how to do yourself. This site sells pretty much everything that has to do with operating an online business, from image software, counters to calculate how often an item is viewed, gallery space, and web hosting for an online store. You can take or leave as many of these aids as you want, but for our purposes, we want to consider their research tools.

Andale has two software packages that you pay a monthly fee to access: Research and What's Hot. What's Hot can tell you what is selling well at the moment on eBay. Research will search all the sites we've listed previously and more to present you with a picture of your item's value. The advantage of the Research software is that it will save you time. The What's Hot software could affect what you choose to buy that month, as well as what you choose to list first, presumably increasing the speed of your sales for only $4 a month.

Should you use any of Andale's online auction tools? At $12 a month for both programs, it's a fairly cheap decision either way, but running a successful online business requires watching every nickel and dime. In general, you can do your own research and pricing, and knowing what's hot on eBay will only be useful if you have a large backlog of items you haven't yet posted online. You might try these services for a month and clock how much time they save you.

 Note: Chapter 14 describes Andale's services in greater detail, and mentions Terapeak, another auction-pricing research service.

Bargaining with Buyers: iOffer

Suppose you really want to sell something, but despite all your research, you don't have a firm idea of how much the item is really worth. You have found descriptions and completed sales prices for similar objects. You know what you'd like to get for an item, but you hate the idea of having to pay a listing fee just to find out if your educated guess matches what someone is willing to pay. And you're actually open to accepting somewhat less than your ideal price.

Sounds like an ideal situation for using an online marketplace called iOffer to make your items available to prospective buyers. In the How to Sell section of its site, iOffer boasts that if you don't know what an item is worth, you can let the buyer make an offer. You pay nothing to create a listing. You either set a starting price and wait for a buyer to either accept that price or make a counteroffer, or simply list the item with the notice "Make an Offer." In the latter case, you leave it up to the buyer to suggest what a reasonable price might be; you can either accept that price or make a counteroffer of your own. Offers go back and forth until a price is agreed upon.

The iOffer site comes in two versions: the regular version and a version called iOffer Lite. The Lite version is intended for items that have a starting price of $4.99 or less. This area of iOffer gives you a chance to sell low-priced merchandise without incurring hefty fees—in fact, there is no Final Value Fee for transactions on iOffer Lite, at this writing. An area called Want Ads enables you to do some "fishing" for items that buyers want—though many of the ads are from sellers looking for wholesale items they can buy in bulk and resell. On the first How to Sell page shown in Figure 5-1, you are given the choice of creating a sales description for your item or searching the iOffer Want Ads to find notices that have already been left. You might be able to find a buyer without taking the time to write a description at all.

Figure 5-1. iOffer lets you choose between creating sales descriptions and searching classified ads from buyers—or both.

© iOffer.

Another feature, Snag a Sale, lets you search the site for transactions that are under way but not completed. The idea is that if a buyer and seller cannot agree on a price, you can "jump in" and offer your own item, if you have one, at a competitive price.

The fees charged by iOffer are shown in Table 5-1.

It's also worth noting that items that tend to have particularly high price tags, such as aircraft, boats, cars, trucks, and real estate, have no Final Value Fee assessed: you can list them for free and sell them for free.

Table 5-1. iOffer final value fees.

Final Transaction Price	Final Value Fee
$4.99 or less (on iOffer rather than iOffer Lite)	$.50
$5.00 to $9.99	$.75
$10.00 to $24.99	$1.25
$25.00 to $99.99	5 percent of transaction price
$100.00 to $1499.99	$5.00 plus 2.5 percent of transaction price
$1,500.00 and over	$40.00 plus 1.5 percent of transaction price

 Tip: An eBay friend of mine, Lu Paletta, wrote a column on Auction-Bytes in which she described her own experience with iOffer and gave it a positive review. Read her comments at http://www.auctionbytes .com/cab/abu/y204/m11/abu0131/s03.

Researching iOffer Buyers

It's true in almost all cases, whether you sell at auction or not, that you don't know what an item is really worth until someone decides how much he or she wants to pay for it. Guidebooks, online search utilities, and price guides can take you only so far. However, can you really expect a buyer to make a reasonable offer for something? Odds are buyers are trying, like everyone else online, to pay as little as possible for merchandise offered on iOffer, just as on other online auction sites. Luckily, iOffer gives you a rating system to research buyers to see if they are really trustworthy. After a transaction has been completed, a positive comment is left for another member, and that person's rating goes up one point; for any negative comments, the rating goes down by one point. Neutral ratings are also available, just as on eBay.

Buyers and sellers who register on iOffer can take an advantage of another feature you won't find on eBay (not at this writing, at least): an online journal called a Web log or blog. Once you register on the site, go to your My iOffer page to begin adding comments to your blog. Your blog can serve as a good public relations tool where you can talk about your experiences on other auction sites and with buyers and sellers.

 Note: Any ratings you obtain through your iOffer transaction are added to your feedback comments that have been brought over to iOffer from

> eBay, using an innovative tool called Mr. Grabber. See Chapter 4 for more information about this utility.

Obtaining Wholesale Merchandise on iOffer

The site iOffer is a useful place to purchase large quantities of merchandise at wholesale prices. In the shoe category, which is an area I am familiar with, you see many vendors from China offering items directly to the public. In this sense, iOffer breaks through trade and language barriers. Browse through the For Sale listings to find the merchandise you normally sell. You won't find a category called Wholesale, as such. You have to search through individuals listings to locate items that are being made available in quantity.

Finding Domain Names at Sedo

There is another marketplace where bargaining and haggling is welcomed and, although you might not have the right merchandise to sell there, it's good to know that it exists. The website Sedo (http://www.sedo.com) is devoted to the buying and selling of domain names, and it is the largest broker of domains on the Web. Listing a domain name with Sedo is free, as it only charges a commission upon the completion of a sale. Most recently, Sedo brokered the sale of the name *website.com* for the impressive price of $750,000.

Although the buying and selling of domain names might appeal only to technocrats, it's good to remember that the nuts and bolts of the Web itself have value to some people, and that names make a difference to a business's success. Another thing that makes a difference is the ability to clear off your inventory shelves and keep products moving through your chosen marketplaces. Chapter 6 will explore strategies for moving stock.

CHAPTER **6**

New Strategies for Moving Inventory

Experienced businesspeople know that, in order to succeed, you have to keep your inventory moving. You need to put as many items as possible up for sale, and you need to sell as many as you can by putting them before the right set of potential buyers. Basically, you have two options: You can "unload" your excess stock as cheaply as possible and hope to make a minimal profit, or you can select the most desirable items and post them where a niche group of knowledgeable buyers will find them.

In either case, eBay may not be the best choice. This chapter will discuss marketplaces that will help you clear off your shelves and help you sell more than you could without having the Internet in the mix.

Liquidating inventory isn't just a way to clear out your shelves while making a few pennies. It's big business. In June 2005, *Entrepreneur Magazine* named Liquidity Services, Inc., the fourth-fastest growing business in the United States. Liquidity Services runs online auction marketplaces such as Liquidation.com. Marketplaces change quickly. Liquidity Services estimates that more than $100 billion of surplus assets must be sold off each year. That doesn't mean you have to take a loss, however. In this chapter, you'll learn the ins and outs of using such marketplaces to sell off your own excess inventory. You'll learn how to use online liquidation services, how to increase attendance at a closeout sale through e-mail, and how to avoid wasting time and money in endless markdowns. Your time and your inventory can work together to your business's benefit.

Using Liquidation Marketplaces

If your primary goal is to sell a single old computer or other leftover item at a cut-rate price, eBay is the ideal venue. Shoppers on eBay are primarily looking for bargains, whether they are hunting for one-of-a-kind varieties or mass-produced consumer goods. However, what if you have one hundred, one thousand, or five thousand things to unload? Although eBay has its Wholesale Lots category, it isn't the most popular category on eBay and was not listed in the eBay Hot Categories Report that was available at the time of this book's printing. If you want to unload excess inventory, you have other options that will be described next.

In the summer of 2005, a website called AppleInsider reported that Apple Computer was preparing to dump its inventory of Macintosh minis and G5 computers through the liquidation site Overstock.com—this effort coming on the heels of a successful effort to clear out previous generation iPods through the same venue. The site claimed that Overstock.com was able to sell several thousand 60GB iPods in a single day by offering a discount of $100 on the devices. Later that summer, Overstock was offering 20GB Apple iPod + HP 4th Generation players for $259, which was less than the $299 Hewlett-Packard was charging on its own website, hpshopping.com.

The point of this consumer reporting is that, if big corporations are willing to move from their own websites to auction/liquidation sites like Overstock.com to unload their excess inventory, you should, too.

uBid

The site uBid.com has established itself as the one of the most reliable online marketplaces around. Launched in 1997 and boasting more than four million registered customers, this site sells brand-name merchandise for a hefty discount. One of the best features of uBid for you as a seller is its Certified Merchant program. By certifying all of its sellers as legitimate businesses, uBid has largely eliminated the problems that come with individual sellers, so that buyers feel as confident in their purchases online as in a department store. In addition, bidders are prequalified in the sense that they have to submit credit card information before they can place a bid.

It doesn't cost anything to join the Certified Merchant program; you need to submit a credit card number, three trade references, a bank account number, and either an FEIN number or social security number. Even if you don't run a brick-and-mortar business, you should have all of those elements from your existing eBay business.

Participating in uBid's merchant program has several advantages. Certified Merchants are not charged a listing fee, only a commission rate plus a 2.5 percent processing fee is due upon each sale (see Table 6-1 for rates). Since uBid itself is a liquidation business, it is familiar with the business and have an interest in helping your sales. You reach a much broader market here than on your own, and the buyers are interested in buying old inventory stock.

Table 6-1. Success rates and fees on uBid.

Winning Bid	Success Rate	Example
$1 to $25	12.5 percent	$20 sell price: $2.50 plus $.50 processing fee = $3 due
$26 to $250	10 percent	$150 sell price: $15.63 plus $3.75 processing fee = $19.38
$251 to $500	7.5 percent	$350 sell price: $33.13 plus $8.75 processing fee = $41.88
$501 to $1,000	5 percent	$750 sell price: $56.88 plus $18.75 processing fee = $75.63 due
$1,001 and above	2.5 percent $2000 sell price: $50 fee plus $50 transaction fee = $100 due	

It is known primarily as a site where businesses sell off used computers and computer accessories as well as other kinds of electronic gear. Categories like Apparel and Collectibles are included on uBid, but they are hardly as well populated with sales listings (and bids) as eBay. When I looked, I found nine pairs of men's shoes for sale. But in the laptops, I found fifteen devices with 2.6GHz or faster processors, sixty-six with 1.6GHz to 2.6GHz processors, seventy-nine with 1.6GHz or below, and so on. The bottom line is that bidders don't go to uBid looking for one-of-a-kind collectibles. They go looking for good deals on laptops, monitors, and other electronics equipment.

 Note: One of the best-known marketplaces for selling multiple items that are considered excess inventory is Overstock.com. (The site is described in Chapter 13.)

Liquidation.com

This site is the largest surplus marketplace in the world. It's a business-to-business marketplace, and not primarily intended for individual sellers to offer single items. Rather, Liquidation.com's sellers tend to be manufacturers, distributors, wholesalers, and public sector or governmental agencies that need to get rid of large quantities of merchandise. Instead of a single designer shirt for sale, you typically find a hundred designer tops for women, five hundred lots of toddler clothing, fifty MP3 players, sixteen digital camcorders, and so on. Although there is no minimum quantity, the site prefers a value of at least $2,000 per lot. All sales start at $100 and there is no reserve. Fees are reportedly higher than on other sites. Liquidation.com does not publish the fees on its website, and requires you to either phone or e-mail for them. However, according to an AuctionBytes article (see the Note below), they amount to a full 15 percent of the winning bid price, with a minimum of $150.

If you are able to provide the lots, Liquidation.com will promote, sell, and ship them. The site can sell any type of merchandise for you, and has a good reputation in its field. While its business model is comparable to most other online market-places, its focus on selling bulk lots makes the site nearly unique.

> **Note:** The eBay PowerSellers discussion board is crowded with comments about problems with Liquidation.com—about poor quality merchandise and poor service. On the other hand, one PowerSeller wrote a positive review about his experiences selling off items that he couldn't move on eBay or Overstock.com at http://www.auctionbytes.com/cab/abu/y204/m03/abu0114/s03.

Sending E-Mail Closeout Alerts

A growing number of companies are using e-mail to alert their existing customers about closeouts. The big retailers do this in an automated way. But small auction sellers like you and me can do this manually. Cabela's Inc. (http://www.cabelas.com), the Nebraska-based sporting goods seller, is able to cut costs and clear out excess and odd-lot inventory by advertising via e-mail rather than using the U.S. Postal Service. Advertising sent via U.S. mail doesn't reflect real-time inventory conditions as e-mail advertisements do.

Donating Your Excess Inventory

By donating your nonmoving merchandise to charity, your company can earn a federal income tax deduction under Section 170(e)(3) of the United States Internal Revenue Code. This can help you cut your taxes substantially, as you can deduct the cost of the inventory, plus half the difference between cost and fair market value. This can be up to twice the cost, actually saving you money. A great group that can help you with this kind of donation is the National Association for the Exchange of Industrial Resources (www.naeir.org). This group has been in existence for nearly thirty years, placing unused merchandise with schools and nonprofits, with a lifetime turnover of over $2 billion. There is no fee to pick up your inventory, and you can be sure of your items going to a good cause.

Cutting Down on Markdowns

All retailers and wholesalers know about the "clearance season blues." This is a state of mind that crops up, often after the holidays, when bales of merchandise have to be marked down and unloaded to make way for new products. It also occurs in late summer, when sellers need to clear out spring and summer items to make way for fall and winter merchandise. These markdowns can cut heavily into your profits. If you reduce the amount of clearance you need to do in the first place, you'll have more first-line goods to sell at auction or on your website. A little planning can help:

- Start with last year's sales histories, and make adjustments for unusual events, such as weather, out-of-stocks, one-time promotions, and so forth. Next, factor in the appropriate increase or decrease based on your current sales trend and your reading of the sales potential for the category for the upcoming season. Finally, for larger categories, it may make sense to break the sales plan down by subcategories, styles, or vendors.

- Try to avoid committing to inventory too far in advance and then bringing it in all in one shot, which is one of the surest ways to find yourself overstocked down the road. For many small retailers, the best way to plan inventories is to plan to have enough on hand at month's end to cover the next two or three month's sales.

- Realize that your plan is dynamic and needs to change along with the marketplace. Use that plan as a dynamic tool to track the progress of the season. As each week goes by, and sales trends begin to develop, adjust future sales plans accordingly, and adjust inventory plans for those updated sales plans. If sales are exceeding plan, you want to be sure you have the inventory to keep the momentum going. Conversely, if sales are coming up short of plan, the sooner you adjust your inventory plans, and thus your scheduled receipts, the less likely you are to end up with excess inventory that needs to be marked down at season's end.

- Make an effort to forecast and track your sales by month and your ending inventories by month. If you keep detailed records, you'll find it is that much easier to calculate how much inventory to bring in each month. You need to bring in enough to cover that month's sales plan and ending inventory, less the prior month's ending inventory. In this way, a buyer can know in January, when preparing for the spring season, for example, how much inventory to plan on bringing in each month of the season.

Selectively Selling a Bookstore's Inventory

Bookworks is a used and rare bookstore that has been in business for more than twenty years on Clark Street in Chicago (see Figure 6-1). Owners Bob Roschke and Ronda Pilon began selling books online in 2001 as a way to supplement the storefront business.

At any one time, Bookworks has 3,000 to 3,500 titles up for sale. But Roschke says they only sell occasionally on eBay. The bulk of the sales come from the following three book-oriented sites:

Figure 6-1. This Chicago bookseller says Internet sales account for 5 to 10 percent of the company's total business.

© Greg Holden.

1. Amazon.com (http://www.amazon.com), which allows sellers to offer used and out-of-print books as well as more current offerings
2. Abebooks.com (http://www.abebooks.com), which specializes in rare, out-of-print books and textbooks
3. Alibris (http://www.alibris.com), which specializes in books but also sells movies and music on its website

Why focus on these sites rather than eBay? One reason is that the buyers Roschke seeks are discriminating collectors who are skeptical about the quality they are likely to get from sellers on eBay. According to Roschke:

"eBay tends to be a great popular marketplace in terms of offering anything or everything someone wants to sell. eBay sales don't turn out well if the condition of a book isn't described properly. And condition has a tremendous impact on a book's value. A lot of rare book dealers wouldn't consider buying on eBay. They expect the condition to be described incorrectly. While eBay is fun, it's 'buyer beware.'"

Bookworks also operates its own website (http://www.thebookworks.com, shown in Figure 6-2) through which customers can view online auctions and search the store's online catalogs.

Knowledge of the market and of the kinds of customers who will pay for rare books is key, according to Roschke. "Being a bookseller is not just about listing books on the Internet. It's about knowing what the market is up front. If you start using sites that are specific to books, you find that the sellers there tend to have more responsibility to their buyers. We tend, because of the labor involved in getting sales online, to limit online selling to better books—things that are more expensive."

Roschke does know of stores that sell as many as fifteen thousand books at a time, and that offer books for as little as one cent each. They are following the strategy of unloading excess inventory on the Internet. "On Amazon, some people sell books for $1 or less and, because shipping costs are fixed, they can still make 50 cents to $1 profit on a book because of the shipping."

For Bookworks, online sales are a separate activity from sales through the brick-and-mortar store. "When I first started selling online, I tried to take books off the shelf and sell them online, and it didn't work. Tracking when something sold and then deleting it from the database proved really difficult." As a result, selling online is a supplement for Bookworks. Online sales account for only 5 to 10 percent of the business's overall income. Roschke estimates that the store sells an average of two to five books a day, although sales can vary widely from two to fifteen items per day. The selective approach to online sales works better than the approach of unloading inventory for the lowest possible price. "There are far more books around than there are saleable books," he says.

Figure 6-2. Bookworks, like many online sellers, uses its website as a base from which to browse sales listings in other venues.

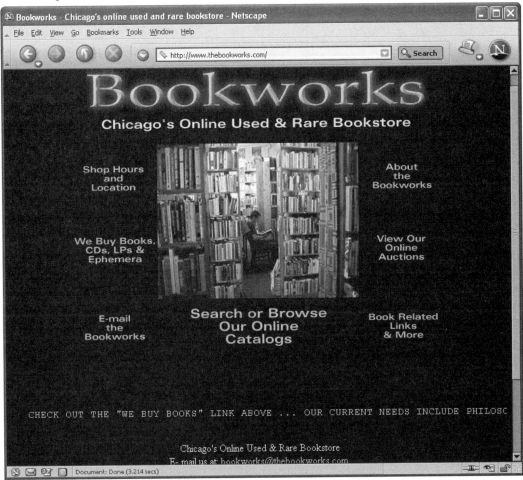

© Bookworks, Inc.

This chapter examined different approaches to moving inventory off your shelves so that you can get new stock for sale. You can unload items in bulk, sell them for as little as one cent each, donate them to charity, or take a selective, targeted approach that tries to attract dedicated collectors. The targeted approach is one you can pursue in many other venues when you start to venture outside of eBay. Chapter 7 will describe some innovative and even unusual ways to match what you have to sell to the buyers who are likely to bid on it or purchase it online.

Finding More than One Way to Sell

Visit eBay, and you will see hundreds of sales categories. At first glance, it seems like you can sell just about anything on the site. However, this is not true, because eBay maintains a long list of prohibited items, each of which is guaranteed to offend some-one. But it's only when you look around at other auction sites and marketplaces that you begin to realize the full range of commodities and services that you can market on the Internet to round out your business.

Once you have some basic experience of selling online under your belt, thanks to eBay, you can extend your knowledge to selling new things in other venues. You can offer things like luxury vehicles, financial instruments, and other high-priced assets at venues that are focused on just those sorts of items. And you can sell on your own website, where you can build trust and retain customers.

You can also sell in unusual ways: you can watch live bidding "stream" within your browser window as auction participants bid on your merchandise; you can cre-ate video that displays your items with live action; you can also go "fishing" for buyers who have placed want ads in reverse auctions. Although eBay also lets you pursue these unusual sales approaches, the sites described in this chapter are dedi-cated to unusual approaches. These sites let you match the merchandise you have for sale with the best marketplaces for making them available to buyers. In this chapter, you learn about the different ways to sell online once you've established a foothold on eBay, such as through a website, through sites that let you sell specialty items, or through sites that let you present your items in unusual and compelling ways.

Deciding Where to Sell: Putting Your Website First

You're used to being part of a larger marketplace that has a built-in audience of shoppers, a customer service area, and user-friendly utilities for creating sales listings and accepting payments. So it's natural, when planning your move away from eBay, to consider a lateral move—a move from eBay to another prominent marketplace such as Yahoo! Auctions.

But sellers who have been in business for a while and know something about the different options say that selling through your own website should be the primary focus of attention. You don't necessarily have to do all the work of e-commerce alone, either. By finding the right business partner, you still get utilities for streamlining sales descriptions and accepting payments.

"Your own website should be at the heart of your channel expansion activities," advises David Yaskulka. David should know what he's talking about. He's not only one of the best-known PowerSellers on eBay but he has also established a major presence as an Amazon Merchant and a Trusted Merchant on Overstock.com. He and his wife, Debbie, operate Blueberry Boutique. They are shown in Figure 7-1 on the About Me page of their website (http://www.blueberryboutique.net).

Nothing encourages customers to return to you on a regular basis like a good deal presented on a business's well-designed website, says David. "It is very difficult to retain customers on eBay or Amazon. At Blueberry Boutique we're among the best in the industry at building customer loyalty. But most people who go to eBay or Amazon do a product search for, say, Zegna ties and then find us. Then they're very pleased, and so repeat their success formula—this time finding a different seller! But a customer who buys from your website will be much more likely to return if they are pleased with the experience."

What kinds of features ensure that a customer will have this sort of experience? Chapter 18 will delve in greater detail into the subject of designing an e-commerce website, but a quick examination of the Blueberry Boutique website reveals the following essentials:

- *Navigational Aids.* A search box and links across the top and left-hand sides of each page help shoppers find their way around no matter where they are on the site.
- *A Shopping Cart.* This utility, which holds items as they are chosen and adds them up at checkout time, encourages multiple purchases. It also makes customers feel they are on a site that is professional and well-organized. The Blueberry Boutique shopping cart and checkout system are provided by the e-commerce host, ChannelAdvisor.
- *Secure Checkout.* Shoppers want options when it comes time to handing over their money. They don't want to be forced into any one choice.
- *Assurances of Safety.* Throughout the site, you see mentions of money-back guarantees, Square Trade seals, and other content that tells shoppers this vendor can be trusted.

Figure 7-1. This husband and wife team sell through many venues, but they value their website first and foremost.

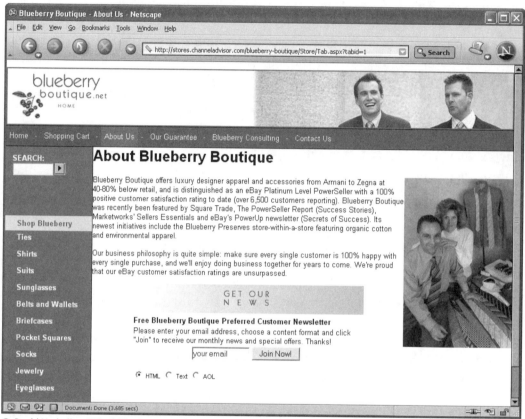

© David Yaskulka, CEO of Blueberry Boutique.

In addition, shoppers also get competitive prices. David does everything he can to make his website a preferred destination for customers who first encounter Blueberry Boutique on eBay, Amazon, or Overstock. On the home page shown in Figure 7-2, you see mentions of dramatic price reductions, last-minute sales, and special shipping deals.

The Blueberry Boutique website doesn't contain glowing statements about the company's feedback level or sales record on eBay—although David says you can use your website to link your past performance on eBay with your current sales activities.

"There are ways to tout your eBay success on your own website, if done right. One is by highlighting quotes (feedback) from happy customers. Another is to build your feedback from a third party, such as Bizrate (http://www.bizrate.com).

"You could also just highlight your eBay success directly, though this is tricky—you may wish to carefully segment your eBay sales from your website sales. Many multichannel retailers use eBay for their end-of-life or bargain basement stock, selling

Figure 7-2. Make your website a destination by offering incentives and special deals.

© David Yaskulka, CEO of Blueberry Boutique.

near or even below cost. In return, they try to use eBay to grow their customer base from eBay and drive it to their own website."

One area on the website, Blueberry Consulting, explores the idea of *strategic philanthropy*—the use of charity auctions to promote the company's reputation, build goodwill, and gain attention.

"We also use higher-profile charity auctions on eBay to build a company reputation that crosses over to other channels. Our customers come to believe in us as not only a great seller but a good corporate citizen. That inspires them to keep with us. And frankly, helping a great nonprofit along the way inspires us to keep with us!"

Deciding What to Sell: Finding the Right Venues for Unusual Commodities

Selling through your own website gives you an important base from which to offer a more varied and extensive variety of items for sale than you ever could on eBay. Once you have your eBay business thriving and your website developed, you can use those venues to sell your core line of products—such as clothing, electronics items, or sporting goods, for instance. But from time to time, you might come across something unusual. Perhaps one of your neighbors comes to you with an unusual item to sell on consignment—a piece of property, or a financial instrument. If you sell on behalf of others, or if you have some unusual things you want to sell for yourself, it pays to know about some venues to sell them—and occasionally, the best place to make them available is outside of eBay.

Government Sales: Liquidating Seized Property

There is a real estate section on eBay, where a few state governments liquidate their seized property. Nevertheless, if you have high-ticket items like homes, timeshares, cars, and other assets to sell, you might want to offer them on a specialty site like Bid4assets.com.

Bid4Assets.com (http://www.bid4assets.com) performs identity verification on each of its sellers to encourage bidders to bid on high-ticket items without encountering fraud. Governmental agencies often require that bidders be qualified—in other words, checked out beforehand to make sure their bid is serious. Bidders on sales of items being offered by the government need to place a deposit for each auction beforehand. If a bidder does not win, the deposit is refunded.

Bid4Assets is particularly popular with government agencies, which need to unload unclaimed property and lots of other assets. If you work for a government agency and you have real estate or personal property to sell, Bid4Assets.com has extensive experience with government regulations. It points sellers to a task order form they can fill out to request that Bid4Assets.com handle their sale.

You can go on this site and sell merchandise as varied as:

- Fleet/Luxury vehicles
- Lab equipment
- Computers
- Furniture

In summer 2005, Bid4Assets.com handled the auction of a mansion seized by the U.S. Marshal's Office when its owner was sentenced to 137 years in prison on racketeering and child molestation charges. It also conducted the sale of a lock purported to be the one used by the Watergate burglars in 1972. But you don't have to have notable items or seized property to sell on the site. Search the listings of jewelry, collectibles, furniture, and household goods offered on the site. You'll find a wide variety of items that have bids and get reasonable selling prices. Bid4Assets is a well-established site, especially because of its connections with governmental agencies. The business it gets from various government offices means it is a stable and reputable marketplace for individual sellers and small businesses, too.

Sale of Financial Instruments

The term *financial instrument* makes it sound like you're selling musical dollar bills, and in fact, selling them successfully can be music to your ears. You won't find financial instruments on eBay. These aren't musical dollar bills, but they are things like:

- Liens
- Note/loan portfolios
- Debt collections
- Receivables

Your assets don't go online immediately. Bid4Assets.com tells sellers to allow one to two days for "quality assurance review" to make sure you are the legitimate owner of what you plan to sell. You must submit a copy of your proof of ownership to the site if you offer something that you value at more than $1,000. You are also required to provide other information such as appraisals, plat maps, and photographs that will help buyers decide whether or not to place a bid.

Financial instruments sell quite well on Bid4Assets.com. The marketplace, at this writing, is allowing the sell-through rates on all categories on its site to be published on AuctionBytes (http://www.auctionbytes.com). The sell-through rates for the first week of October 2005 indicated that all the financial instruments offered on Bid4 Assets.com that week were sold. The following other categories had good sell-through rates, too:

- Apparel & Accessories: 41 percent
- Artwork: 35 percent
- Coins & Stamps: 63 percent
- Computer Equipment: 37 percent
- Financial Instruments & IP: 100 percent
- Jewelry: 65 percent
- Real Estate: 60 percent
- Sports Memorabilia: 100 percent

- Timeshares: 59 percent
- Toys & Games: 33 percent

While it's likely that many of the sales reported here are coming from government liquidations and the sale of seized property, they still indicate that buyers who use Bid4Assets trust the site and are willing to place bids on a large percentage of the items offered—something that can't be said for other auction marketplaces.

Deciding How to Sell: Exploring New Sales Techniques

There are many different auction formats on eBay. And, at this writing, it recently purchased the Internet telephony company Skype, a purchase that carries with it the promise of real-time voice communications between eBay members. But its Live Auctions site (the result of a purchase made several years ago) isn't nearly as popular as the regular auction site. You might be better off turning to specialized auction sites if you have especially valuable jewelry to sell, or if you have a valuable and unusual object that is visually interesting and a video presentation would be far better than taking ten to fifteen separate photos of the object. You can find these and other offbeat ways of connecting with prospective buyers on specialized auction sites.

Three-Minute Live Auction Excitement: Bidz.com

The Live Auctions area of eBay does get some visitors, but it certainly isn't the most user-friendly part of eBay's universe site—especially for people who have something to sell and who aren't already in the trade. You have to be a licensed dealer to put anything up for auction; if you aren't, you need to consign your item to a registered dealer. The dealer will sell in large quantities called lots, and the bidding goes by at lightning speed.

Bidz.com (http://www.bidz.com) takes the live auction concept to a new level and makes it accessible to individuals like you and me who aren't necessarily dealers in antiques and collectibles. One idea behind the site is simple: Many people don't like to bid on online auctions until the last minute anyway. Why not hold the sale on a last-minute basis so bidders don't have up to a week or more for that "last minute" to come and the sale to end? When you connect to the site's home page, you are greeted by a group of sales that are going to end in the next few minutes—and because the site is configured in such a way that it refreshes your Web browser contents, you can see the time for the sale tick down, second by second.

You can list items for three to seven days on Bidz. However, one of the most intriguing parts of the site is the category called Three-Minute Auctions. Sales last only three minutes; however, there's a big problem. There's no explanation on the site as to how individual sellers can put up their items for sale in this particular category. The site Epinions.com posts a number of negative comments about the site, such as:

- Comparison prices are listed for each item that supposedly suggest the retail price, but there's no way to check that these prices are accurate.
- There is no feedback system on the site.
- Most of the merchandise sold on Bidz.com is of poor quality (at least in the opinion of the Epinions posters).
- Customer service can be slow to respond, or does not respond at all.

 Note: The website Bidz.com charges flat fees for conducting sales. You are charged $1 for each listing, and if your item sells, you are charged a Final Value Fee of 10 percent of the final sale price. You should only sell items on Bidz that you really want to sell, regardless of the price. All sales start with an opening bid of $1. There are no reserve prices, and no starting bids that you can choose yourself.

Watch Out for Fly-By-Nights

Not all of the sites that exist off eBay are reputable. The site mentioned previously, Bidz.com, has some innovative features, but there are plenty of caution flags as well. In the course of looking for marketplaces where you sell specialty items, you're bound to run into lots of sites that seem to be out to get your personal information. One bargain real estate site I visited attempted to get my e-mail address on the very first page. I entered a bogus address, and was taken not to a page where real estate was actually listed, but one that immediately asked for my contact information and my credit card number before anything else. At that point, I moved elsewhere.

By all means avoid sites that require you to disclose sensitive personal information right off the bat. You should, at the very least, be able to shop for items on a site without making any commitment beforehand.

Fishing for Buyers at Reverse Auctions

Several sites promote reverse auctions—sales in which buyers post ads describing items they want. It's up to the sellers to respond with offers. If more than one seller responds, the buyer is in the happy situation of having prospective suppliers compete. The best-known reverse auction services (at least, the ones that have the highest profile through advertising) include Priceline.com, which specializes in travel, and LendingTree, which specializes in mortgages and other loans.

If nothing else, browsing through the ads on eWanted.com (http://www.ewanted .com) gives you an idea of what kinds of merchandise are in high demand—demand that is so high people will go beyond searching auctions and actively put out ads seeking those same items. There's a chance that you might find someone who is posting an advertisement for something you actually have for sale, of course.

Adding Video to Your Auctions: EZ2Stream.com

If you are willing to pay a $14.99 per month fee, you can use your Webcam and microphone to create a video presentation of the items you have for sale. When you see the example video on the EZ2Stream.com website (http://www.ez2stream.com), you immediately understand the value of including video instead of (or perhaps along with) a series of still photos of your items for sale: a set of hands holds the item to be sold and turns it around before the camera so each side is visible. Immediately, the viewer has a point of reference from which to judge the size of the item, which is something you don't always get with still photos. As a seller, you are also able to display all sides of the item in a matter of seconds. Rather than having to take six or eight photos and post them online, you post a single video file. By including video, you make yourself stand out from the crowd and show buyers that you are willing to go through some extra expense and effort to include video of what you have to sell.

In this chapter, you learned about some innovative ways to sell your items that become available to you when you look around the Internet for new places to sell. It's all about making profits, and profits are maximized when the merchandise you have to offer is of especially high value. You'll learn the ins and outs of selling large and high-value equipment and other items in Chapter 8.

CHAPTER **8**

Selling Off High-Value Assets and Equipment

Like eBay, most other online auction sites work best when you have something small to sell. Golfballs are the classic example. Websites like Golfballs.com thrive because their product is relatively inexpensive, easy to ship, and comes in many varieties.

What do you when the merchandise you have to sell fits none of those categories? In other words, you have a large and expensive item you need to sell, and you are unable to reach buyers through traditional outlets such as the local paper. You know there is a market for that thresher, bulldozer, or boat somewhere in the world, but you're not sure how to get your item before the people who need it.

Although eBay allows you to sell vehicles and heavy machinery such as farm and construction equipment, imagine the selling fees on an item that is worth, say, $22,000. (You don't have to imagine; for vehicles, the fees typically range from $60 to $80; for business and industrial equipment, the insertion fee is $20 and the Final Value Fee is 1 percent of the closing value, with a maximum fee of $250. Not only that, but your buyers then have to either pick the item up in person or possibly pay hundreds of dollars to have it shipped.) Other auction sites specialize in sales of heavy equipment; they have lower fees, attract specialized buyers, and will even help with the process of listing and shipping. You just have to make sure you prepare what you have for sale and that you present it in a way that prospective buyers will find attractive.

What You Need to Know About Selling Heavy Equipment

The bigger the item, the bigger the problem when something isn't described correctly or the buyer is dissatisfied in some way. It is one thing to have a customer return a piece of clothing in the mail because it doesn't fit. It is quite another when you ship a two-ton vehicle and the buyer decides not to accept it for some reason. You need to make sure everything works properly the first time.

Inspections

You should get the vehicle or other piece of equipment inspected before you sell it, and you should have the inspection report available for people to read online. A site like IronPlanet (http://www.ironplanet.com) has trained inspectors who will evaluate your equipment onsite and add their report to your listing. The U.S. General Services Administration also provides an inspection form through its website (http://w3.gsa .gov/web/c/newform.nsf/0/12DEA1036CFF1C7085256521004BAEA1? OpenDocument).

 Tip: If you manage a fleet of vehicles and expect to sell them online at some point, consider using the Vehicle Record System or Fleet Vehicle Record System to track their maintenance history. Having such records available to sellers (not to mention the IRS) will come in handy. Find out more about these products on the K-Jon Software LLC site (http://www.kjon.com).

Photos

The bigger the item, the more photos you need to take. If you take photos of two sides of a vehicle, people are going to ask you for photos of the remaining two sides so they can assure themselves that dents and other flaws aren't being concealed. You might want to include links to photos of the same model in new condition, to allow comparison.

When you create a Premium Ad on the Point2UsedIron website, you have the ability to list as many as eight photos of your equipment. The photos are presented in thumbnail format, as shown in Figure 8-1. Click on a thumbnail, and a full-size image appears on the right.

A related site, Point2Homes (http://www.point2homes.com, shown in Figure 8-2), offers real estate for sale. Roger Noujeim of the parent company, Point2Technologies, says the site is growing rapidly with some five hundred new listings added everyday. "It displays listings from thirty-seven countries and is the world's first unified real estate search site that is fully controlled by real estate agents."

Figure 8-1. Be sure to include multiple photos of your heavy equipment for sale.

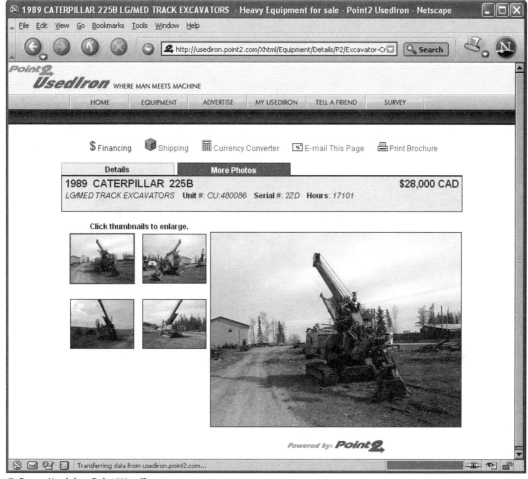

© Roger Noujeim, Point2UsedIron.

Tax Advantages

If you are selling off business equipment for a capital gain, your transaction may qualify as a tax-free exchange. This type of transaction is provided for in U.S. Internal Revenue Code section 1031. A tax-free exchange allows you to defer the federal income tax you owe after the sale of a piece of equipment if the money made by the sale is being used to purchase a replacement property. In order to qualify for a tax-free exchange, you must use a qualified intermediary, purchase the replacement asset within a certain amount of time, and the new asset must be of "like kind" to the asset that was sold. Check with your accountant if you have one.

Another first-class site for information about exchanges is the Federation of Ex-

Figure 8-2. This site is becoming increasingly popular for buying and selling real estate in Canada and the United States.

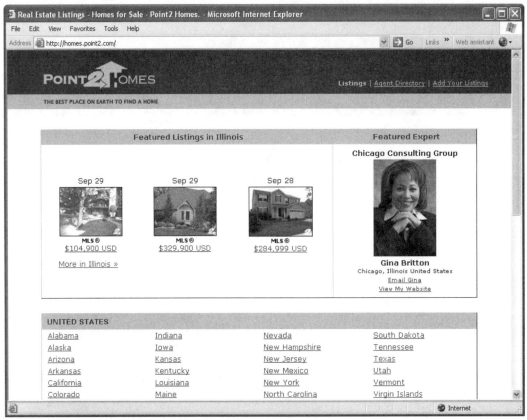

© Point2 Realty Solutions.

change Accommodators (http://www.1031.org). This site provides a listing of qualified intermediaries, essentially the people who hold the money until the transaction is completed, and breaks down the different kinds of tax-free exchanges in a clear and simple manner.

The Title

Some sites, like IronPlanet, will hold the title for you when you agree to have them sell it on consignment. You will need to either sign the title and send it to the site before the auction or send the unsigned title with a notarized power of attorney form. The form will authorize the auction site to sign the form for you after the sale, and it will only apply to one piece of equipment at a time. Unless you have a compelling reason to choose the power of attorney form, it's faster and simpler to sign the title and send it by insured mail. Talk to your local IronPlanet representative for advice if you're not sure what to do. Go to the Sell Your Construction Equipment Quickly and Easily page (http://www.ironplanet.com/sell/how2sell.shtml) and choose your home state from the drop-down list on the left-hand side of the page.

 Note: If you don't have the title to the vehicle or machinery, you will probably have to get a manufacturer's statement of origin (MSO) in order to sell it online. Also called a manufacturer's certificate of origin (MCO), this document was originally created to help simplify international trade that has now become a part of online business. You'll need to contact the manufacturer to get this document, and since the manufacturer needs to get the certificate from the state, allow plenty of time to acquire your MSO before putting your equipment up on the listings.

Refurbishing

Some businesses that deal in used machinery and lab equipment need to take the time to refurbish it. Medical equipment can fetch high prices, but only if it is in good condition. ReadyMedical does this as an eBay Store (http://stores.ebay.com/READY-MEDICAL). This business has employees in its warehouse who take the time to reupholster and repair equipment so that it is in "like new" condition when sold. This will obviously create a longer interval between the time you list an item and the day you receive payment, so don't try to sell well-used goods if you're in a hurry.

Marketplaces for Vehicles and Heavy Equipment

Sites that specialize in selling construction equipment and other sizeable assets take into account the fact that their clients may not be Internet-savvy. These sites often provide customer service representatives who can be reached by toll-free telephone numbers and who can explain exactly what sellers need to do to create a sales description. You know all about sales descriptions—but if a construction company or an individual gives you a forklift or a boat to sell on consignment, you might not know how to handle the title transfer or the shipping, for instance. If that is the case, it makes sense to choose a marketplace that already has a full set of resources to help sellers, such as the ones listed next.

IronPlanet

IronPlanet (http://www.ironplanet.com) is the leading auction site for heavy equipment in the United States. The site holds two types of sales:

1. *Featured (Consignment) Auctions.* These auctions are held every two weeks where equipment is sold from all over the United States. Sellers place their items on consignment with IronPlanet, which then conducts an inspection at your place of business and posts the report and photos online two weeks before the auction. IronPlanet markets the equipment and answers buyer's questions for you, accepting bids on your behalf. Once the auction is over, the title is transferred, and IronPlanet takes its commission, which can range between 6.4 and 12.5 percent of the final sales price. The buyer arranges for the transportation of the equipment. It's a good model and it's been very successful.

2. *Owner Auctions.* Owners who want to create their own sales listings and deal directly with buyers can create their own descriptions. Owner auctions are held on a daily basis.

There are two important differences between owner auctions and featured auctions. Owner auctions are held on the seller's schedule; they can be put up for sale at any time. Featured auctions are held every two weeks. The other difference is the listing fee: in featured auctions, the owner is not charged a listing fee unless the equipment sells. In owner auctions, the owner is charged a nonrefundable listing fee. For inspected equipment, the listing fee is $500 for a single item and $425 per piece for multiple items. For uninspected equipment, the listing fee is $75.

IronPlanet has a strong industry presence, allying themselves with some of the largest construction equipment companies in the world. The site's representatives also regularly attend conventions and trade shows, seeking new customers.

There are two key reasons to use IronPlanet as the auction site for your property. The first is the inspection process. IronPlanet sends trained appraisers to you to prepare the report on the equipment, and in fact, you don't have to move the equipment at all during the whole auction process. IronPlanet's reputation is trusted, and buyers are comfortable relying on its assessment of the equipment's condition, so you will receive the full value for your listing. The second reason is the knowledge and assistance that IronPlanet provides for the sale itself, helping you navigate the title transfer and tax ramifications of each sale with experienced professionals. You want to know what you're doing with expensive merchandise and IronPlanet can help.

Bid4Assets

As mentioned in Chapter 7, this site can auction just about anything, but it specializes in high-value assets such as real estate, vehicles, and even financial instruments. Federal and local governments uses Bid4Assets to auction off property. It is a truly all-inclusive auction site.

For sellers who have high-value vehicles or other property to sell, Bid4Assets offers three different types of sales formats. You're sure to find a format that fits your needs from the following options:

1. *Online Auction*—This is the traditional type of auction, where the highest bid wins after the reserve price is met, if there is a reserve price.
2. *BuyNow Auction*—Just as on eBay, if the buyer pays the BuyNow price, the auction ends immediately, but if a bid is placed first, the option to BuyNow disappears.
3. *Sealed Bid Auction*—An auction where buyers submit sealed bids to the seller for review. The seller reserves the right to accept or reject bids based on his or her own criteria.

If you're not sure what your item is worth, it makes sense to offer it in the traditional online auction format. If you are definite about the price you need to get for the item and don't want to let it go for a lower amount, choose the BuyNow auction format. If you want control over who makes a purchase, choose the Sealed Bid auction (but be prepared to receive fewer bids because of the secrecy involved).

Because the assets sold on this site are often expensive, there are higher fees to purchase Bid4Assets's premium services. Consider the following services:

- *Featured Auction*—Your listing appears on the homepage along with other auction listings throughout the day: $150 per week
- *Special Opportunity*—Your auction is listed in the Special Opportunity column on the right side of the homepage: $400 per week
- *Featured Auction/Live on the Auction Block*—Your auctions are featured prominently in the appropriate category of the website: $50 to $150 per week

There are also two package deals that include two or three of these ads together at a reduced rate. Because of the expensive fees, you should be certain that your item's value merits this much attention, but don't be too cautious. Spending a little to market your item could set up that bidding war you've always wanted.

Because of its partnership with government agencies, Bid4Assets serves a community of serious buyers. Typically, you'll find that many of the businesses that sell on Bid4Assets also buy there, such as Neimans Jewelry. Private collectors and investors of every kind come to the site, so you can trust that your item will be noticed here. Giving high-value items good exposure is why Bid4Assets is worth the higher-than-average fee structure (8 to 10 percent of the sale price) and worth investing time and energy in the description and maintenance of the item.

TraderOnline.com

TraderOnline.com (http://www.traderonline.com) is a collection of twenty websites that offer vehicles and equipment classified ads. These sites see millions of visitors every week, so this is a very high-exposure site. Sellers place ads with the site that matches their listing, and purchase an ad package that varies from the simple description-and-a-photo to the featured-item-six-photo-bold-text extravaganza.

The primary advantage of using TraderOnline is that all the advertisements are shared by all twenty sites, so you simply reach more buyers out there than with a single site. TraderOnline is owned by a company that publishes advertising magazines (such as Cycle Trader, Equipment Trader, Truck Trader, and so on), so your ad can run in print as well and reach buyers who don't go online. There is a large collectors and specialized vehicles market on this site, and your unusual 1960s convertible will receive more attention than on a more general site.

PlaneBid.com

This auction site devoted solely to airplanes is small but unique. PlaneBid.com (http://www.planebid.com) was launched as a marketplace where sellers and buyers could meet without intermediaries to save money and time for both parties. There are no fees to list and sell here, and the buyers and sellers make all arrangements for inspection, pricing, and shipping among themselves. Although an auction site, most of the listings are at a fixed price, and you get the sense that the people who use PlaneBid already know what their vehicles are worth. PlaneBid can help you find a qualified aircraft appraiser to assess the value of your plane, but the site does not require it. This is a good, simple site for aircraft professionals.

Other Sites

The websites mentioned in this section are only a few examples of online venues buying and selling construction equipment and other big vehicles. Table 8-1 provides pointers to other sites that specialize in construction equipment, building supplies, and other big commodities.

Table 8-1. Online construction equipment marketplaces.

Site	URL	What It Does
AssetLine.com	http://www.assetline.com	A global marketplace for construction equipment; content is in Japanese and English; provides inspection services.
digitalEPC.com	http://www.digitalepc.com/index2.asp	An online marketplace for surplus construction equipment and materials; listing is free; sales commission is 5 percent.
EC Online	http://www.econline.com	A sourcing site for electrical contractors: you can sell power supplies and many other electrical components.
Point2UsedIron	http://usediron.point2.com	This Canadian site has been buying and selling used construction equipment since the late 1990s. You can create five premium listings with eight photos each for no charge.

Lab and Medical Equipment

Medical equipment can be expensive to purchase new, which is why many hospitals and other institutions purchase refurbished equipment from some of the venues shown next. For sellers who are able to find a supply of medical equipment, this is a potentially lucrative category. The key is condition, because most medical institutions require used equipment to be in top condition and safe to use before they'll consider buying it.

LabX

For used medical and scientific equipment, LabX (http://www.labx.com) is the premier site on the Internet. With four hundred thousand visitors a month, this site offers auctions and for sale postings for every variety of lab equipment. There are no special requirements to sell lab equipment online, although you should make sure that your state doesn't have any special laws regarding the shipping of your item. Except for its focus on scientific hardware, LabX is much like any other niche auction site. It offers listing enhancements, the full range of selling styles and categories of auctions, and assistance in organizing your ad to best effect. The major strength of this site is that so far, it is pretty much the only game in town. Everyone comes here and everyone buys here. Take good photos of the item and make sure you're describing it accurately and succinctly, and take the time to communicate fully with the buyer and make sure it is what he or she needs.

DotMed.com

DotMed.com (http://www.dotmed.com) is a classified site where you can post used medical equipment for sale, buy parts, and start auctions. You can also post your wants for parts and equipment, which is a handy resource for sellers who want to match their inventory to customer need. Posting is free, with the option of purchasing a featured posting or starting an auction for a small fee.

Most sellers purchase some form of premium exposure on this site, which sees approximately two thousand new listings a month. DotMed.com offers a free certification process to boost buyer confidence and many companies use the site to advertise their services and merchandise. This is not a large site, but it is reliable and serves a genuine need.

 Tip: Another medical equipment marketplace, MEDmarketplace (http://www.medmarketplace.com), lets sellers keep their listings online for up to thirty days. Sellers are charged a flat monthly fee rather than a sales commission.

Industry Directories

If you sell medical or laboratory equipment, you have to take into account the fact that many hospital purchasing agents or administrators aren't automatically going to look for you on eBay or one of the auction sites listed in this chapter. You'll cast the widest possible net if you make sure your company is listed in industry directories. These are lists of medical suppliers that hospital and laboratory managers turn to when they need a piece of equipment. Here are a couple examples:

- Lisa's World of Health & Wellness Industry Directory (http://www.lisa.com/trade/index.html)
- OBGYN.net Vendor Database (http://www.obgyn.net/cfm/suppliers/suppliers.cfm)

In this chapter, you learned about options for selling heavy and expensive equipment on a variety of specialty websites. All the types of merchandise mentioned in this chapter, including airplanes, construction equipment, and medical equipment, are sold occasionally on eBay. However, by choosing a specialty website, you target your audience more narrowly. In some cases, you can obtain personal help with shipping and other issues. And you take advantage of inspection services. It's all a matter of matching your merchandise to the clientele that frequents your chosen marketplace—a subject explored in greater detail in Chapter 9.

CHAPTER **9**

Connect with Collectors at Specialized Auction Sites

You probably know from the auction sales you've done to this point that selling is a matter of matching each item you have to offer with someone who has been looking for just that item—or something exactly like it. If you are lucky enough to find a collector who feels passionately about something and needs exactly that item to fit into his or her collection, you'll get eager bidding for your item, and higher prices than you probably ever imagined. This is what happened with the woman who found the can of Clipper Beer, which had been sitting under her house since it was constructed in the 1940s. She found some collectors on eBay who needed this rare can to complete their beer can collections, and they drove the final sale price up to an amazing $19,000.

By moving your sales activities beyond eBay to auction sites that cater to a special niche market, you increase your chances of finding the collectors, enthusiasts, or devotees you've been looking for. In some cases (like firearms and alcohol) you have to search for niche marketplaces, because eBay won't allow the sale of these items unless they have value as antiques. This chapter discusses some of the reasons to sell with a niche auction site, what you need to run a successful business on such a site, and a few examples of auction sites devoted to specific collector's markets.

Why Move to a Specialized Auction Site?

Because eBay attracts collectors of all sorts, it's a safe bet that just about anyone who collects anything avidly has searched on eBay for items to round out their collections. Why take the trouble to learn new sales systems and try special niche auction sites? Here are some reasons to consider the move:

Some Collectors Prefer Their Niche Communities to eBay

A niche auction site often has a small but devoted community of buyers and sellers who prefer to support each other's businesses first before going to eBay. Items you post on these sites will get a more thorough look from the buyer than on eBay, and the feedback you receive from purchasers, whether approving or not, will be more constructive than the cursory "Good, timely" comment that makes up most eBay feedback. This means you can customize your business and inventory much faster through the niche site than through eBay, thereby saving time and energy.

Niche auction sites often have additional features that are useful to the online business owner. News and industrial press releases related to your market can be found there, and discussion forums allow you to get a better sense of what other sellers are buying. Personally, I collect fountain pens, and I'm familiar with a niche site called PenBid.com (http://www.penbid.com) (see Figure 9-1). PenBid's members occasionally sell on eBay, but they know each other well from attending pen collectors' conventions around the world, and they want their own place to congregate and share their thoughts about their shared passion. When they connect to the PenBid website, they get much more than a place to buy and sell pens. The link COMMUNITY takes them to an area of the site (http://www.penbid.com/Auction/Community.asp, shown in Figure 9-1) where the editorial director Michael Fultz, who is a well-known collector, has assembled a wealth of background information for pen collectors, including the following:

- An archive of articles for "insiders" on pen- and writing-related topics
- A bookstore full of books for collectors that have been chosen by the PenBid staff
- A set of member links to other collectors' websites
- A link that enables visitors to subscribe to the PenBid newsletter
- A link to community forums where pen collectors can answer questions from newcomers and share their thoughts on the state of the pen industry

Used wisely, information like this can tell you when to post a specific item for sale and when to wait on it. Discussion forums also can sharpen your use of the site itself, and give you early warning of problem buyers from other sellers.

Using multiple niche auction sites is an exciting opportunity to streamline your sales. Sometimes eBay sellers find that entire categories of their inventory aren't selling well. A presence on one or more niche sites can give you flexibility in sales, and even aid in the organization of your inventory.

Figure 9-1. Niche auction sites frequently offer community resources for their members.

© Penbid.com, Inc.

Some Niche Sites Charge Lower Sale Fees than eBay

You probably won't be surprised, given eBay's fee increases, to discover that smaller niche auction sites are often cheaper than eBay for the seller. Consider Ticket-Auction.net (http://www.ticketauction.net), a site that guarantees its fees will be half of eBay's. I have even found sites that don't charge any sales fees at all, such as Writerspace (http://writerspace.com/auctions), a book auction site. It's possible that the dollar or two you save per transaction at these sites will provide you with your only profit on the sale, especially for small-ticket items like used books.

Your Merchandise Stands out Better in a Small Venue than a Large One

No matter what kind of rare or unusual item you find, it is either posted on eBay or will be in a week. On a small niche auction site, your unusual and high-quality merchandise has a better chance of being noticed by both buyers and sellers. This can lead to your business developing a reputation on the site, with buyers maintaining greater loyalty to your business and sellers referring customers to you for items they consider your specialty. You can use your good reputation to refer shoppers to your website, where you can sell to them directly in a way that builds customer loyalty. (See Chapter 7 for more information on the importance of developing a fully functional e-commerce website.)

What Do You Need to Start Selling on a Niche Auction Site?

Every e-commerce website, including eBay, requires you to climb a learning curve. But niche sites are less crowded and generally less complex to use. Ideally, it will help your sales and your morale if you are prepared to use the niche auction site you have chosen immediately, rather than spending many frustrating days learning its policies, responding to vague technical questions from buyers, and generally feeling like it was a mistake to leave eBay's comforting familiarity. This is why you shouldn't begin working with a new auction site until you have thoroughly equipped yourself with all the information and techniques that you will need. Get the following "ducks" in a row before you start.

Knowledge of the Field

You don't have to be an expert to sell on a niche auction site, but it helps if you are at least familiar with the specialized lingo that the enthusiasts who frequent these sites use to talk to one another. Here are a few examples of special terms collectors on these sites use:

- *Appellation* and *horizontal collection* are terms used on WineBid.com.
- What are *trade beads*? What are *jewelry findings*? It will help if you know such terms before you start selling on Just Beads.
- *Slip cap, plunger filler*, and *brassing* are terms casually used by pen collectors who frequent Penbid.com.

In fact, WineBid.com has a full page full of wine and auction terms (http://www .winebid.com/buy_wine/wine_terms/index.aspx) that can help you understand the often mystifying terms that are thrown around by dedicated collectors.

You don't necessarily have to be a collector to sell on a niche auction site. But if you manage to turn up an especially rare bottle of wine or a fine old fountain pen that's covered with gold or sterling silver, your description will sound more knowledgeable if you do a little research beforehand. If knowledgeable collectors feel you are an amateur, they will try to bid as low as possible in order to win, because they're sure you don't know what the item is worth. If you sound like you know what the item is worth, they're more likely to bid higher at the outset—even if you don't have any idea of the item's true value.

Knowledge of Site Policies

It's vital that you master a niche site's selling policies and fees as soon as possible, so that you can start building a good reputation and a returning customer base. Most sites are very helpful toward this end, because they want to avoid problems as much as you do. Also, do some research into the common practices on the site, like shipping and payment trends. Many auction buyers use the payment service PayPal, and will avoid your listings if you don't offer it. The auction site may also have unusual standards you need to meet—for example, GunBroker.com (http://www.gunbroker .com) requires you to check the license of the gun dealer who makes a purchase from you against the GunBroker.com database of approved sellers after each sale to make sure the people who buy from you have legitimate business reasons for doing so.

Familiarity with the Site's Community

This is the area of business knowledge that will probably take the longest to acquire, but in the long run, it can turn out to be the most profitable. The more you learn about the kinds of buyers the site serves, the more you will be able to tailor your descriptions and listings to their needs and wants. Individual collectors pay a great deal of attention to detail, so they will appreciate a lengthy factual description of an item without extravagant prose and exclamation points. Dealers or small businesses can be more complicated to deal with, but they will often be the source of that big sale you want. Pay attention to any requests or trends that appear on discussion boards. Sometimes, media events can bring amateurs to a site looking for a specific item, as happened with sales of Pinot Noir on WineBid.com after the release of the movie *Sideways*. Keep your inventory and business contacts as diverse as possible.

Examples of Niche Auction Sites to Visit

There are dozens of niche auction sites around the Internet. Many are listed in Appendix A. The sites listed next are only a small sampling of the options available to you. My assistant, Ben Huizenga, and I are personally familiar with these sites and have discovered that, in some cases, these sites let you sell items you simply couldn't sell on eBay.

WineBid.com

Founded in 1996, WineBid.com is the largest online auction site for wine, with more than thirty thousand registered users. Buyers can use a user-friendly search engine to locate auction lots of wines, which they may either purchase or track on their Lot Tracker page. WineBid.com offers shoppers an Autobid feature that resembles eBay's proxy bidding system, so that buyers aren't glued to their computers day and night. Buyers pay their bid, a premium fee, and insurance, to cover accidents in handling or shipping. WineBid.com maintains a staff of experienced professionals at climate-controlled facilities to ensure the quality of its product. WineBid.com's weekly auctions have more than four thousand lots of consignment and rare wines.

Sellers have it even easier. A registered seller simply e-mails a consignment list to WineBid, which responds with an appraisal report of the wine's value. The seller arranges to ship the wine to WineBid a month before the auction, so that the lot may be inspected. The seller receives a detailed report on the progress of the auction, and a check thirty days after the auction's close.

The distinguishing feature of WineBid.com for a seller is the turn-around time between shipping your merchandise and receiving payment. Two months is standard, and the time involved can take longer. However, given the complexity of shipping a perishable and delicate substance like wine, WineBid.com's facilities and expertise are invaluable. Once you get used to the longer process, you'll see how buyers, especially in this market, appreciate the extra time and care spent to ensure a quality product.

Penbid.com

Penbid has become known as the premier Internet auction site for writing instruments. One of Forbes's Best of the Web, PenBid offers fountain and antique pens at prices that range from two dollars to several hundred dollars. This site was launched in 1997, and it is extremely easy to search. The site's selection is well organized and clear, with the major categories of pens tabulated for quick searching. The Penbid community section is a great strength to this site, with articles by experts and an active collector's forum. This site is an excellent example of the advantages a smaller niche auction site can offer over eBay.

Sellers on PenBid have many of the options available to sellers on eBay to make their merchandise stand out. A seller can add a thumbnail photograph of the item, have the text of the item bold-faced or highlighted, or even list the auction as a featured or premiere auction. These options all come with fees, ranging from $.25 to $24.95, but the chance to draw increased attention to your auction is well worth it. Penbid also offers the chance to leave and receive feedback—a useful tool to avoid problem customers and to identify weaknesses in your sales technique.

PenBid is not a very large site, with listings that include about a thousand items at any given time, but its organization and community make it worth your time. Don't expect huge numbers of sales, but do expect to receive the full value of your offers.

JustBeads.com

This is the top bead auction site on the Internet. Launched in 1999, Just Beads (http://www.justbeads.com, shown in Figure 9-2) offers a comprehensive array of features to the bead seller and buyer, supported by an active community of enthusiasts. Sellers pay a small fee to list an item, can purchase optional premium services to make their item more visible, and then pay a small (usually between 2 and 6 percent) sales commission rate. Feedback ratings help protect the seller from problem customers, and a chat forum provides a convenient place for buyers to list their needs.

Just Beads is a true collector's site, so be sure you've done your homework before selling there. *Lampwork* and *annealing* are just a couple of the terms you'll need to become familiar with as a seller. With such a visual product, having good pictures of your listings is crucial, and the more succinct the description the better.

Just Beads recommends a piece of software called Auction Tamer, which is an auction management tool that can support several different sites, including eBay. Unless you're seriously getting swamped with the details of your business, I'd recommend against this software. The features it offers are largely ones that organized people can perform for themselves, like a countdown to when your auction ends. Some of the automated post-auction tools seem neat, like an automatically generated winning bidder form, but it's easy to set that up yourself on your home PC.

GunBroker.com

Firearms are one of the items that are prohibited on eBay unless they're being sold as antiques. If you have a firearm you want to sell, it's logical to turn to this venue, which bills itself as the largest online firearms auction site. GunBroker.com (http://www.gunbroker.com) auctions everything from modern rifles to antique pistols, including accessories and stuffed animal heads. This site is excellent at helping a seller learn the value of an item, linked to the Blue Book of Gun Values and also to a

Figure 9-2. This specialty site for bead enthusiasts includes discussion boards and notices of upcoming bead shows.

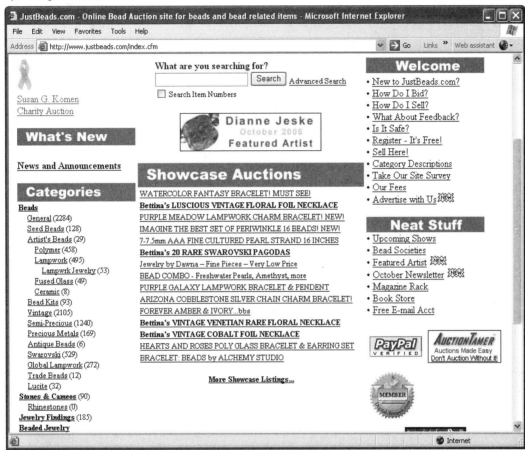

© JustBeads.com.

partner site that performs cheap appraisals. GunBroker is also meticulous about following the federal laws that govern gun sales.

 Note: Only federal firearms license (FFL) gun brokers buy from this site, and all sellers are required to verify these licenses with GunBroker.com before completing a sale.

The advantage to selling with GunBroker is its reliability. Firearms are difficult to sell online without help, and GunBroker provides it, along with an established network of clients. The condition of items is of first importance with this site, so take the time to learn about the details of muzzle-loaders, caliber sizes, and engraved holsters. Make sure your photographs are first-class, and include any details of the item's history that seem noteworthy.

Where the Booksellers Go: Abebooks.com

You probably already know about Amazon.com (see Chapter 12), but Amazon has its limitations. It's a convenient venue for textbooks and recent releases. But when it comes to obscure, rare, and long-out-of-print books, there's a better option.

Abebooks is not an auction site, but it *is* the largest online seller of used and rare books. Abebooks is where thousands of booksellers list their merchandise, so that the buyer can search all of the site's inventories through one engine. Almost 40 percent of all books bought online are bought here, so even if you don't use it to sell, you'll want to use it as an information resource to find the best price and match condition with other sellers. Sellers pay a flat monthly rate depending on the number of books they have listed, (4,000 to 10,000 would be $42), and then pay 8 percent of the selling price in commission. Abe's search engine is great, and its software for listing to its database is easy to use.

Online sales of books have become enormous in recent years, so competing successfully depends on knowing which books are worth listing and which aren't. Get to know the rare and unusual publishers, and learn about evaluating book condition. For example, that rare old *Tarzan* novel isn't worth nearly as much without its dust jacket. The number of books that you sell compared with the number of books you list should always be growing.

By using Abebooks and Amazon in tandem, you can come up with an accurate assessment of a book's value online, and an idea of how many copies are available. With time, you'll be able to avoid buying books that are always available, and narrow your inventory to the truly unusual items that dedicated collectors will be eager to buy from you.

When you change your approach to business from thinking of yourself as an eBay seller to regarding your operation as a full-fledged online business, you've got to take niche marketplaces into account. If you are already an enthusiastic collector, you'll not only find more buyers for what you have to sell, but you're quite likely to strike up some fruitful friendships as well. The Internet is all about connecting small, dedicated communities of individuals. That includes potential buyers in your own local community—a subject you'll examine in the next chapter.

CHAPTER **10**

Reaching Local Buyers

The ability to reach buyers around the world is one of the best things about online auctions. But there are times when you need to reach bidders across the street or across town rather than across the globe. The most obvious reason is when you have something big and bulky to sell such as a car, a piece of farm equipment, a major appliance, or a couch. It's not a piece of construction or medical equipment like the items covered in Chapter 8, but a single heavy household object. You either don't know how to ship the big item or don't want to bother with the considerable expense and trouble.

At one time, eBay used to have special resources for local buyers. The site offered special local versions of eBay that gathered together merchandise offered in various major cities in the United States. Now, in order to reach people in your own area, you need to specify your location in your listing and make it clear in the description that you want buyers to pick up their purchases in person. And you have to hope that buyers will search for what you have to offer by zip code, using the Advanced Search form. It just isn't reliable, so even the professional eBay drop-off store owners mentioned in Chapter 18 use Craigslist when someone has a couch to sell, for instance.

The ability to conduct transactions with people in your own neighborhood is one of the best reasons to try sales venues other than eBay. By placing simple classified ads on Craigslist or other sites, you can sell items that are hard to ship. If you specify that buyers have to pick up from you in person, you make them do the work after the transaction, not you; you save yourself the time and trouble of packing and shipping. You can also use Craigslist to offer your professional services, put up notices seeking personal items you've lost, and plenty of other things. This chapter examines options for local auctions that exist outside of eBay and how to use them to your advantage.

Pickup in Person: LiveDeal.com

At LiveDeal.com (http://www.livedeal.com), buyers search by location. Sellers don't want to deal with shipping. They offer their merchandise at a starting price, but they also invite buyers to make offers with them, just as at a garage sale or flea market. And, just as in those venues, it's up to the buyer and seller to negotiate shipping and payment. Picking up in person has many advantages for you, the seller, such as the following:

- You don't run the risk of having the shipper lose or damage merchandise in transit.
- You don't have to deal with insurance claims.
- You don't have to pack and haul your boxes to the shipper.
- You don't have to deal with postage mix-ups and mistakes, which can occur frequently on eBay—especially if you didn't estimate the shipping weight accurately before the sale. When you hand over an item in person, you know it was in good condition, so the buyer can't falsely claim that it was damaged in transit.

LiveDeal doesn't offer a payment service directly through its site, although you can list PayPal as a payment option on your listing if you're a verified seller. Negotiating with the buyer can take patience and time, and you might consider listing your payment guidelines along with the item. Many LiveDeal listings are as short as possible and contain no payment information. A typical set of guidelines might look like this:

- I accept PayPal (provide the e-mail address you use with PayPal).
- Escrow.com (http://www.escrow.com).
- Postal money orders.
- Western Union BidPay.
- Personal checks (but allow seven to ten days for checks to clear before shipping).

Stick with the payment services you're comfortable with, and kindly request that the buyer comply with your guidelines.

LiveDeal.com is simple to use. After taking a minute to register an account, you can immediately begin posting your items. The best part of working with this site is that there is no listing fee. LiveDeal.com offers a number of premiums to make your item more noticeable, but posting your item with a description and a photo is free. Listings are removed after thirty days on LiveDeal.com, but there is no charge for reposting an item. If you use a free Web-based e-mail account, like Yahoo!, or if you wish to be listed nationally, you will have to pay a $5 fee to have your identity verified with LiveDeal.com.

 Tip: LiveDeal describes its fees at http://www.livedeal.com/about/ fees.jsp. Notice the $.10 per image fee; you'll probably want to post images on another website and make links to them.

Selling Household Goods

The key to selling household goods on LiveDeal.com is learning to recognize what is worth posting and what isn't. Ideally, a pleased buyer will click the button that says SEE SELLER'S OTHER ITEMS, and you want to be sure that those other items look attractive. Take advantage of LiveDeal's first-photo-free policy, be honest about any defects in the product, and be willing to come down a little in the price. By far the most popular categories on LiveDeal.com are electronic appliances, stereo/computer hardware, and luxury items like watches and collectible coins. Make sure you're not posting anything that people can acquire more cheaply at the store next door.

Selling Household Pets

LiveDeal.com offers an entire category of merchandise that eBay does not: pets. You can list any type of pet or household animal here (such as the puppies shown in Figure 10-1), as well as pet services, such as grooming for dogs.

There are no special requirements for listing and selling the animals on LiveDeal .com, although most buyers will want to meet the pet in person and be satisfied as to its health and behavior before following through with the purchase. (However, many of the pet listings on the site include a shipping fee for buyers who simply want their animals sent to them rather than picking the pets up in person.) A detailed description of the pet is a good idea, including age, brief history, and any chronic problems.

 Note: Chapter 19 examines the ins and outs of using another offline sales venue: an auction in your local area held by a live auctioneer.

Just the Facts: Craigslist

Craigslist is a national phenomenon. The site was founded in 1995 by Craig Newmark, a programmer in San Francisco, California. Essentially, Craigslist is a commu-

Figure 10-1. LiveDeal allows breeders and other pet owners to advertise their animals online.

© LiveDeal Inc.

nity classifieds and forum page, with sections for jobs, housing, services, personals, and pretty much everything else. There are now 175 Craigslist sites, serving all 50 states and major cities in 34 countries. The site is a tremendous success, as evidenced by the following figures:

- 2.5 billion page views per month
- 10 million users per month
- 5 million classified ads and 1 million forum postings per month

The reasons for this popularity are straightforward. There are no pop-up or banner ads on Craigslist, there are no charges for posting an ad, and the listings are constantly refreshed by new users. The site is also designed for simplicity and efficiency, without any distracting graphic elements.

Craigslist became a for-profit site in 1999, but so far, the site has been able to maintain its simplicity by generating revenue from modest job posting fees in a few cities. It supports a nonprofit foundation that helps other nonprofits gain attention and organize events.

Craigslist's For Sale section is the third-most popular section of the site, so it is a great place to list those unwieldy items you want to sell. Craigslist suggests that you make sure the item you want to sell doesn't fall under any trade restrictions in your state. (For most users, this means not selling things that require a license, such as tobacco, alcohol, and firearms.) The listing process is fast and easy. You create a title for your posting, usually a simple statement of what you're selling, assign a price and a location, then create a more detailed description. People won't see your description without clicking on the title, so make sure your title is clear and straightforward and save the details for the description.

> **Caution:** Many individuals who post on Craigslist have a bad habit of using capital letters and exclamation marks to get attention, and the community of buyers generally looks down on that tactic. Be honest and friendly, and you will get all the responses you need.

After you finish your description, you enter your e-mail address to complete the posting. Craigslist can assign you an anonymous forwarding number so that your address is protected from casual viewing. You will receive an e-mail address from Craigslist to complete the posting, and you can edit the description and title at any time. Craigslist is different from most selling sites in not offering any kind of premium service to increase the visibility of your item, but that is part of why people come here, so enjoy not having to consider such options for a change.

There is no cost—I repeat, *no cost*—to post sale listings on Craigslist. The only fees for this site are for job postings in New York, San Francisco, and Los Angeles, and even in those cities the fees are below the industry standard. Craigslist also uses a popular "flagging" method to weed out spam and other ads that are outside their guidelines. Visitors to the site can flag an ad that they feel is miscategorized or otherwise inappropriate. Although Craigslist acknowledges that it removes some legitimate postings, so far the system had been very successful, with only 2 percent of flagged postings turning up as legitimate. This largely responsible, and free, use of feedback allows Craigslist to function as the free, populist site that it is.

> **Caution:** It might be tempting to post classified ads for that couch or coffee table on more than one classifieds site at the same time to cast the

widest net. If you do multiple listings, you run the risk of double-selling an item and incurring the wrath of a disgruntled buyer. It's more likely that you'll sell the item in one location and then have to remember that you had the same thing posted elsewhere so you can remove the listing early. If you don't remember, you could end up selling something that is no longer there. It's simplest to avoid trouble by selling one item in one venue at a time.

Yahoo! Classifieds

Yahoo! is one of the most popular websites, and if you already enjoy using its e-mail, yellow pages, and search services, you'll have no problem learning to use its classified ad service (http://classifieds.yahoo.com) as well.

Like other services on Yahoo!, Yahoo! Classifieds has its pros and cons. On the plus side, it's free for most household goods. You do have to pay a listing fee for certain categories, however. The classifieds categories listed in Table 10-1 carry fees for a thirty-day listing. You are assessed the fee whether or not your item sells.

The "For Sale" category is a fairly inclusive one. It means you can post basic (not featured) ads for things like antiques and collectibles, boats, books, computers, furniture, office supplies, pet supplies, and video games for free. As you might expect, a featured ad is placed prominently at the top of a Web page full of search results.

On the downside, it's not clear how many of your neighbors are going to turn to Yahoo! Classifieds in order to find your ad. Among tech-savvy individuals, Craigslist is highly popular. If you live in a rural area where relatively few locals have Internet access, they're not going to look on Craigslist or Yahoo! at all. You're better off using your local paper to reach them.

Table 10-1. Yahoo! Classifieds paid listings.

Category	Basic Ad	Featured Ad
Autos	$24.95	$34.95 (includes two free 21-day renewals)
For Sale	Free	$9.95
Residential Real Estate	$49.95	$62.90
Rentals	$34.95	$54.95
Pets	$12.95	$19.95
Commercial Real Estate	Price Varies	N/A

Note: Another downside to Yahoo! Classifieds is that the basic listings let you post only a single photo. Featured listings can include up to six photos.

Newspaper Classified Ads

Despite the popularity of the Web and the Internet, the fact remains that millions of people simply don't have any way of going online. Chances are you can name a few people off the top of your head who don't have an Internet connection at home or who just don't know anything about the Internet. They may not have the technical know-how to get connected, or they may not have the means to purchase a computer and get an account with an Internet provider. How do you reach this huge potential market of consumers in your area? One effective strategy is to use newspapers.

Newspapers are still a trusted and popular medium for selling big-ticket items such as homes, new or used cars, furniture, or major appliances. Many large cities have a selection of alternative weeklies that list classified ads as well, often for a cheaper rate than the big dailies, or even free. Pick up as many different kinds of papers as you can find, and read their classifieds to see if what you're selling is offered there.

Turning to Your Local Newspaper's Website

Every newspaper has a website these days, and most of them post their classifieds online as well as in print. Posting a classified ad is usually simple, but there are two basic things to keep in mind. Newspapers still run by deadlines, so get to know exactly what hour they close their classifieds postings for the next day. Also, the rate for ads is either by line or by word. Usually a paper offers a flat rate for a certain number of lines or words, and then an extra dollar or two per line or word after that. Learn to describe your item in the minimum amount of space, but don't leave out anything pertinent. Reading a few ads in the paper should give you the sense of how to write your posting.

The most important thing with running a classified ad is to check it immediately for typos and errors. One mistake on the telephone number or description and your work is wasted. Be aware of how long you've ordered the ad to run, and whether this is a good time of the week or year to sell your item. Most miscellaneous items for sale get the biggest response over the weekend from garage sale shoppers and the like, but vehicles do well throughout the week. Also, make sure you include a telephone number. It seems obvious, but you're trying to reach people who don't go online, so an e-mail address is worthless to them.

Turning to an Advertising Network

There are many advertising networks online, like the Advertising Network of Florida, (http://www.national-classifieds.com) that offer the chance to post your classified ad in many different newspapers all around your community. Usually these include the major dailies in your area, as well as many of the local or alternative weeklies. Each state, for example, can sell you classified space in newspapers on a daily, weekly, or monthly basis with prices adjusted accordingly.

Needless to say, using a large advertising network can only be justified if you are selling a truly expensive or exotic item, like a home or expensive industrial equipment. However, there are usually networks that can be tailored to your needs on a more modest level. For example, some statewide networks can place your ad just in campus and college newspapers, or just in the free weeklies around the state, at a reduced cost. You can use these networks to reach millions of people for a few hundred dollars, so it should be considered an extremely powerful weapon in your sales arsenal, worth using only when the potential gain is high.

If you really need to reach a nationwide audience with a single, simple ad, try the National Advertising Network (http://www.nationwideadvertising.com). They offer many different packages of advertising at fair rates, including the full national package that reaches more than ten thousand newspapers. This is certainly not the most expensive newspaper advertising offer, but it is quite possibly the most thorough, and you should bear it in mind for when your business really begins to expand.

Offering Your Professional Services

When it comes to some professions like psychiatry or medicine, the Web may not be the best choice. Consumers still turn to print media such as their local yellow pages when they are looking for professional help. As there are multiple yellow pages companies, you should shop around to compare prices and readership. Consider using an advertising agency that specializes in yellow pages ads to increase your exposure. If possible, keep track of how new customers reach your services. Your ad in the yellow pages should be one of their main reasons. Otherwise consider scaling back on the ad or eliminating it.

Online yellow pages are often popular, such as Yahoo! Yellow Pages (http://yp.yahoo.com), so don't ignore them entirely. You will probably not want to purchase advertising, but at least make sure that you are listed. There are also a large number of sites that let people post reviews about their experiences with different kinds of businesses, like Yelp.com. Many of these have very small databases, but it's an online phenomenon that seems to be growing, so it's probably worth your while to at least check if you are listed and see what people are writing about you. The way you present yourself online is important; one of the best ways to build trust is to partner with a big name company to host your storefront or your website, and options for finding a prominent host are described in Chapter 11.

PART **III**

Opening an Online Storefront

Partnering with a Big Name

When you're out shopping for an important household item, such as a refrigerator or other major appliance, how do you decide where to spend your money? Price is certainly a consideration; you're looking for the best deal possible. But when you set price aside, what do you look for? Chances are you want to shop with a retailer you can trust—a seller with a good reputation, known for providing customer service. Bigger and better-established sellers have extra benefits such as their own credit cards, rewards programs, and extended warranties, too.

It's the same with auction sites. Although there is nothing wrong with small, niche websites (like the ones described in Chapter 9) that aim for a narrowly defined clientele, when you choose a well-known organization, you get extra benefits you wouldn't find otherwise. You get access to customer service staff who might be difficult to reach on smaller sites; you also gain a reputation as a professional who is "worthy" of participating with the major players in the field.

This chapter examines options for expanding your sales operations beyond eBay while aligning yourself with some of the biggest names in e-commerce. You'll explore two well-known companies that streamline the process of setting up your own websites: Yahoo! and Microsoft. You'll also learn how to include your sales information in the shopping database maintained by Google's consumer search service Froogle. You'll even learn about eBay's ProStores option, in case you want to expand your eBay auction sales to eBay's website-hosting service. I'll explain why you might want to consider selling on each of these sites as well as potential problems to watch out for, too.

Setting Up Shop with Yahoo!

As I write this, Yahoo! is making some big moves in the online auction space. Although eBay may be dominant in the United States and Europe, Yahoo! is poised to become the dominant auction seller in all of Asia. Its Japanese version of Yahoo! Auctions already has 90 percent of market share in that country. In 2005, it purchased the Chinese auction site Alibaba (which is described in Chapter 21), which dominates the potentially huge Chinese market. What does this mean for you, the lone auction seller or small business manager hoping to start selling at auction? If you speak Japanese, you can start buying and selling on Yahoo!'s Japan auction site. The acquisition of Alibaba probably means that it will be progressively easier to interact with Chinese merchants as well as consumers, who number in the billions.

What is the main reason to consider Yahoo! Auctions as an alternative, or addition to, eBay auction sales? That is a reasonable question, given the fact that Yahoo! Auctions attracts far fewer buyers than eBay. There are two reasons: It doesn't cost anything to sell on Yahoo! Auctions; you aren't charged a listing fee or Final Value Fee. The second reason is that, when you sell on Yahoo!, you gain access to a network of related services that include:

- *The Yahoo! Newsgroups (http://groups.yahoo.com).* Yahoo! has a network of discussion groups that is lively and heavily used. It is free to set up a discussion group, and lots of people use it.

- *Yahoo! Shopping (http://shopping.yahoo.com).* If you sell consumer merchandise in bulk, you can submit your product listings so they can be included in this part of Yahoo!, which resembles an online shopping mall. You can submit listings to Yahoo! Shopping by going to http://searchmarketing.yahoo.com/shopsb/index.php and clicking the link PRODUCT SUBMIT in the left-hand column. You are assessed a small fee if someone clicks on a product listing on Yahoo! Shopping and goes to your site.

- *Yahoo! Classifieds (http://classifieds.yahoo.com).* See Chapter 10 for more information about this part of Yahoo!, which allows you to post a classified ad that you want local buyers to be able to find.

- *Yahoo! E-Mail (http://mail.yahoo.com).* Yahoo! is one of the few service providers on the Internet to provide free e-mail accounts for anyone.

The truth is that you don't have to sell on Yahoo! Auctions in order to use Yahoo!'s e-mail or shopping services. Anyone can make use of those services. But if you have an account with Yahoo! and are comfortable using the site to find online resources, you'll probably also be comfortable with putting some merchandise up for sale on its auction site as well.

Registering at Yahoo! Auctions

Yahoo! Auctions works and looks pretty much the same as eBay's own auctions. The differences are relatively trivial when it comes to the way the sales are presented on the page, and the way you create the descriptions. One difference is that Yahoo! Auctions presents lots of ads along with auction listings: these are paid listings by businesses to include on the site. The ads make Yahoo! Auctions search results more difficult to read than eBay's search results because a good part of the page is taken up by ads, and the search results are presented in a narrow column in the middle of the page.

In order to put something up for sale on Yahoo! Auctions, you first need to make sure you are registered as a seller. If you already have an account with Yahoo!, you may already be registered to sell. Go to the help page at http://help.yahoo.com/help/us/auct/asell/asell-01.html, and click on the link REGISTER. You'll either see a page entitled Registration Completed or a form that requests more information. Once you are registered, you need to sign up for the Yahoo! Wallet service (http://wallet.yahoo.com), which records your credit card information.

Once you are registered and signed up for Yahoo! Wallet, you need to agree to the terms of service presented at http://auctions.yahoo.com/phtml/auc/us/legal/additionaltos.html. After that, the process of selling should be straightforward because it is very similar to the process of selling on eBay. First, you choose a category; you'll notice, furthermore, that there aren't nearly as many categories and subcategories as on eBay. I often sell shoes, for instance, and if I were to sell on Yahoo! Auctions, I would not have a subcategory actually called Footwear or Shoes. I would have to sell in the following category: Clothing & Accessories -> Men's -> Accessories -> Other.

Next, you go to the Submit an Item form. Right away, you see one difference between eBay's auctions and Yahoo! Auctions, because you are allowed to post three photos to accompany your description at no charge. You also are required to describe the condition of your item from the "Condition" drop-down list (the options are Acceptable, New with Tags, New without Tags, Like New, Very Good, or Good).

Other differences between Yahoo! Auctions and eBay auctions are summarized in Table 11-1.

There's no doubt that many of Yahoo!'s auction features—particularly the automatic extension at the end of the sale, and the wider range of sales lengths—would be welcomed by many eBay sellers. These unique features make Yahoo! Auctions worth a try—especially since there's no charge for listing items. The problem is obvious to anyone who has done a search on Yahoo! Auctions for either current or completed

Table 11-1. Differences between Yahoo! and eBay auctions.

Item	Yahoo!	eBay
Length of Sale	2, 3, 4, 5, 6, 7, 8, 9 10 days	1, 3, 5, 7, 10 days
Shipping Cost	Buyer usually pays, though seller can offer free shipping	Buyer or seller can pay
Shipping Start	Seller usually ships on receipt of payment	Seller can ship on auction close or on receipt of payment
End of Sale	Sale ends exactly 1, 3, 5, 7, or 10 days after start	Seller can specify that the sale can be automatically extended by 5 minutes if a bid is placed near end of auction.
Relisting	You must relist sale yourself and pay another listing fee	You can specify that Yahoo! will automatically relist the auction for up to five times.

sales: the range of items offered, the number of bids received, and the number of sales is nothing like that on eBay.

 Note: If you want to sell items in bulk, Yahoo! Auctions offers its users a tool called Seller's Manager (http://auctions.yahoo.com/phtml/auc/us/promo/ysm.html). This tool is a software program you install on your computer; it works with Windows 95 or later operating systems. The Mac OS is not supported.

Microsoft's Small Business Center

If you are familiar with Microsoft FrontPage and have used this powerful Web design software to create and edit Web pages, you should consider having Microsoft Small Business Center host your website. That's because FrontPage is specially designed to help you create an online sales catalog, complete with Buy It Now buttons and an online shopping cart—as long as you host your business site with Small Business Center, of course. FrontPage has a special bit of software called an e-commerce add-on that lets you create a sales catalog that is connected to a database.

Besides its integration with Microsoft Office and Small Business Center, Front-Page gives you the ability to create forms that actually receive visitors' input and process it so you can work with it. You don't need to host your site with Microsoft just because you use FrontPage, of course. Plenty of Web designers create their sites with FrontPage and find a Web-hosting service that supports the FrontPage Server Extensions, the software components that help you create forms, and other features such as discussion groups. But if you do choose Small Business Center, you can take advantage of the fact that it provides its customers with services that can help them track who visits their site so that you can develop ongoing relationships with them. These include Traffic Builder, which automates the process of listing your site with different Internet search services; Customer Manager, which helps you manage contacts with your customers; and ListBot, which helps you assemble a mailing list from your customer names. Once you have a mailing list, you can market to people who have already made purchases from you.

Small Business Center has several different levels of hosting, which are described in Table 11-2.

Delta Pecan Orchard is operated by a husband-and-wife team, Mike and Suzanne Powers, who moved to the Mississippi Delta from Cincinnati. They resurrected a pecan orchard with the goal of selling pecans on the Internet. The market for pecans in Louisiana is limited, so it's essential for them to reach a worldwide audience through their website. Their site, hosted by Small Business Center, is shown in Figure 11-1.

When shoppers make an order for a chocolate-covered pecan mix or other pecan-related product from the Powers's online catalog (a catalog they created with Front-Page), they go to a checkout area provided by Microsoft Small Business Center and shown in Figure 11-2.

Become a Google Froogle Merchant

You've probably heard of Froogle (http://froogle.google.com), the Google search engine that is especially designed to help shoppers find consumer goods. If you operate

Table 11-2. Microsoft small business center hosting options.

Level of Service	Monthly Cost	Yearly Cost	Features
Introductory (Web hosting only)	$12.95	$119.40	100MB of storage space
Standard	$24.95	$239.40	200MB of storage; includes Commerce Manager, which lets you set up shopping card and credit card payment system
Professional (e-commerce)	$49.95	$455.40	350MB of storage; Commerce Manager included; database access included

Figure 11-1. Delta Pecan Orchard has been a Microsoft small business site since the early 2000s.

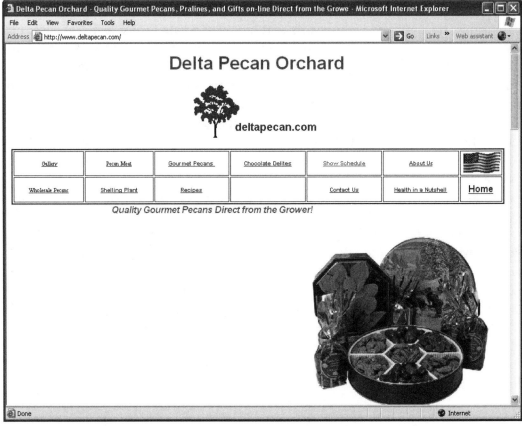

© Delta Pecan Orchard.

an eBay Store, a Yahoo! Store, a Microsoft Small Business, or a brick-and-mortar business you, too, can have your store listed on this popular search tool. Froogle, like Google, uses computer programs called spiders to assemble content. The spider scours the contents of millions of Web pages, indexing their contents and storing them in a huge database. Web pages that offer products for sale are automatically indexed in Froogle; eBay Stores pages are indexed as well.

However, the very fact that you operate a small home-grown business means that you're not necessarily going to have your pages indexed by Google. You'll increase the chances of being included by Google or Froogle if you make the effort to make Froogle aware that you exist—and not only that, but transfer your sales catalog listings to Froogle.

Note: You cannot pay a fee to have your store listed on Froogle, or on Google, for that matter. You can, however, pay to purchase advertising space on the right-hand side of a page of Google search results. You place a bid on keywords that you think your customers will enter in order to find your products. If yours is the high bid, your ad appears in the advertising column. The program is called AdWords, and it is described in Chapter 17 along with other marketing strategies.

Figure 11-2. Microsoft provides its small business customers with shopping carts and other functionality.

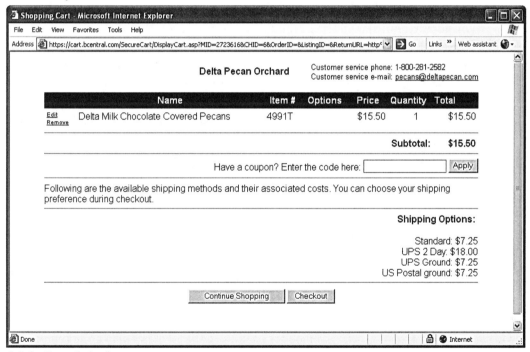

© Delta Pecan Orchard.

Creating a Feed for Data-Hungry Froogle

Google, like the other websites described in this chapter, requires individuals to create a user account to use its services. To list your site so that it is included in Froogle's search results, you need to create an account as well. If you already have an account to use other services such as Google's free e-mail service Gmail, you can use that account's user name and password. Otherwise, you get started by following these steps:

1. Connect to the Internet and point your Web browser to the Froogle Merchant Center page (https://www.google.com/froogle/merchants) where you can read general information about the program.

2. If you don't have a Google account yet, click the link CREATE AN ACCOUNT NOW. If you do, sign in with your e-mail address and password in the Merchant Center Sign In box on the right-hand side of the page, and click SIGN IN.

3. After you have signed in, go to the Merchant Center home page (https://www.google.com/froogle/merchants/home) and click the link CREATE AN FTP ACCOUNT. You go to a page where you select a new login name and password so you can transfer your site feed to Froogle using file transfer protocol (FTP). You won't need a special FTP application to carry out this transfer because the service is Web-based. When you're done, click the CREATE FTP ACCOUNT button. A page labeled Success should appear when your account has been created.

4. Click the SHOW FTP ACCOUNT button. This page asks you to fill out a variety of information about your store, including:
   • *Store ID.* This is a new ID that you create for your Froogle store. It's an ID you need to remember but the public doesn't see.
   • *Store Name.* This is your store's name—the name the public *will* see.
   • *Store URL.* This is the Web address for your store.

5. When you are finished, check the box that indicates you've read and accepted Froogle's terms of service. Then click the REGISTER A PRODUCT FEED link.

6. You go to a page that indicates you've created a name for your feed and that your store has a home on Froogle. Make a note of the name of your feed; you'll need to save the data as a text file and give it this name. Click the RETURN TO MERCHANT CENTER HOME button.

Once you've set up Froogle to receive your feed, the next step is to actually *create* a feed that you can send to the site. If you have a sales catalog, this is basically a matter of exporting the information to a text file that includes the fields shown in the following list:

- ***Product_URL.*** This is the URL for the Web page on which the product appears.
- ***Name.*** This is the product name.
- ***Description.*** This is your product description.
- ***Image_URL.*** This is the URL of the image that illustrates the product.
  category. You need to list the category or subcategory in which your product appears. (If your products aren't divided into categories, you need to create at least one with a generic name such as *products*.)
- ***Price.*** This is the price of your product.

Make sure the data fields are separated by tabs. Save the file with the name indicated in Step 6 in the preceding set of steps. Then, you can upload the file as described in the following section titled "Upload Your Feed."

If you run an eBay Store, you already have an easy way to create a feed for your store; but your store settings don't allow you to save your data in the format desired by Froogle. You need to open the file in Excel, adjust the data, save the file as a tab-delimited text file, and upload it to Froogle. Go to My eBay (http://my.ebay.com), log in with your eBay user ID and password, and click Sign In Securely to view your My eBay page. Click the Manage My Store link, log in again and, when the Manage My Store page appears, click Export Listings. Make a note of the URL where your data feed will be listed, click the button next to Make a file of my Store Inventory listings available, and click Apply. Go to the URL to view your file, click Save As, and save the file on your computer.

Once you have saved the file (which is in extensible markup language, or XML, format), open it in Excel. The file appears with each type of data separated into columns. Some of my store's data is shown in Figure 11-3. For instance, I need to change name of Column E to "Name" and reorder it to fit Froogle's format.

 Note: Whether or not you are registered as a Froogle merchant, you can participate in the Froogle Merchants discussion group, where you can ask questions and compare notes with other businesspeople who are trying to get more exposure for their merchandise.

Uploading Your Feed

The phrase *upload your feed* sounds like what happens after you eat something that your stomach finds disagreeable. But don't worry; I'm just describing the process of

Figure 11-3. You can save your eBay store's data in XML format, open it in Excel, and edit it for Froogle.

/StoreExport/Products/Product/Caption	/StoreExport/Products/Product/Category	/StoreExport/Products/Product/Country	/StoreExport/Products/Product/Description	/StoreExp
New for 2004! Latest Edition Absolute Begin	Books:Nonfiction Books	United States	Absolute Beginner's Guide to Online Dating Sign	Nonfiction
New for 2005! Latest Edition Collector's Guid	Books:Nonfiction Books	United States	Collector's Guide to eBay Signed by Author For	Nonfiction
New for 2005! Latest Updated Edition Degun	Books:Nonfiction Books	United States	Degunking eBay Signed by Author Greg Holden	Nonfiction
Includes CD-ROM Domino 5 Web Programm	Computers & Networking:Technology Books:F	United States	Domino 5 Web Programming with XML, Java, Ja	Programmi
640 Pages full of eBay buying and selling tip	Books:Nonfiction Books	United States	eBay PowerUser's Bible Signed by Author For Y	Nonfiction
Faster Smarter Microsoft Office FrontPage 2	Computers & Networking:Technology Books:\	United States	Faster Smarter Microsoft Office FrontPage 2003	Web Devel
New for 2005! Latest Updated Edition How t	Books:Nonfiction Books	United States	How to Do Everything w/Your eBay Business 2n	Nonfiction
Get started on eBay buying and selling How	Books:Nonfiction Books	United States	How to Do Everything with eBay Signed by Auth	Nonfiction
New for 2004! Latest Edition Internet Babylo	Books:Nonfiction Books	United States	Internet Babylon Signed by Author For You	Nonfiction
Latest Updated Edition Karma Kids: Answer	Books:Nonfiction Books	United States	Karma Kids Signed by Author Greg Holden For	Nonfiction
See Chicago through the Eyes of its Writers	Books:Nonfiction Books	United States	Literary Chicago Signed by Author Greg Holden	Nonfiction
Latest Edition Norton Internet Security for D	Computers & Networking:Technology Books:I	United States	Norton Internet Security for Dummies Signed by	Internet
Nine Books in One!Red Hat Linux All-In-One	Computers & Networking:Technology Books:I	United States	Red Hat Linux All-in-One Desk Reference for Du	Networking
New for 2005! Latest Updated Edition Startin	Computers & Networking:Technology Books:I	United States	Starting an Online Business for Dummies 4th ed	Internet
DIMITRI Men's Leather Loafers Size 9.5W H	Clothing, Shoes & Accessories:Men's Shoes	United States	Dimitri Brown Leather Loafers Size 9.5W Hand	Men's Brow
RALPH LAUREN COUNTRY Men's Shoes E	Clothing, Shoes & Accessories:Men's Shoes	United States	Ralph Lauren Country Men's Brown Leather Sho	Men's Sho
ALLEN EDMONDS Richmond Wingtips Col	Clothing, Shoes & Accessories:Men's Shoes	United States	Allen Edmonds Richmond Sz 14A Wingtips XLN	Men's Sho

© Greg Holden.

transferring the data file containing your current sales listings to Froogle so that your products can be included in its database. Once you have created your feed and saved it as a tab-delimited text file, you upload it to Froogle by following these steps:

1. Open the Froogle Merchant Center—FTP Instructions page (https://www .google.com/froogle/merchants/ftp_instructions.html.

2. If you are familiar with using an FTP application, you can click Option 2; if you are comfortable with the MS-DOS language, you can click Option 3; for the purposes of these steps, I'll assume you want to use your Web browser to do the file transfer, so click Option 1.

3. Follow the steps shown in the page to enter the URL for the Froogle FTP site (ftp://Hedwig.com), log in, and transfer the file you saved earlier.

Once you upload your data to Froogle, you need to keep doing so on a regular basis. If your product list changes every week, you need to upload your data every week. Froogle itself requires you to upload at least once every thirty days to keep your site in its database.

 Tip: Do a search for your store's name on Google; see if your store's name turns up, and if so, where it appears in the search results. If your site appears, you probably don't need to go through the effort of listing your site with Froogle. If it does not, review the section about creating an RSS feed and uploading it to Google. If your site appears but it is many pages down in Google's listings, you need to make more links to your site's home page. Get your friends and business colleagues to make links to your site; the more links your site has, the better your chances of being listed higher up in the search results.

Back to eBay: ProStores

Since the title of this book is *Selling Beyond eBay*, it might seem like a violation of my entire premise to discuss creating a website called a ProStore with eBay as your Web host. But my point is to demonstrate options for selling beyond eBay auctions, fixed-price sales, and eBay Stores. The option of eBay's ProStores (http://www.pro stores.com) gives you a way to sell through a website that is just as valid as the hosting solutions provided by Yahoo! or Microsoft. And eBay is certainly a well-known name.

One advantage of choosing ProStores, if you already sell through an eBay Store, is that you get a 30 percent discount on the usual hosting fees. Those fees are shown in Table 11-3.

That's right: If you are already used to having eBay charge you a Final Value Fee on each auction or fixed-price sale, you won't be surprised to find that, even though you're being charged a monthly fee to have a store, you have to pay a successful transaction fee of 0.5 or 1.5 percent of each sale that is completed. You are also charged a Bandwidth Quota coverage of 4 cents for every megabyte of bandwidth. (Bandwidth refers to the amount of data that moves along a network connection. In this case, you pay for the amount of data your visitors view.)

It's not uncommon for Web-hosting services to charge you for bandwidth. But

Table 11-3. Hosting fees for eBay ProStores.

Store Level	Monthly Fee	Successful Transaction Fee
Express Store	$6.95	1.5 percent
Business Store	$29.95	0.5 percent
Advanced Store	$74.95	0.5 percent
Enterprise Store	$249.95	0.5 percent

they don't always charge you a monthly fee for each transaction you conduct. Personally, I think you pay enough to eBay already, and you can find less expensive hosting options elsewhere. See Chapter 15 for suggestions of affordable Web hosts; Chapters 12 to 14 examine some well-known e-commerce operations that will provide you with storefronts, new auction systems, and other ways to get your products and services before the public.

CHAPTER 12

Leveraging Amazon.com's Customer Base

When you move beyond eBay to explore new sales opportunities, the key is to avoid reinventing the wheel. Rather than starting a new storefront or e-commerce website from scratch, build on what you have already done or take advantage of what others have accomplished in advance. In the case of a storefront, you will be better off if you choose a host or an online mall that already is well-known and has a lot of traffic. If you join a marketplace that already attracts millions of customers, you can skim off only a small percentage of them, and you are still likely to generate substantial income.

When it comes to well-known and highly trusted websites, you can't do much better than Amazon.com. According to an article in the journal *The Economist* (http://www.economist.com/displayStory.cfm?Story_id = 2646123), Amazon took in more than 2 million orders in a single day during the holiday season of 2004. The same article cited a study by the American Customer Satisfaction Index (ASCI), which reported that Amazon lead all competitors with a customer satisfaction rating of 88 out of a possible 100.

You can't just sell anything on Amazon, however. You have to pick your merchandise carefully. If you want to sell in the popular Marketplace area of the voluminous Amazon.com site, you can't sell jewelry or clothing unless you have been invited to do so and been approved to sell beforehand. You're best off if you sell merchandise that Amazon already sells, such as books, CDs, DVDs, electronic games, household goods, and any kind of high-tech gadget you can lay your hands on. Although Amazon allows individuals to conduct person-to-person auctions, this part of its site is hardly the most popular. Where Amazon excels is in letting individuals like you and me piggyback on to things that they are already selling. It is like a college bookstore: the store will sell new textbooks at full price, but invite students to sell back their used textbooks alongside the new ones at a reduced price. Both the students and the bookstore benefit. If you do the same on Amazon, you can sell with less effort than on eBay or other sites. The key is to match what you have to sell with Amazon's options for putting your "stuff" online, as you'll learn in this chapter.

Exploring Amazon.com's Marketplace Sales Options

Amazon.com provides individuals and businesses with many different options for piggybacking their own merchandise onto Amazon's seemingly limitless inventory. The first problem, when you connect to the site's well-traveled home page (http://www.amazon.com, shown in Figure 12-1) is to decide which option to go with. When you scan the home page, it can leave you scratching your head. When you look under the heading "$ Make Money," you see the following options:

- *Marketplace.* This is the option that lets you sell your own books, CDs, and other items alongside products that Amazon.com is already listing.
- *Associates.* This is Amazon's term for its well-known affiliates program. You place a link or ad on your Web page, and if someone clicks on your link and makes a purchase as a result, you make a percentage of the purchase price.
- *Advantage.* This is for publishers, labels, studios, or those few artists who own the rights to distribute their own creative works. If you have a band and create CDs that you sell on your own, theoretically this would be the category for you. However, for the most part, Amazon works with well-known music, book, and other publishers.
- *Web Services.* If you develop software, you can create tools to help other people find what they want on Amazon—or to help sellers sell more effectively on the site. Some of the products, such as SellerEngine and ScoutPal, are described later in this chapter.
- *Paid Placements.* If you produce books or music, you can have your products offered along with complementary titles already listed on Amazon.

So far, for individual sellers like you and me, the Associates program and the Marketplace are the most practical options. However, if you dig a little further you can find some different ways to set up shop on Amazon's turf. If you click on the link SEE ALL SERVICES under the heading "$ Make Money," for instance, you go to a help page that lists other options for publishers, such as Amazon's well-known Search Inside the Book feature. That's not for you. However, if you go back to the home page and look under the heading Bargains, you find two links that are worth investigating:

Figure 12-1. Amazon.com carries a wide variety of options for individual sellers as well as buyers.

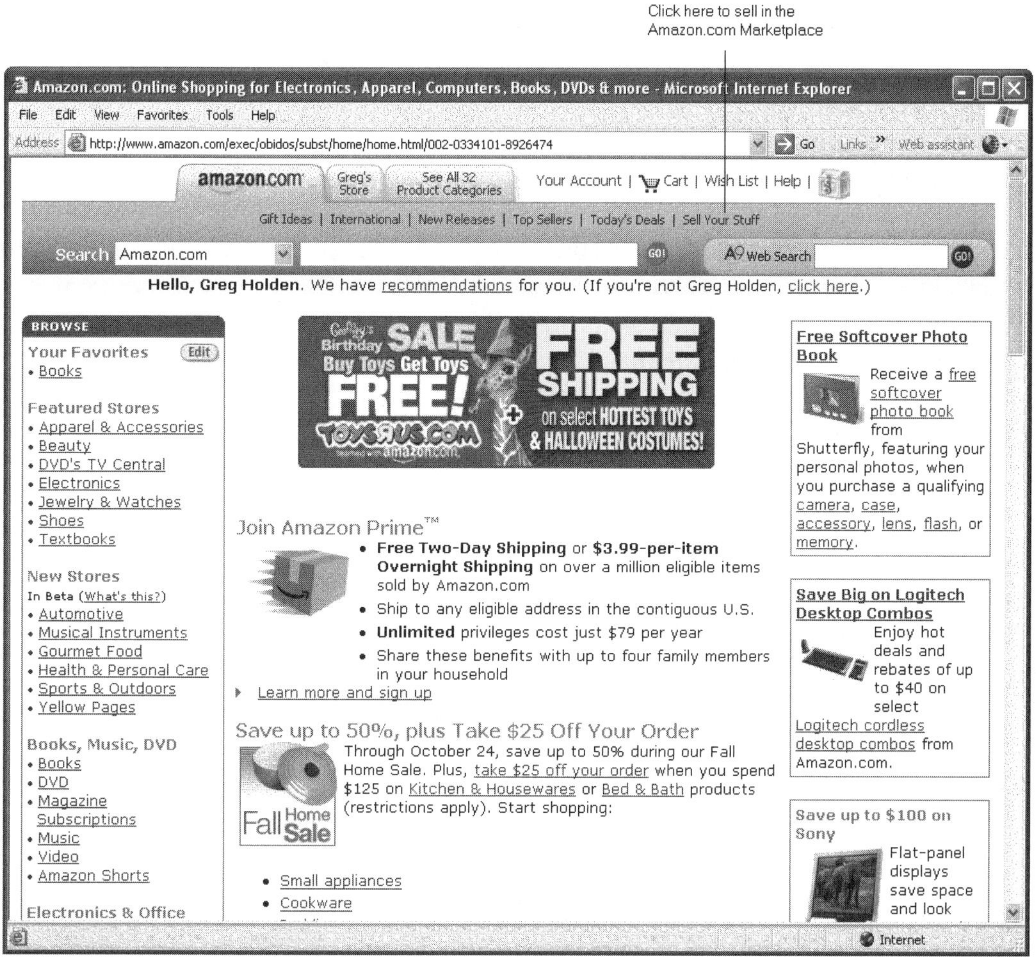

© Amazon.com, Inc.

- *Auctions.* Although Amazon.com has its own auction area, it is not nearly as wide-ranging and offbeat as eBay's. Unlike the Marketplace, sellers are allowed to list in any of the categories. Once again, the best things to sell are books, CDs, and electronics, because those are the items that most people want to buy on the site anyway.

- *zShops.* Amazon lets you set up your own storefront with items for sale, in a fashion similar to eBay Stores. The executive I spoke to at Amazon frankly admitted that this part of the site doesn't get much traffic, however, and suggested that individual sellers are better off listing in the Marketplace.

Auctions and zShops have been part of Amazon's website for several years. They don't get as much traffic as the Amazon.com Marketplace, and certainly not as much as eBay. In my opinion—and the opinion of the Amazon.com executive I interviewed—the Marketplace is the best option for individual sellers and small sellers to make money when they move beyond eBay.

If you're not a small seller but have a large-scale business on eBay or on your own website, you may be able to gain entry to a more exclusive program on Amazon called the Amazon Merchant program. "It was our success on eBay that allowed us to sell on Amazon," says David Yaskulka of Blueberry Boutique, a prominent and successful business on eBay, Overstock.com, and Amazon.com. "But it's challenging to get into the Amazon Merchant program. We're the largest shirt and tie sellers on eBay, and one of the smallest on Amazon. Amazon vets its sellers in much the same way that a highly successful shopping mall does. But it's worth the effort—most buyers assume (correctly) that if you're selling on Amazon, you're a professional and they have little risk."

Jumping on the Amazon Marketplace Bandwagon

You can participate in the Amazon Marketplace in two different ways: as an individual seller or a business. The difference is in how much you are charged when you successfully complete a transaction. In either case, you are essentially adding one or more of your own items to existing Product Detail pages on Amazon. One of those detail pages is shown in Figure 12-2. As you can see, the book being advertised sells new for an already deeply discounted price of $16.47. However, if you don't mind reading a used book, you can choose from fifty copies of the same book that various individuals are offering for as little as $12.99. You'll learn how to add your own books to Amazon's product pages in the sections that follow.

Selling Individual Items

You've probably got lots of books lying around the house that you no longer need. You have lots of options for getting rid of them. You can donate them to your local resale shop; hold a garage sale (don't expect to get more than a dollar for each; you'll probably get less that that); or sell them on eBay.

Think about the steps involved in selling a book on eBay. If the book you want to sell is recent, you can enter its ISBN (International Standard Book Number) in the Product Detail form. If you're lucky, eBay will be able to use that number to pull up a stock photo of the book that you can use in your description, along with basic

Figure 12-2. You can add your own copies of books or other products to listing product detail pages in the Amazon.com Marketplace.

© Amazon.com, Inc.

information about the book such as its size, publication date, and number of pages. If not, you'll have to take your own photo and note all that information yourself. You also have to choose the category in which to sell your item. And it's up to you to work out payment and shipping arrangements.

If you sell your book on Amazon.com, several of those steps—the photos and details, and the payment and shipping options—are streamlined for you. You don't have to make those choices because Amazon.com gives you the stock photo and basic product information on its Product Detail page. It also handles the payment question by requiring you to use its Amazon Payments system. As far as shipping, Amazon doesn't give you an option, either: it determines how much shipping will cost and requires you to ship your book out within two days of purchase; later, it reimburses you.

Although selling on Amazon.com gives you less control than selling on eBay, it also saves you some time and trouble. Think about all the questions you receive from prospective buyers:

- "Why is your shipping so expensive? Can you ship another way?"
- "Can you pack in an envelope instead of a box to save on shipping?"
- "Do you accept money orders or checks instead of PayPal? Do you accept cash or Western Union wire transfers?"

When you're selling on eBay, you have to answer each of those questions yourself. On Amazon, the questions never arise. You have to do things Amazon's way or not at all. Sam Wheeler, Amazon's Director of Strategic Partnerships for Amazon.com Services, sees this as an advantage for sellers. Wheeler states:

> Time is money, and you save time on Amazon because you don't have to have so many discussions with your buyers. They buy something; you ship it out, and that's it. As far as using our payment system, we believe that if every transaction flows through our transaction pipeline, there is more trust between buyers and sellers. Fraud is a problem for everyone on the Internet. As far as shipping, we believe that you're not here to make money on the shipping, you're here to make money on the product. Buyers don't have to play the game of wondering how much it is going to cost to ship your product.

It's easy enough to try out the system for yourself, especially if you have ever purchased anything on Amazon.com in the past and already have an account with the site. You only need to look around for a textbook or other item to sell, and then follow these steps:

1. Go to the Amazon.com home page and click SELL YOUR STUFF if you haven't done so already.

2. Once the Sell Your Stuff page appears, choose the category in which your item should appear from the drop-down list labeled Select category. The options in this list (shown in Figure 12-3) give you a good idea of the kinds of merchandise for which Amazon.com is ideally suited.

3. Search for the book you want to sell on Amazon.com. You can enter either all or part of the title in the Search by Title or Keyword box, or enter the ISBN number (for a book) or UPC or ASIN number (for another product). Then click START SELLING. For this example, I'll use one of my own books, which is shown in Figure 12-4.

4. Fill out the Select Condition page and click CONTINUE.

5. When the Enter Price page appears, enter the price at which you want to sell the item. Since I have a new book and I am willing to sign it for the purchaser,

Figure 12-3. It's a good idea to sell merchandise that Amazon.com already has listed for sale.

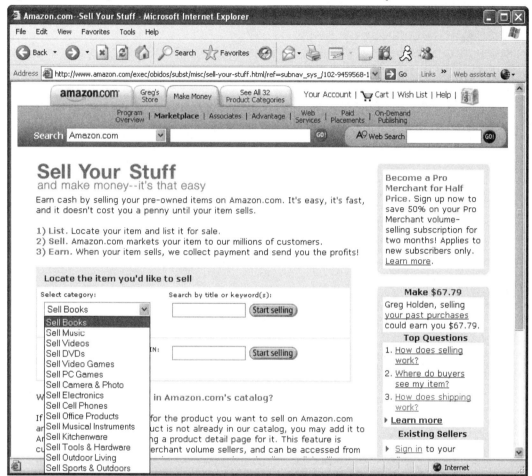

© Amazon.com, Inc.

I presumably have an advantage over the other sellers. But should I advertise the book as new or collectible? My feeling is that people shop on Amazon.com for convenience and value; they're looking for bargains. If the book is signed, so much the better. I decided to offer the book for $9.99 and inscribe it personally to the buyer. I enter the quantity, my location, and my shipping methods, and click CONTINUE.

 Note: Shipping methods are described next, but keep in mind that Amazon.com is reimbursing you for the least expensive Media Mail shipping option. For a book, your standard shipping method is U.S. Postal Service

Media Mail. The seller also has the option to choose expedited shipping (not overnight, and not Media Mail), or the international shipping option (delivery in three to six weeks).

Figure 12-4. Accurately describe the condition or special features of the item you want to sell.

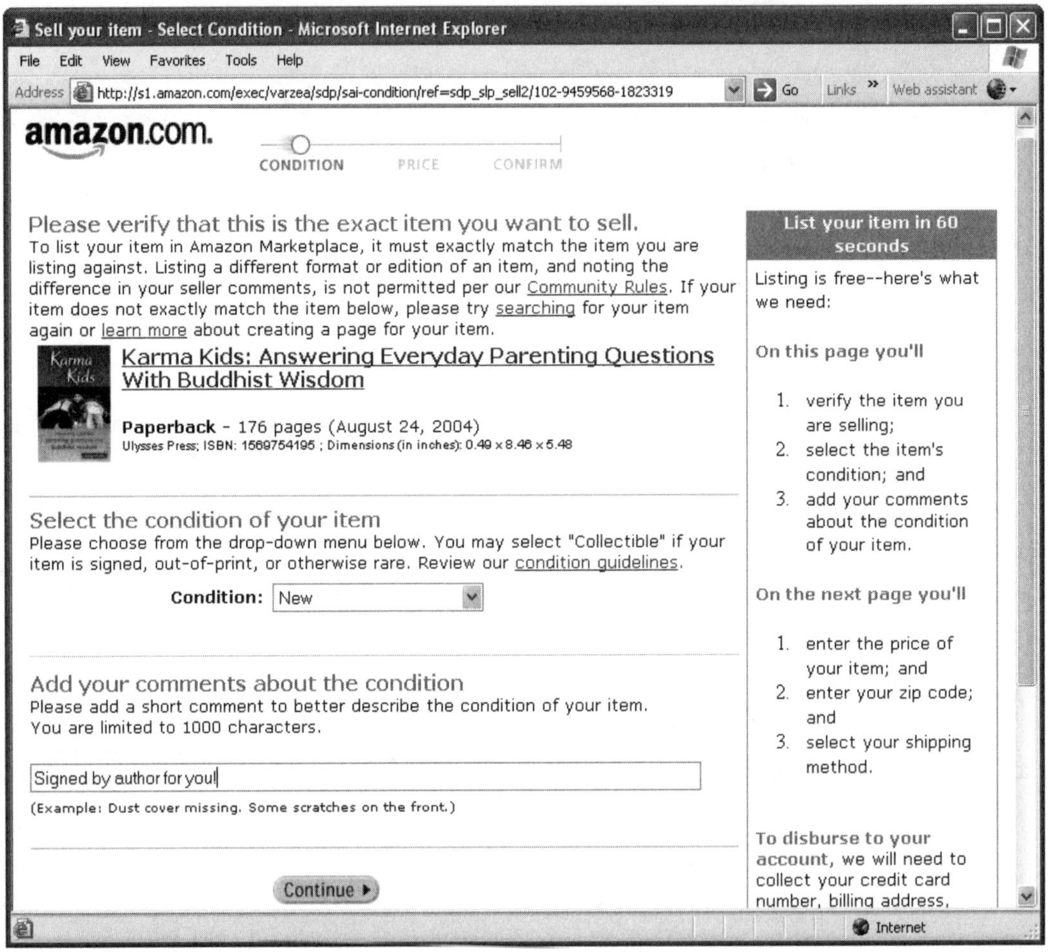

© Amazon.com, Inc.

6. Click CONTINUE. On the Confirm Listing page, review the terms of the sale carefully. You don't want to get surprised when the sale is made. Amazon doesn't charge for listing merchandise, but it takes a commission when the sale is made. (See Table 12-1, Amazon Marketplace Commissions, for details.) In this case, Amazon will take 15 percent of the sale, or about $1.25 on a sale of $9.99. I will make $7.74 on my sale.

Table 12-1. Amazon Marketplace commissions.

Type of Item	Commission	Example
Computers	$0.99 plus 6 percent	$1000 sale; $60 commission
Camera and photo equipment, cell phones, cell phone service, and electronics	$0.99 plus 8 percent	$150 sale, $12.50 commission
Everything else	$0.99 plus 10 percent	$250 sale, $25 commission
Musical instruments	$0.99 plus 12 percent	$300 sale, $36 commission
Books, CDs, DVDs, other products	$0.99 plus 15 percent	$50 sale, $7.50 commission

7. If the terms are acceptable, click SUBMIT your listing to list your book for sale. That's all there is to it.

Once an item goes up for sale on Amazon.com, it stays online for sixty days. If the item doesn't sell, you will receive a message from Amazon with instructions on how to relist it.

 Note: In order to use Amazon Payments (and thus make purchases from you in the Marketplace), you must live in a country where Amazon.com Payments is allowed. Residents of many Eastern European and Asian countries, including China, India, Russia, and the Philippines, are not allowed to use Amazon.com Payments at this writing. If you are selling merchandise that might appeal to residents of these countries, you might want to use eBay or another auction site instead. To access a complete list, click HELP, ORDERING FROM AMAZON MERCHANTS, AMAZON MARKETPLACE, AND MARKETPLACE SHIPPING TIMES & RATES.

Shipping Do's and Don'ts

If someone does buy your item, it's up to them to pay you using Amazon Payments. Amazon requires all buyers to pay immediately using the credit card associated with their Amazon.com account. Once the buyer's credit card has been charged, you receive a message from Amazon.com entitled "Sold—Ship Now!" Be sure to verify the order in your Payments Account to make sure the transaction is marked "Completed." If it is, you need to be on your toes (or more accurately, in town and near your merchandise). The reason is that you are required by Amazon.com to ship your item out within two days of the e-mail message. If your package doesn't arrive in the time that Amazon.com allows, it's up to the buyer to ask you about the status of the shipment. Time estimates are as follows:

- Standard delivery within the United State: four to fourteen business days after shipping
- Expedited shipping in the United States: two to six business days after shipping
- International Standard: three to six weeks (though buyers are made aware that delivery may take as much as eight to twelve weeks due to customs restrictions).

Of course, you can add two business days to each of those estimates, since you have two days to pack and ship—a generous amount of time, considering that many eBay buyers expect the package to fly out the door within a day after an instant PayPal payment is received.

Which option should you choose? It's up to you whether to pay for Domestic Standard, Domestic Expedited, or International Standard shipping. It's still up to you to pick the shipper: the United States Postal Service (USPS), United Parcel Service (UPS), Federal Express (FedEx), or DHL International. No matter which shipper you choose, you get the same shipping allowance from Amazon.com. The exact amount of the allowance depends on what you're shipping and what service is chosen. Some examples are shown in Table 12-2, Amazon.com Shipping Allowances.

There are at least two obvious flaws with this system. First, suppose you sell a book and it's really heavy? I mentioned to Sam Wheeler that I once sold a Bible that weighed 9 pounds and cost $7.70 to ship in a USPS flat-rate box. If I get an allowance of $5.39 for that book, I'm losing $1.31 on the deal. "Clearly the allowances don't cover everything, but you would have to add the extra cost to your purchase price," he acknowledged.

Second, what if you sell something to someone overseas and that person wants to receive the item faster than three to six weeks? Typically, Air Parcel Post and Global Priority, the USPS's two expedited overseas shipping methods, cost more than $20 for a package of 3 pounds or more. How could you add more than $10 to the purchase price to cover international buyers when there's an even better possibility that a domestic buyer will make the purchase? In that case, it's a good idea to restrict your item to domestic buyers only, which you can do when you list it in the Marketplace.

Table 12-2. Amazon.com shipping allowances.

Type of Item	Domestic Standard	Domestic Expedited	International Standard
Books	$3.49	$5.39	$9.79
CDs, Cassettes, Vinyl Records	$2.49	$4.99	$5.49
DVDs	$2.49	$4.99	$9.79
Video Games	$3.49	$4.99	N/A
Camera & Photo	$4.49 + $0.50/lb	$6.49 + $0.50/lb	N/A
Electronics	$4.49 + $0.50/lb	$6.49 + $0.50/lb	N/A
Musical Instruments	$4.49 + $0.50/lb	$6.49 + $0.50/lb	N/A
Everything Else	$4.49 + $0.50/lb	$6.49 + $0.50/lb	N/A

Note: You can view the entire table of shipping allowances by going to Amazon.com and clicking HELP, ORDERING FROM AMAZON MERCHANTS, AMAZON MARKETPLACE, MARKETPLACE SHIPPING TIMES & RATES.

Which Amazon.com Categories Are Best for You?

You probably know the site is good for books, CDs, DVDs, computer games, and video games. It's not as well known that the following additional types of items are already contained in the site's product catalog:

- Camera and photo equipment
- Electronics, including radios, portable CDs, iPods, and so forth
- Cell phones
- Office products, including printers, toner, paper, pens, and much more
- Musical instruments
- Kitchenware
- Tools and other hardware
- Outdoor living items, such as gas grills, mowers, bird feeders, and outdoor furniture
- Sports equipment

If you click the tab labeled SEE ALL 32 PRODUCT CATEGORIES at the top of the Sell Your Stuff page, you'll notice that there are many more sales categories on the site. The ones that aren't in the Select category drop-down list are the ones for which you have to be approved by Amazon. These include jewelry, clothing, pet supplies, health and beauty care, baby items, and many more. In these additional categories, the items don't include used merchandise offered by individuals.

"There are categories where we require approval before you sell," says Wheeler. "Amazon has a $2,500 guarantee for every item we sell. We want to make sure sellers in selected categories are reputable and offer merchandise that's in good condition."

Becoming a Book Seller with the Book Loader

The easiest and most practical way to supplement your eBay sales with Amazon.com sales, in my opinion, is to gather all the books in your house in one big pile and list them in the Amazon.com marketplace. Everyone has books lying around the house that they don't read any more. Even if your books qualify as antique and don't have an ISBN number, you can list them easily using the Book Loader. (Amazon lists millions of pre-ISBN titles in its catalog and you may already find your older book described there.)

Unlike eBay's Turbo Lister, the Book Loader isn't software you download and install on your computer. It isn't a tool you access online with your Web browser. It's the Microsoft Excel spreadsheet shown in Figure 12-5, which you download and

Figure 12-5. To upload books in bulk, you need to fill out and upload a Microsoft Excel spreadsheet.

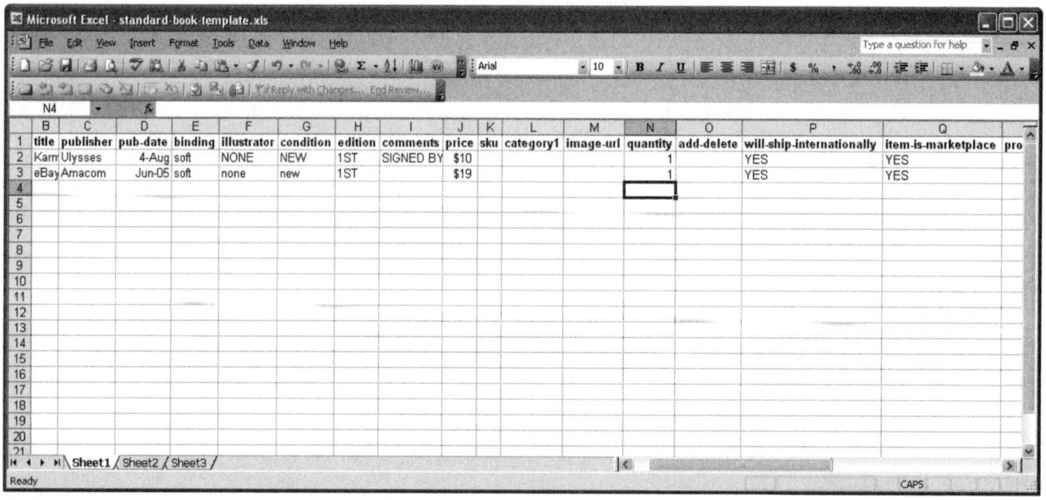

copy to your computer. (It assumes, of course, that you have Excel installed on your system.)

> **Note:** A variety of developers have created software tools that help sellers find items to sell that will be profitable on Amazon.com, and to help create sales listings on the site. See Chapter 14 for more on Monsoon, SellerEngine, and ScoutPal.

Once you have filled out the file, you save it in Excel's default .xls format, tab-delimited. Go to your Seller Account page, click LIST SINGLE ITEMS OR UPLOAD MULTIPLE ITEMS, and follow the instructions for using the Book Loader.

> **Tip:** To download the Book Loader file or to find out more about using it, perform the following steps:
>
> 1. Click HELP
> 2. Click SELLING AT AMAZON.COM
> 3. Click EXPERIENCED AND VOLUME SELLING
> 4. Click VOLUME LISTING TOOLS
> 5. Click BOOK LOADER

Selling Merchandise as a Pro Merchant

The goal of any successful auction or fixed-price seller is to build volume. When you build volume, you build revenue. Anyone who sells at volume on eBay—either as a PowerSeller or an ambitious and hardworking amateur seller—will want to know how to sell at volume on Amazon. The Marketplace is still a great place to sell at volume; those who sell at bulk are in the Pro Merchant program. As Amazon boasts, it has "no such thing as a nonpaying bidder" because it passes through only valid payments that are charged to the credit card that is already on file for a buyer.

Becoming a Pro Merchant is easy: you only have to commit to paying a monthly fee of $39.99 to sell in the Marketplace. If you are an individual seller you pay no listing fees; if an item sells you are charged $1 plus Amazon's commission. In contrast, Pro Merchants are charged only the commission. If you are a Pro Merchant, your item stays listed until it sells; if you are an individual seller, your item is taken down if it does not sell after sixty days. Some examples of Pro Merchant profit-and-loss margins appear in Table 12-3. As you can see, Pro Merchant status puts you ahead if you make numerous sales and have a steady revenue stream. For occasional sellers who complete only a handful of transactions per month, Pro Merchant monthly fees don't make sense.

Many Pro Merchants on Amazon list thousands of items at a time, so the monthly fee is justified for them.

Table 12-3. Pro Merchant profit margins.

Type of Item	Number of Sales/Month	Total Gross Revenue	Commissions	Profit if you pay commissions	Profit if you are a Pro Merchant
Computer-related equipment	6	$325.00	$28.44	$296.56	$285.01
Computer-related equipment	20	$550.00	$52.80	$497.20	$510.01
Books, CDs, DVDs	5	$92.00	$18.75	$73.25	$52.01
Books, CDs, DVDs	25	$310.00	$71.25	$238.75	$270.01

Using Volume Listing in the Marketplace with Inventory Loader

There is a volume listing tool for Pro Merchants and other Marketplace sellers who need to upload many items at once. If you read about the Book Loader in the previous section, you're already familiar with Inventory Loader and how it works. It is not a Web-based tool or a piece of software, but an Excel spreadsheet you download and fill in with your product information. You'll need to enter the identification number for each product you want to sell, such as:

- International Standard Book Number (ISBN)
- Universal Product Code (UPC)
- Amazon Standard Identification Number (ASIN), a number assigned by Amazon.com itself
- European Article Number (EAN)

You can take the number from the product packaging, or search for the item on Amazon.com to retrieve the number there. If you don't have Excel or are simply resistant to working with spreadsheets, you'll have to add each item to the Marketplace individually as described earlier in this chapter.

Tip: To access the Inventory Loader or find out more about it, perform the following steps:

1. Click HELP
2. Click SELLING AT AMAZON.COM
3. Click EXPERIENCED AND VOLUME SELLING
4. Click VOLUME SELLING TOOLS
5. Click INVENTORY LOADER

See Chapter 14 for descriptions of third-party selling tools, such as Monsoon and ScoutPal, that help sellers manage their listings on Amazon.

Tracking Your Inventory

If you sell on eBay, you're probably used to going to the My eBay page or your account page for a sales management tool such as Seller's Assistant. With a few clicks, you can check what is for sale at any particular time. Things work in a similar way on Amazon.com. Amazon allows not only Pro Merchant subscribers but zShops owners or regular Amazon Marketplace sellers to download their current inventory information for the previous fifteen, thirty, or sixty days. But you can also view the information online. You go to your Seller Account page (click the YOUR ACCOUNT link that appears at the top of nearly every page on the Amazon.com website, then click the link YOUR SELLER ACCOUNT) and click the link that applies to the action you want to perform.

If you are a Pro Merchant and have a product to sell that is not listed with a product detail page in Amazon.com's current inventory, you can create your own product detail page for that item. The page you create becomes a permanent part of Amazon.com's catalog. At this writing, items must be in one of the following categories:

- Books
- Camera and photo
- Electronics

- Kitchen
- Home and garden
- Music
- Musical instruments
- Pet supplies
- Sporting goods
- Tools and hardware
- Video & DVD
- Everything else

Before you start taking photographs, looking up the applicable ISBN or UPC numbers, searching for categories, looking up publishers, and all the steps required to create a product page on Amazon, keep in mind that you could do the same on your own website and not have to pay Amazon.com's sales commissions and monthly Pro Merchant fees. If you become big enough and successful enough that Amazon .com is a regular source of income, you may want to consider branching out to your own e-commerce website to maximize profits even further. The product detail page will be used not only by you but by other sellers who want to offer similar items in the Marketplace. In other words, you're creating a product detail page so you can sell an item and give competitors a chance to sell the same item. Before you go through the work, ask yourself: Do you want to help your competitors in this way? If the answer is yes, you can follow the online walk-through that explains how to create a Product Detail page: click HELP, click SELLING AT AMAZON.COM, click CREATE A PRODUCT DETAIL PAGE, and finally click CLASSIFY A PRODUCT.

 Tip: At this writing, Amazon.com was offering a reduced monthly fee of $19.99 to new Pro Merchant subscribers. To find out more about selling on Amazon.com as a Pro Merchant, go to http://www .amazon.com/promerchant or click HELP, click SELLING ON AMAZON.COM, and then click EXPERIENCED AND VOLUME SELLING.

Selling at Amazon.com Auctions

I've spent a good deal of time discussing how to add your books, CDs, and other household merchandise to Amazon.com's existing Marketplace because I think it's the most practical way to expand your sales beyond eBay. By selling in the Market-place, you gain access to the millions of shoppers who visit Amazon.com every day. With Amazon.com Auctions, things are different. The auction site is a separate entity from the main Amazon.com marketplace. In other words, if Amazon.com has a book for sale in the Marketplace, you may find a variety of sellers offering new, used, and collectible examples of that same item in the Marketplace. But if you offer the same item at auction on Amazon.com, a link to the auction won't appear on the Product Detail page.

To reach Amazon.com Auctions, you either click Auctions on the home page or go to http://auctions.amazon.com. Unfortunately, it's not obvious how to get started, because you don't see a link like SELL YOUR STUFF, which appears on the Amazon .com homepage. After some hunting around, I found two pages that serve as good gateways to auction selling on the site:

1. The Auctions Help page. The URL is too long to reproduce here, but click HELP, click SELLING AT AMAZON.COM, and then click AUCTIONS.
2. The Sell an Item form (http://s1.amazon.com/exec/varzea/auction-new). This is the form you fill out to create an auction listing on the site.

Once you find your way into the Sell an Item form, you'll find it easy to use, especially if you are familiar with eBay's Sell Your Item form. You write a title, a description, and you upload photos you have taken of the item—if you need to, that is. You might not need to if you are selling books or other products that are being sold in the Amazon.com Marketplace. If you enter the product number of such items, Amazon adds the images for you. One difference between Amazon.com auctions and those on eBay is that you have the option to list your sales for a full fourteen days, which is four days longer than the maximum time allowed on eBay.

Creating a Member Profile

Amazon.com, like eBay, lets sellers in its auctions or zShops areas create a type of About Me page. In this case, it's called a Member Profile. To create this page, go to the Auctions homepage (http://auctions.amazon.com), click SELLER ACCOUNT, and click CREATE or EDIT YOUR AUCTIONS/ZSHOPS MEMBER PROFILE. Your browser connects to the form shown in Figure 12-6, which you fill out to create the page.

Amazon's Member Profile form doesn't provide you with a choice of layouts; you simply fill out the form with your contact information, presumably so prospective or current buyers can look you up. You have the option of making a link to your home-page and including a single image, as well. It's difficult to make your store, or your

Figure 12-6. Be sure to fill out the member profile form so prospective buyers know you're "legit."

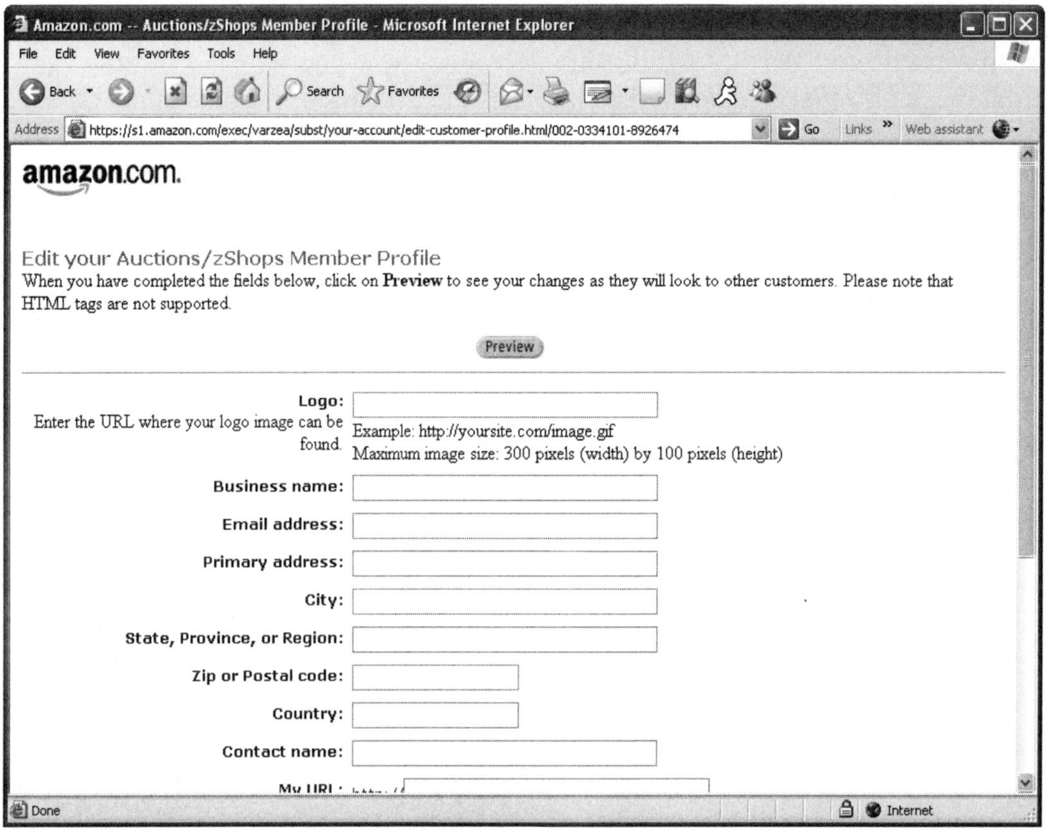

© Amazon.com, Inc.

company, stand out from the crowd on Amazon.com. You won't find the equivalent of an eBay Stores page—a place where you can see all the seller storefronts in one location. For many big-time sellers, that's probably just fine as long as they continue to be profitable on Amazon.com.

Former eBay PowerSeller Finds Success on Amazon.com

Tom Hawksley was once a prominent PowerSeller on eBay. He was, and still is, a member of the Professional eBay Sellers Alliance. But he no longer sells in great quantity on eBay because he was unhappy with eBay's fees and the number of nonpaying bidders he encountered there, and because he is so satisfied with his level of success with his company Global Media Direct on Amazon.com. He also sells on his Global Media Direct website (http://www.globalmediadirect.com, shown in Figure 12-7).

Figure 12-7. This seller offers tens of thousands of items for sale through Amazon.com.

© Thomas W. Hawksley, owner of Global Media Direct.

Q. What made you decide to set up a storefront there rather than Overstock or Yahoo!?

A. I have been on Amazon for about a year and half. With the help of Sam Wheeler and a few others at Amazon, I have grown my business to be very profitable and much more enjoyable than other venues. Their philosophy of letting me list and then pay the fee when and only when the item sells made a world of difference.

Q. What advantages does Amazon provide for you as a merchant?

A. More money, more money, more money! With my software/management program AMAN, I can sell, process, and pack several hundred items a day and be done in only a few hours. The customer base is better than eBay and customer service is second to none. Average selling prices are significantly higher than other sites and payment is guaranteed with commission not being due unless and until the item sells.

Q. *What do you sell on Amazon?*

A. I specialize in media products—things like CDs, VHS tapes, DVDs, and books. I also have a Seller Central Account with Amazon that I have started and will be selling over thirty-five hundred SKUs of video games. (This is exciting as they have greatly reduced the number of sellers approved to sell video games on their site.) I also have an Amazon.UK [United Kingdom] account. My computer guy has just now implemented a tool that will let me list all my items on both sites and when it sells on one site it is removed from the other. I expect this to significantly increase my sales volumes.

Q. *How many items, approximately, do you have there at any one time?*

A. I just did an Amazon search and I have about thirty thousand unique items currently listed. I have about fifty thousand that are literally sitting in a warehouse that I am entering in as time allows. By the end of the year, I hope to have in excess of a hundred thousand unique items listed at any given time.

Q. *Are there kinds of merchandise that sell especially well for you on Amazon?*

A. I had a unique opportunity last year to purchase over fifty thousand Columbia House tapes of old television shows. eBay was the only sales market for those as these items were not in the database at Amazon. Their category management team was very helpful in getting the items on the site and when they did my $5 Average Sale Price (ASP) on eBay, it turned into $25 to $40 ASP with a higher sell through rate than on eBay. This one deal turned my business around from a job to a career. I will owe my start to eBay but I will credit my first million to Amazon. I now find great success in rare and hard-to-find CDs and other media products.

Q. *What advantages does Amazon provide for you as a merchant?*

A. With Amazon, I can list an unlimited number of items and not pay a cent for commission until it sells. This allows me to list items that I would not otherwise be able to do with eBay's weekly fee.

Q. *When you moved from eBay to another venue like Amazon, were you able to build on your reputation as an eBay PowerSeller?*

A. I had a huge following on eBay and my screen name had much familiarity. I also had many thousands of customer's e-mails so I e-mailed them all to tell them I was now on Amazon. I also mention in my comments section that I was a major PowerSeller on eBay. By sending out newsletters to my customers as well as thank-you notices and follow-up notices (each with a sales pitch and a link) I tend to retain more customers than most sellers.

Opening a zShop

As eBay Stores are to eBay, zShops are to Amazon.com—with one significant difference. The difference is that zShops are hardly as well known and not nearly as widely used as eBay Stores. In theory, sellers can offer anything from computer equipment, food, collectibles, and many other types of merchandise on the site—anything that doesn't fit in the Marketplace. In practice, most sellers stick with the Marketplace or auctions when they want to offer something unusual.

Becoming an Amazon.com Associate

In the language of e-commerce, an *affiliate* is someone whose website acts as a referral service for another website. The site that receives the referral pays a fee to the referrer if the referral produces a purchase or another specified type of activity, such as a registration. Amazon.com has one of the best-known affiliate programs on the Internet. You can create links to specific books or CDs on Amazon's site on your own website and refer your visitors to Amazon by clicking on those links.

Amazon calls its referrers *associates*. To join the Associates program, click the link ASSOCIATES on the left-hand side of the site's home page. When the next page appears, click JOIN NOW. You'll be asked to register for the program by filling out forms; you'll have to decide whether you want to receive a deposit into a checking account or a paper check when you receive a referral fee. You go to a page called Associates Central, where you have the choice of making several kinds of links to Amazon: you can make a link to a CD, book, or DVD you like, a product you want to recommend, a text link, or you can even post an Amazon.com search box on your site. If someone makes a purchase after clicking a link or making a search, you receive a referral fee of 4 to 5 percent of the value of the items that are sold.

Amazon.com is perhaps the single biggest marketplace on the Internet after eBay itself. Another marketplace that is often mentioned in the same breath as a prominent alternative to eBay is Overstock.com, which also offers various sales opportunities for sellers. It is described in Chapter 13.

Overstock.com

As I write this, the online auction site with the highest profile in·terms of television advertising is not eBay, Yahoo!, or Amazon.com, but Overstock.com. "It's all about the O," the woman in the advertisements says—though what the letter *O* has to do with selling my excess inventory at a profit isn't clear to me. On its website, Overstock's CEO Patrick Byrne says the company also prepared a series of ads that blatantly encourages sellers to consider them as an alternative to eBay. However, he notes with more than a little frustration that the big commercial networks refuse to air the ads.

For individual sellers who are eager to reach out to new buyers beyond the confines of eBay, Overstock.com offers an attractive alternative. If you have large quantities of business supplies or merchandise that you can't sell, Overstock gives you a way to liquidate them at a bargain. Shoppers, in fact, come to the marketplace expecting to find cut-rate inventory that businesses have to clear out. If you can't sell items on eBay, you can offer them here. Overstock.com, for its part, almost certainly wants to present itself as a marketplace of first choice for sellers who have current consumer goods or merchandise. Whether you're turning to Overstock as a first choice or as an alternative to eBay, you'll find a well-established and easy-to-use sales system.

Understanding the Female Factor

Identifying your ideal customers and targeting them in the places where they shop online is one of the primary strategies to follow when moving beyond eBay. The need to reach your targeted market is one of the reasons for expanding your sales to other marketplaces in the first place. When it comes to eBay, the site reportedly attracts about the same number of male as female customers: 55 percent male to 45 percent female.

If you deal in women's clothing or accessories, however, it's worth taking a look at Overstock.com. "We skew a little more female than eBay does," says Holly Mac-Donald-Korth, Overstock's senior vice president for auctions. "In fact, Overstock is fully two-thirds female." According to Korth, Overstock.com's best-selling items include:

- Women's shoes and handbags
- Fashion jewelry
- Small electronics
- Cell phone accessories

The Jewelry & Watches home page, shown in Figure 13-1, presents prospective buyers with plenty of categories, subcategories, and options for shopping.

Two links near the upper right-hand corner of the page shown in Figure 13-1 (and other category pages on Overstock) provide both buyers and sellers with specialized

Figure 13-1. If you sell jewelry or other accessories for women, Overstock.com may be a good choice.

options. The link LIQUIDATION BINS enables businesses that have large quantities of items (such as a bin full of towels, or a set of watches that have been discontinued) to put them up for sale at cut-rate prices. The CLEARANCE BIN link takes buyers to items that have been offered by sellers at "deep discount."

Getting Started with Overstock.com

The moment you want to do anything other than casually browsing for items to purchase on Overstock, you are required to set up an account. After you click the HOW TO SELL link, you are prompted to enter your e-mail address and password. Click the link NEED AN ACCOUNT to set up the information necessary to put up items for sale.

Using the Sell Item Form

Once you have an account and have logged in, you go to the Sell Item form. If you have sold anything on eBay, you'll recognize all of the information requested on the form. First, you choose a main sales category; the categories are similar to eBay's. Selecting a second category doubles your listing fees. However, Overstock.com does not charge an additional fee for a subtitle. (Remember, eBay charges a sizeable $.50 for a subtitle.)

The rest of the form is similar to eBay's own Sell Your Item form. One nice feature is that as you specify a starting price, the fee associated with it appears next to the figure you enter.

Adding Images

Adding images to Overstock.com isn't as straightforward a process as it is on eBay, which gives you the option of either using its Picture Services to host your images online or uploading your images to your own Web server space and linking to them in your auction descriptions. The Sell Item form doesn't immediately present you with the option to host your own images. Instead, you click an Upload Images button and locate the image you want to display on your own computer. An Overstock Auctions Images preview page appears with your images displayed (see Figure 13-2).

You choose one small and one larger version of your image—click SAVE SELECTION, and the image is added to your description. That first image is free; each additional image you want to show is $.10. In order to add additional images, you need to make links to them from the body of your description. Click the YOUR OWN HTML tab, and enter the links in the following format:

Figure 13-2. Overstock.com lets you upload one image for free; subsequent images cost $.10 each.

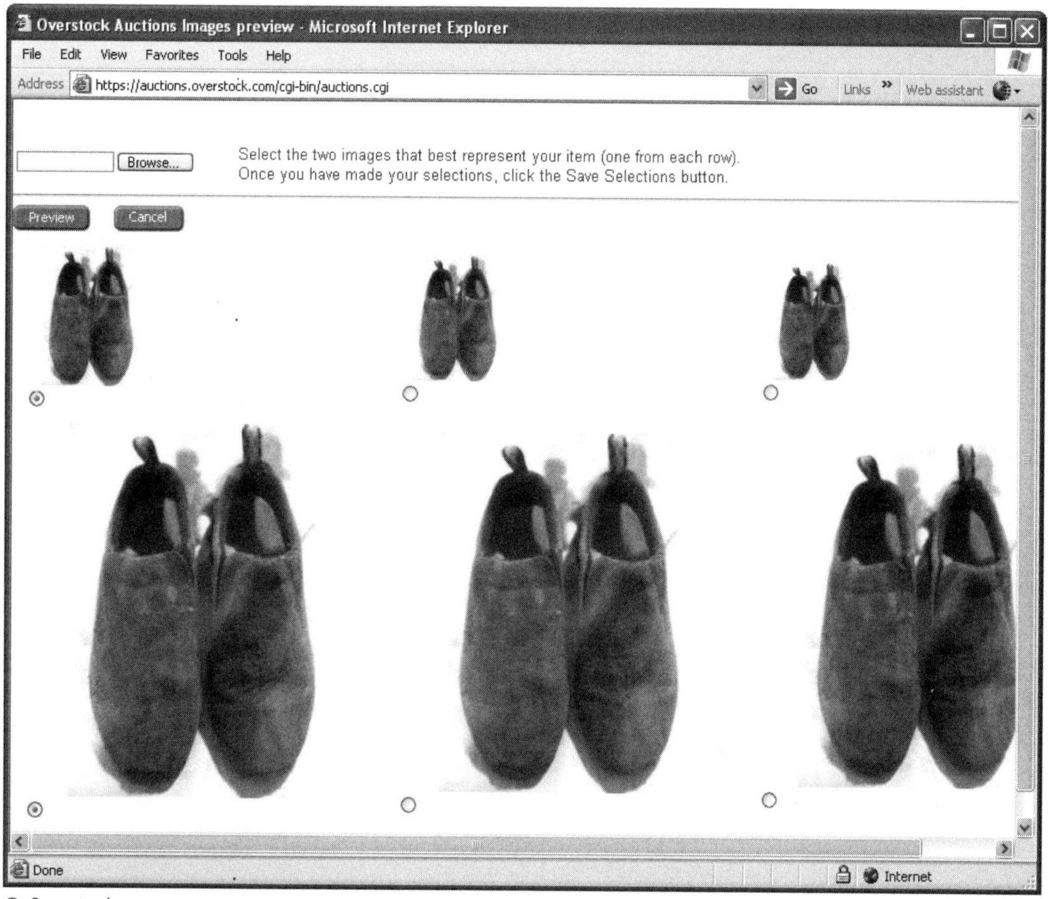

© Overstock.com.

Format as Code:

```
<P><A href = "http://www.gregholden.com/ebay/22/22-12-02.jpg"><Img
src = "http://www.gregholden.com/ebay/22/22-12-02.jpg"></A></P>
<P>A href = "http://www.gregholden.com/ebay/22/22-12-03.jpg"></A>
<img src = "http://www.gregholden.com/ebay/22/22-12-03.jpg"></P>
<P><A href = "http://www.gregholden.com/ebay/22/22-12-04.jpg"></A>
<Img src = "http://www.gregholden.com/ebay/22/22-12-02.jpg"></P>
```

End Code

This causes your subsequent images to be displayed in a single column under your description, just as on eBay. The difference is that you have to enter the links using the HTML <A></A> anchor tag; there is no user-friendly way of adding the links without having to type the code—unless you use Overstock's automated listing tool, O Lister, which is described later in this chapter. The HTML code as shown in the Sell Item form is shown in Figure 13-3.

When you're done, click the PREVIEW YOUR LISTING button. Check your listing carefully: even though I specified a flat shipping rate for the shoes I put up for sale, the shipping fee came up as $0 when I did the preview. I had to add the shipping fee

Figure 13-3. If you want to post more than one image, you have to make links to them using HTML.

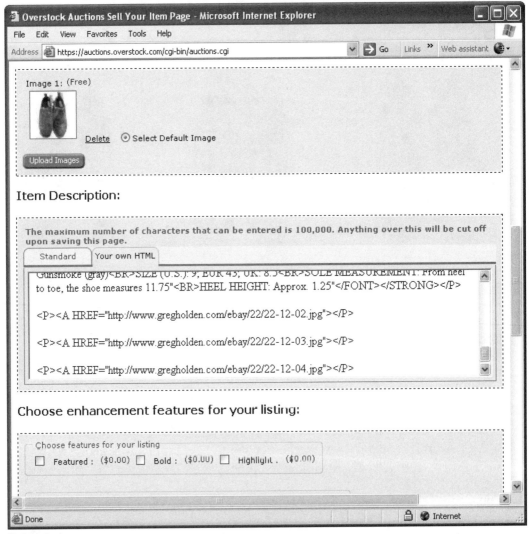

to the item's description; I'm not sure why. When you're done, click NEXT; then review the listing fees and click AGREE AND SUBMIT ITEM to get your sale online. My sales description is shown in Figure 13-4.

Note: Your sale starts the moment you upload the listing from the Sell Item form; there is no option in this form to schedule your sale for a different starting time. If you use Overstock's O Lister software, you can schedule your sale to begin at a later date and time.

Figure 13-4. Make sure your shipping rates and other essentials appear in your description before it goes online.

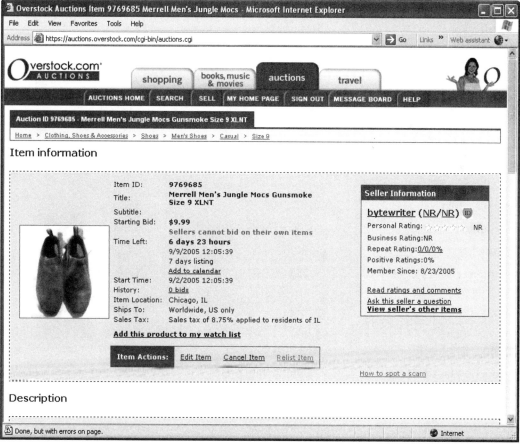

Understanding Overstock.com's Fees

When you are preparing your sales description, it pays to know how much features like reserve prices and bold highlighting cost. You can see from the comparison in Table 13-1 that Overstock.com is making an effort to keep its fees about 30 percent less than eBay's.

Two things are worth noting in Table 13-1: Overstock.com's fees are the same if you want to upgrade your sales description by highlighting it in a graphical way. However, Overstock.com charges no fees for fixed-price sales. If you want to sell your

Table 13-1. Selling fees for eBay and Overstock.com.

Fee	eBay	Overstock.com
Insertion Fee ($.01–$.99)	$.25	$.17
Insertion Fee ($1.00–$9.99)	$.35	$.23
Insertion Fee ($10.00–$24.99)	$.60	$.40
Insertion Fee ($25.00–$49.99)	$1.20	$.79
Insertion Fee ($50.00–$199.99)	$2.40	$1.58
Buy It Now Fee ($.01–$9.99)	$.05	N/A
Buy It Now Fee ($10.00–$24.99)	$.10	N/A
Upgrade: Bold	$1.00	$1.00
Highlight	$5.00	$5.00
Featured	$19.99	$13.17
Additional images after first free image	$.15 each	$.10 each
Reserve Price ($.01–$49.99)	$1.00	$.66
Reserve Price ($50.00–$199.99)	$2.00	$1.40
Transaction Closing Fee (Sale Price $.01–$25)	5.25% of sale price	3.25% of sale price
Transaction Closing Fee (Sale Price $25.01–$1,000	5.25% of initial $25 ($1.31), plus 2.75% of remaining balance	3.25% of initial $25 ($.81), plus 2% of remaining balance

items at a fixed price rather than inviting auction bids, you'll save on fees by moving to Overstock.

 Note: You are immediately prompted when you register to put a credit card number and billing information on file. You don't have to do so immediately, but you'll be prompted to enter it when you put an item up for sale or create your home page on Overstock.com.

Using O Lister

Overstock.com has a software tool that enables you to design listings, upload sales descriptions in bulk, and schedule sales to start at the same time, much like eBay's Turbo Lister. Called O Lister, this tool is freely available for download at http://auctions.overstock.com/cgi-bin/auctions.cgi?PAGE = STATIC&PAGENUM = 601.

 Note: O Lister works with Microsoft Windows 98 or later and requires Internet Explorer 5.01 or later. The Mac OS is not supported.

Using Overstock to Find Merchandise

The whole idea behind Overstock.com is that it serves as a place where businesses can liquidate excess merchandise at a low price. But it's hard to find merchandise on Overstock.com that you can then resell on Overstock.com, or on eBay. You'll have better luck if you search for big lots of wholesale merchandise on a separate site that's run by Overstock: Overstock Unlimited Closeouts (http://www.overstock unlimitedcloseouts.com). You have to be very selective and knowledgeable about what you buy on this site. You might have the opportunity to buy 12,528 child safety scissors for $.76 each, for instance (a deal I saw advertised at the time I was writing this chapter), but you need to make sure you'll be able to sell them for a profit, or your investment of nearly $10,000 will turn out to be unwise.

Becoming a Trusted Merchant

Trust is a problem for sellers, no matter which auction site you use. Those sellers who fail to deliver on merchandise that has been purchased reduce the trust level for everyone. A 2004 report by the National Fraud Information Center, in fact, reported that a full 51 percent of the complaints it received were related to auction goods that were purchased but never delivered. Overstock.com has partnered with the auction bonding service buySAFE to create a Trusted Merchant program for Overstock sellers. Buyers on the site are able to check a box on the search form (shown in Figure 13-5) so they can only search for sellers that have been bonded by buySAFE.

In order to become a Trusted Merchant, you must have buySAFE verify your identity and your financial stability. The company does an extensive review of your background as a seller so it can give you the Trusted Merchant seal of approval. It also reviews the following:

- Your payment history on Overstock.com: how reliably you pay for items you purchase, and how you pay your Overstock.com fees.

Figure 13-5. If you sell on Overstock.com, you should strongly consider becoming one of its Trusted Merchants.

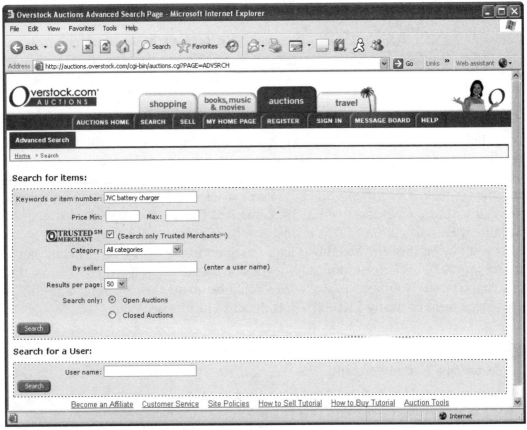

- The number of Overstock.com auction transactions you have conducted. You must have completed multiple billing cycles on Overstock.com.
- Your sell-through rate: the number of items you put up for sale compared with the number of items you actually sell.
- Your seller rating on Overstock.com; you must exceed the "minimum required rating," a rating that Overstock.com does not disclose.

In other words, you can't apply to be a Trusted Merchant when you're just starting out on Overstock. You need to have a track record. And even if you had the buySAFE seal of approval or were a PowerSeller on eBay, buySAFE evaluates your sales performance on Overstock.com, so your status doesn't carry over to the new venue.

"It's your success on eBay that will help you gain entry to this highly featured Trusted Merchant program," comments David Yaskulka of Blueberry Boutique, a successful business on both eBay and Overstock. "On Overstock, as on eBay, it's a good idea to buy a dozen or so auction items to build your initial feedback before you begin selling."

Once you are approved as a Trusted Merchant, you are charged a 1 percent transaction fee for each of your sales. What do you get in exchange for this fee and all of the scrutiny? First, buySAFE assures you that you get higher bids, as well as more bids. Second, you get a Trusted Merchant and a Bonded Seller icon that appears beside your listings on Overstock.com. And your customers have the knowledge that your sales are bonded up to $25,000. That means if you cannot or do not fulfill a transaction, buySAFE will compensate the buyer for the loss.

Securing Volume Discounts

Sellers on eBay struggle to put fifty, one hundred, or even a thousand items up for sale each week. They do so in the hope of building up sales volume: the more you put up for sale, the more you tend to sell, as long as your merchandise is desirable to enough people. These volume sellers don't expect to get a discount simply for putting items up for sale: the more items they put online, the higher the fees eBay collects from them. Because eBay hasn't led them to think they're going to get a discount, they don't expect one.

Overstock.com gives volume sellers a break: the more listings you have on the site at any one time, the more of a discount you get. The discounts are applied to both listing fees and closing fees. The discounts work as follows:

- Once you have 100 active auction listings on Overstock, a 2 percent discount is applied to the fees on active auctions 101 to 200.

- Once you have 200 active auctions on Overstock, a 3 percent discount is applied to the fees on active auctions 201 to 500.

- Once you have 500 active auctions on Overstock, a 5 percent discount is applied to the fees on active auctions 501 to 1000.

- Once you have 1,000 active auctions on Overstock, a 7 percent discount is applied to the fees on active auctions 1001 and higher.

This isn't an earth-shattering discount unless you sell a lot of items at a high price. Suppose you manage to put two hundred items online at one time on Overstock.com, each with a starting price of $9.99. (For a retail or wholesale business with a team of employees available to handle the work, this is not out of the question.) For the first one hundred items, you'll pay the usual listing fee of $.23 for each item as well as the transaction closing fees shown in Table 13-1. For items 101 to 200, you'll save only $.46 in total listing fees. But the real savings come in the transaction closing fee. If you sell all of items 101 to 200 for $9.99, you'll pay not the usual 3.25 percent closing fee on each item ($.32) but a 1.25 percent closing fee ($.12). Your total savings in transaction closing fees would be $20. Your total savings overall would be $20.46.

Understanding How Overstock Outdoes eBay's Feedback System

There is a simple feedback system on eBay. People leave positive, negative, or neutral comments for members with whom they conduct transactions. Overstock has a feedback system as well, but it's supplemented by many other ways in which buyers and sellers are rated:

- *Business Ratings*. This rating is the sum of each comment you have received from an Overstock member with whom you have been involved in a transaction. You can give the other member a rating ranging from +2 to −2.

- *Personal Ratings*. Personal ratings don't have a direct connection to your transactions on Overstock. They are given to you by your "friends" on Overstock; you can receive a star rating of zero to five stars.

- *Positive Ratings Percentage*. This figure is the result of a complicated calculation: the ratio of your average positive rating to your average negative rating.

- *Repeat Ratings*. Overstock also reports on the number of repeat customers a seller has had—something else eBay ignores. The information is presented in this format: 145/125/20. This indicates that the seller has sold 145 items to 125 customers, 20 of whom are repeat customers.

Repeat customers are a sign that a business is well-established and highly trusted. Overstock also recognizes this with a red LL icon next to the user's feedback rating: the LL stands for "Loyalty Leader."

Overstock Customers Affluent, Yet Value-Conscious, Seller Finds

A successful seller on Overstock.com who also happens to be one of the largest sellers on eBay was happy to comment on the differences between the two sites but preferred to remain anonymous.

Q. Did you have any problems making the transition from eBay to Overstock.com and building a reputation at the new venue?

A. It was a lot faster for us to gain a foothold in the Overstock marketplace. The folks at Overstock gave us a lot of support as well [as] a jumpstart.

Q. What advantages does Overstock provide for you as a merchant?

A. Overstock provides an alternate channel that reaches out to a different clientele base than eBay. Most of Overstock's customers are a little more affluent yet still trying to find a good deal.

Q. Do you still sell on eBay?

A. We will continue our operation at eBay without a doubt. Overstock is simply another venue that will complement the overall selling strategy.

Q. What kinds of merchandise do you sell on Overstock that you don't sell elsewhere?

A. We sell value-added combinations of items that are specifically catered to Overstock's clientele base. These combos may not be the lowest priced items. However, it usually offers the best value on the Web. The name, Overstock, itself simply implies a bargain place. We wanted to offer the best value to our customer.

Q. Overstock doesn't have a built-in payment system. Is that a problem?

A. So far, it's working out just fine as we are offering all payment methods such as PayPal, merchant services, and paper payments. The good side that Overstock doesn't associate with any particular payment processor is that we can make the best decision on offering the most preferred payment method to our customer.

Q. How do most of your Overstock buyers pay for what they purchase?

A. Paypal and credit cards via independent merchant services.

Q. What do you do, if anything, to market to a predominantly female clientele?

A. It's true that Overstock has more of a female-oriented client base. We make our product description template a bit more user friendly for browsing as well as our payment instructions.

If you're looking for a place to expand your sales beyond eBay while saving on selling fees, Overstock.com is a viable option. Don't use the site as a dump for items that won't sell elsewhere, however; you'll be better off if you choose merchandise and settle on prices that represent a good value for your customers. Just as with eBay, the more items you put up for sale, the more difficult and time consuming it becomes to manage your auctions—and by extension, your business—on your own. Overstock.com counts third-party auction management providers like ChannelAdvisor and Market-Works among its solution providers. Overstock members get special deals when trying out or using their software. You'll find out more about these and other auction service providers in Chapter 14.

CHAPTER **14**

Finding the Right Operational Partner

When I attended a convention of eBay PowerSellers in early 2005, those in attendance seemed to be divided into two camps. First, there were the PowerSellers who actually belonged to the group that was conducting the meeting. Second, there were eager visitors who wanted to sell something to those PowerSellers, write about them, or do business with them. It was hard to tell which group was larger than the other. The bottom line was clear: As a successful eBay seller, you are a highly sought-after commodity. And there are many companies that offer you useful resources and are ready and willing to provide you with assistance.

For example, there is a wealth of options available when it comes to service providers. In fact, you may think that you need a scorecard to tell the players apart. There are auction service providers who focus on utilities designed to make auction buying and selling more effective. They are different from marketplace managers who enable you to set up e-commerce storefronts that can supplement your auction sales.

You'll learn about both kinds of providers in this chapter. You'll also learn the pros and cons of each so that you can decide which will best meet your needs. Ideally, the service provider you choose will function more like an operational partner—a resource that will provide you with software tools as well as support and advice to help you make a smooth transition to the world beyond eBay.

Reasons for Turning to an Auction Service Provider

Anyone who tries to sell seventy-five to a hundred or more items per week knows what happens—suddenly, you have something to do every minute of the day and long into the night. You have to field questions from prospective buyers; you have to keep track of checks and money orders received from current buyers; you have to gather new items, write text, and take photographs to create more sales listings; you have to leave feedback. The amount of work can quickly become overwhelming. Auction management software can automate many of the steps involved. You do, however, use some of your hard-earned profits to pay subscription fees to the auction service provider you choose to make your work go easier. What can you expect to get in return for your investment? Some of the goals you should be shooting for are mentioned next.

Essential Features to Look For

All of the many auction service providers differ in the details. One might offer more image storage space than another. One might have a slightly different monthly fee. However, there is a set of must-have features that every auction seller needs, including the following:

- *Formatting Descriptions*. Make sure the software you use streamlines the process of adding colors to your descriptions, choosing typefaces, and arranging photos and text in a user-friendly way.

- *Providing E-mail Management*. It is a very impressive touch to send automatic e-mails to customers telling them their items have shipped, or thanking them when a purchase is completed. However, it is a drain on time and energy to compose a new message each time off the top of your head. Look for an auction service provider that can automate the process for you.

- *Hosting Images*. For your subscription fee, you should get space on a server where you can post images of the items you have for sale. That will eliminate the need to pay eBay's hosting fees.

- *Helping with Feedback*. Feedback is an essential part of every transaction, but it can be difficult to remember to leave it when so many other duties are pressing. A service provider should be able to leave standard comments automatically. Although not as personal, it is better than leaving feedback that is poorly written or not leaving any feedback at all.

- *Uploading Multiple Descriptions*. A service provider's auction tool should let you create and list multiple items, as well as let you schedule them so they start at the same time.

Ideally, an auction service provider will help by providing reports that track your income, expenses, and profits. You should be able to track sales for a longer period than the sixty-day limit on My eBay, for instance.

Tip: Go on the discussion boards run by various auction sites described in this book, such as AuctionBytes (http://www.auction bytes.com/forum/phpBB/index.php), to ask for opinions on the reliability of a service provider before you sign on the dotted line.

Boost Your Productivity

When you have identified a sales niche as well as a supplier of merchandise, the challenge is simple: You need to get as many sales online as you can, and complete as many transactions as you can to ensure a profit.

Any auction sales tool you use should increase your productivity. I once interviewed an eBay PowerSeller who told me he counted thirty-six separate steps involved in creating a sales description and completing a transaction on eBay. He also said that, after a great deal of effort in collaboration with a software developer, he created a software program that reduced the number of steps to fewer than ten.

Sell Smarter Through Better Research

Your sell-through rate depends in large measure on the quality of the research you do beforehand. Doing extra work to look up brand names and original retail prices can mean the difference between a sale and a zero in the bids column. Although this book focuses on marketplaces other than eBay, the millions of sales records on eBay make it by far the best place to do research. Looking up completed auctions on eBay is useful up to a point—up to about two weeks, which is when the sales records stop. You can get a more complete picture of the completed transactions for an item that is similar to the one you want to sell when you subscribe to some services that provide more extensive background information than you can get on eBay.

Terapeak

Terapeak (http://www.terapeak.com) is an auction service provider with a specialty. It focuses on mining eBay's rich database of sales information and presenting the data in different ways. As you might expect, Terapeak lets you search eBay's completed auctions for a long time—the previous three months' worth of sales. You can study when the best times are to start a sale, and what the best starting bids are, based on the final sales price. An example of a search result is shown in Figure 14-1.

You can also mine eBay's information in other ways. Consider the single most popular question asked by prospective sellers: What is the best thing to sell on eBay—

and, by extension, on other websites? Well, Terapeak has an answer in the form of its What's Hot lists. These lists go beyond eBay's simple listings of "Hot," "Very Hot," and "Super Hot." They provide percentages indicating how many of the items offered for sale actually sold (see Figure 14-2). The figures are available for a single day or a week. You can then do a search for one of the items on the list, clicking on it to get the particulars about sale prices, starting bids, and especially popular models within a particular brand.

Figure 14-1. Terapeak search results present up to thirty days' worth of eBay completed auction results.

© Terapeak Marketing Research.

Auction Service Providers

Auction Service Providers are primarily concerned with helping you to format sales descriptions and complete transactions more quickly. You have the usual choice be-

Figure 14-2. Terapeak's service reports on sales categories on eBay that have been "hot" in the recent past.

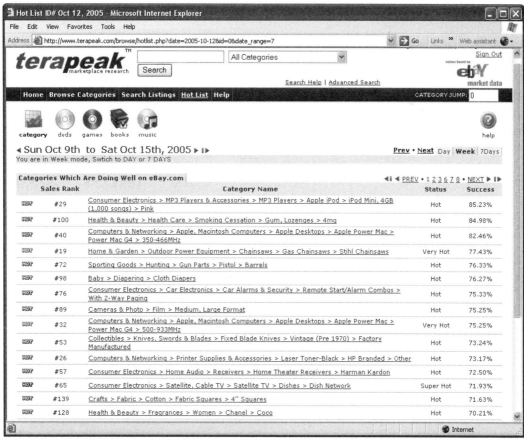

© Terapeak Marketing Research.

tween downloading and installing desktop-based software that runs on only one computer or subscribing to a service that you can access from any computer that is connected to the Internet.

Some of the best-known auction service providers are listed in Table 14-1.

With so many choices, it can be difficult to pick the right service. Most of the aforementioned service providers allow customers to try out their software for a thirty-day trial period. It's also a good idea to look around the Web to see what software tools are used by the sellers you know or whose listings you admire. My personal impression is that many PowerSellers choose Vendio or Zoovy to be their provider.

In any case, be sure to take into consideration the uptime of the provider. Because service providers aren't always forthcoming about reporting service outages on their

Table 14-1. Auction service providers.

Service URL	Monthly Fees	Features
AAA Seller (http://www.aaaseller.com)	$8.95 to $44.95.	Fifteen to more than a thousand listings per month; unlimited image hosting; compatibility with eBay Motors.
Andale (http://www.andale.com)	Research tools $7.95; Image hosting $3 to $55; Customer Manager $5.95 per month.	Counters, listing tools, automated e-mails.
AuctionHawk (http://www.auctionhawk.com)	Charges a flat monthly fee rather than a commission on sales. For 110 listings per month, you pay $12.99 per month, 250 listings for $21.99 per month, and so on.	Customers can use a simple one-page listing form, can add a scrolling showcase of images to their listings, automatically send invoices and e-mail messages to winners, and bulk relisting.
Auction Tamer (http://www.auctiontamer.com)	Version for sellers costs $12.95 per month or $99.95 per year.	Has tools for buying and watching sales as well as selling. Enables sellers to sell not only on eBay U.S. but on many of eBay's international sites, Yahoo!, Amazon .com, uBid, Bidville, and others.
Auction Wizard 2000 (http://www.auctionwizard2000.com)	License costs $75 for the first year, $50 for each year thereafter.	Includes a complete e-mail system with an unlimited number of e-mail accounts. Provides templates for e-mail addresses; sorts e-mail automatically. Works with eBay, eBay Stores, Overstock.com auctions, Yahoo! Auctions, and Player Auctions.

Vendio (http://www.vendio.com)	Several plans are available for Sales Manager: annual listing for $250 per year and $.06 per listing; pay as you go for $.10 per listing; $12.95 per month, $.05 per listing and 1 percent final value fee to flat rate of $39.95 per month and $.10 per listing.	Its Sales Manager Merchandising Edition works with Amazon.com, eBay, and Froogle. It includes free image hosting, listing templates, an HTML editor, reports that display your revenue, costs, profit, and sales. Has its own marketplace, Vendio Stores.
Zoovy (http://www.zoovy.com)	Auction Seller package: $49.95 per month, $399.95 setup fee. Other add-ons such as customer relations management package range from $9.95 to $35.00 per month.	Zoovy Auction includes automatic relisting, and instant checkout; integration with PayPal; upselling and cross-selling; label and packing slip printing.

own websites, this can be difficult to track. It is also important that the software provided is updated on a regular basis. Zoovy, for instance, includes its own user forum where you can discuss Zoovy's offerings with other customers.

Marketplace Managers

A marketplace management provider offers all the functionality of the auction service providers listed in the previous section: they give their customers image-hosting space, help with automating e-mails, have a selection of tools for designing sales descriptions, and so forth. But they go beyond auction sales to help businesses expand into other locations as well. They provide software for tracking inventory, creating marketing, providing customer support, and hosting online storefronts and websites—in short, all the things that longtime auction sellers do on a piecemeal basis are consolidated in a single location by a marketplace manager. Look for the following essential features that go beyond the standard set supplied by auction service providers:

- *Sales Tax.* The tool should keep track of the sales tax you have collected from buyers who live in your home state, which will be a big help when it comes time to file your taxes.

- ***Tracking Inventory.*** The marketplace manager should let you keep track of inventory so you can provide a replenishment before you run out of a particular model or item.
- ***Shipping.*** The manager should streamline the process of printing mailing labels and packing invoices.
- ***Branding.*** Some managers, like Marketworks, help you create unique logos that you can use on your Web pages and your printed materials.
- ***Overseas Business.*** Some managers will provide translation services and help you fulfill tax and customs requirements, which can often be confusing.

The two big players in the field of auction management (and online business management) are ChannelAdvisor (http://www.channeladvisor.com) and Marketworks (http://www.marketworks.com). They offer expensive and complex packages designed for large businesses, but they also provide entry-level packages to individual sellers. Some of the best-known marketplace managers are listed in Table 14-2.

As stated previously, there is considerable overlap between the services I am describing as auction service providers and those that are marketplace managers. ChannelAdvisor deserves a special mention: the company was founded by an eBay PowerSeller named Scott Wingo. Vendio, in particular, can be described as a marketplace manager, while AuctionHelper has plenty of auction service tools. Don't be reluctant to investigate companies listed in both categories when you're looking for your own provider.

Amazon.com Selling Tools

Amazon.com offers its own bulk listing tool, Bulk Loader, but it is only an Excel spreadsheet, and cannot help with tasks such as quickly capturing order and description data, inventory information, or shipping procedures. It's not well known to outsiders, but individuals and companies that sell in volume on Amazon.com know that they can take advantage of a variety of third-party software that helps them manage sales on Amazon.com and even do research to find books and other products that will fetch particularly strong prices.

AMan

One of the Amazon.com sellers described in Chapter 12, Tom Hawksley, uses AMan to manage his Amazon.com sales descriptions. AMan, by Spaceware, keeps track of orders you have received on Amazon and maintains a list of which items have been

Table 14-2. Auction service providers.

Service	Monthly Fee	Features
AuctionHelper (http://www.auctionhelper.com)	After fourteen-day free trial, you pay 1.95% of sales price with a minimum fee of $.15 and maximum fee of $1.25, plus $.02 eBay API fee for each item (eBay's Application Programming Interface or API allows service providers to connect to its database).	Inventory management: you can enter your inventory into Auction-Helper's database; the service tracks your sales, inventory numbers, invoices, and sales history.
ChannelAdvisor (http://www.channeladvisor.com)	The least expensive option, ChannelAdviser Pro, starts at $29.95 per month or $270 per year.	ChannelAdvisor Pro works with eBay, eBay Stores, Overstock Auctions, Amazon.com, Yahoo! Auctions. Customers get customer care advice, discussion boards, newsletters, and more.
Infopia (http://www.infopia.com)	N/A; You have to consult with an Infopia salesperson.	Separate software modules are available for managing inventory, keeping in touch with customers, online branding, and more.
InkFrog (http://www.inkfrog.com)	Each software package has its own monthly charge; or you can purchase all four for $17.90 per month.	i-Images is an image-hosting plan; i-Lister lets you list and schedule auctions; i-Showcase lets you display a preview of all your items for sale in each listing; i-Checkout handles the e-mails and tracks payment at the end of the transaction.

(continues)

Table 14-2. Continued.

Service	Monthly Fee	Features
Marketworks (http://www.marketworks.com)	Image Hosting ranges from $29.99 for 100MB and up.	Marketworks charges a minimum $29.95 image hosting fee (three other plans ranging up to $119.95 are available), plus 2% of the final price of a successful transaction with a $.20 minimum and a maximum of $3 per auction sale. No insertion fees are charged. (Source: AuctionBytes)
SpareDollar (http://www .sparedollar.com/corp)	No listing fees, insertion fees or final value fees; $8.95 per month lets you use all the company's services.	Auction management service gives you 50MB of storage space, a listing designer, automated feedback, reports of your sales history, and more.

shipped and which remain to be sent out—data that become important if you sell dozens or even hundreds of separate items at a time.

Seller ratings are especially important on Amazon, especially when you might have a half a dozen or more individuals selling the same used or "collectible" book in the marketplace. You'll stand out from the others if you have a better seller rating. As you know from your eBay selling, the best way to improve your seller rating is to ship quickly. AMan helps you with shipping by letting you print out shipping labels and packing slips that can bear your business name or user ID. AMan also generates U.S. Postal Service bar codes so you can print out your own postage and avoid waiting in line at the post office.

Monsoon

Monsoon (http://www.amazon.com/gp/browse.html/102-8416412-8597724?_encoding = UTF8&node = 3472421&no = 3435361&me = A36L942TSJ2AJA) is a bulk listing tool for Amazon. It enables you to "grab" the sales information for a group of items and prepare multiple sales listings. You can schedule your sales so they all start at the same time if you wish.

SellerEngine

SellerEngine (http://www.sellerengine.com/) is software that enables you to search Amazon in a way that the site itself doesn't permit—by the names of individual sellers. You can search through all the items sellers currently have for sale. That way, you can adjust your own prices to make sure they are competitive. SellerEngine, like Monsoon, also lets you upload sales listings in bulk.

ScoutPal

ScoutPal (http://www.scoutpal.com) is an amazing hardware device lets you scan the bar code of an item you see in a secondhand store, a flea market, or a resale shop. ScoutPal records the ISBN (for books) or other number of the product and automatically looks up the price of the item in the Amazon.com marketplace. It is a great way to do on-the-spot research to see how likely you are to be able to resell the item for a profit on Amazon.

● ● ●

One of the most important service providers you can choose is, of course, the service that provides you with the ability to process payments sent to you by your buyers. If you use a service like Amazon.com, which processes payments itself, you don't have to worry about this. However, if you create your own website to support your sales in various marketplaces, you'll need to sign up with a payment processor you can trust, as described in Chapter 14.

CHAPTER **15**

Handling Payments

Ever since eBay purchased the payment service PayPal in 2002, payments on eBay have been an easy matter—in theory, at least. PayPal is convenient and well integrated with eBay. You can jump to your PayPal payments directly from My eBay, and you can print shipping labels by clicking on a link in My eBay that takes you to the appropriate part of PayPal's website. To be sure, PayPal has had its share of service glitches; it was offline for several days at one point, and at the time I was writing this book, it was forced to admit that it had mistakenly double-charged a few of its debit card users. And PayPal doesn't come cheap for merchants—it's frustrating to see several dollars being deducted from a payment that a buyer has sent to your PayPal account.

PayPal has more positives than negative points, however. The big asset is that PayPal is so well established as a payment system that most of the marketplaces profiled in the book include it among their suggested payment options for sellers. Nevertheless, it is to your advantage to accept other payment options as well, whether you're selling through your own website or through an auction site.

In this chapter, you'll learn about the different payment options available to you when you sell outside of eBay. You'll learn how to add PayPal to your website, how to obtain a merchant account so you can receive credit card payments directly, and about the pros and cons of other options such as money orders, checks, wire transfers, and—shudder—*cash*.

Using the Easiest Option: Piggyback onto Your Merchant's Payment System

If you don't want to have to determine the types of payments you'll accept from your customers once you move away from eBay, there is one option that doesn't require any work on your part: taking advantage of your merchant's existing payment system. The primary examples here are Amazon.com and uBid. Anyone who wants to buy or sell on such sites must register with these sites beforehand. As part of registration, you are required to submit a credit card number. All payments are deducted from that number. No other option is allowed. It's a transparent and easy-to-use system and one that doesn't require any overhead on your part. In return, you're free to focus on creating listings, shipping out your merchandise, and other tasks.

 Note: Other marketplaces that have their own payment systems include Liquidation.com (which lets buyers submit credit card payments).

Working with Online Payment Services

Because you're used to selling on eBay already, you're familiar with the speed and convenience of electronic payment systems. They enable a buyer to make a charge to a credit card account or a debit from their checking account. The funds are then transferred to your own account with the payment service—after the service deducts a fee for receiving a payment, of course. The two options in this area are PayPal and Escrow.com.

Using PayPal

The fact that eBay owns PayPal might make it seem like only eBay members can use it. But anyone can sign up for an account and use it for any auction service. On a non-eBay marketplace, you just don't get the convenient level of integration you are used to with eBay and PayPal; you can't jump from your personal home page on Amazon.com to PayPal, for instance, and you can't print shipping labels from your page on your My iOffer page. Nevertheless, it makes sense to accept PayPal for auction purchases no matter what marketplace you use. Most online shoppers expect to pay using PayPal. And PayPal can handle the virtual "card swipe" (the submission of customer purchasing data) and the verification of customer information. The customer can use a credit card number to make a purchase, and PayPal debits the customer's credit card account and transfers the payment to you.

Adding PayPal to Your Website

PayPal isn't just for auction and personal payments. If you sell on a website, PayPal offers three types of merchant tools. These tools give your customers various ways to pay you using their credit cards or by making debits from their checking accounts. You can find the options described at https://www.paypal.com/us/cgi-bin/webscr ?cmd = _merchant. They are:

- ***PayPal Website Payments Standard.*** If you already have a shopping cart integrated into your website, PayPal provides the back-end functions that enable customers to pay you. You add a PAYPAL SECURE CHECKOUT button to one of your catalog or shopping cart pages. The customer fills out a form on PayPal and transfers payment to you. If you don't have a shopping cart, you can install one provided by PayPal itself. You pay no setup fee, but you are charged a 1.9 to 2.9 percent transaction fee and $.30 per transaction.

- ***PayPal Website Payments Pro.*** This solution lets you control the payment process yourself. Buyers aren't directed away from your site to PayPal's in order to complete the transaction. You process the payments on your site and PayPal handles the transfer in the background. You pay a $20 setup fee and transaction fees from 2.2 to 2.9 percent plus a $.30 per-transaction fee.

- ***PayPal E-Mail Payments***. You send your customer an invoice by e-mail; the customer clicks on a link and is directed to the PayPal website to complete the transaction.

With all the warnings about clicking links in e-mail, the third option might turn off some customers. The best option is the second one, which keeps the customer on your site at all times. The longer you can keep customers in your domain, the more likely they are to make subsequent purchases or to interact with you in other ways—by subscribing to an e-mail newsletter or mailing list your might offer, for instance.

Joining PayPal's Online "Mall"

I had been using eBay and PayPal for quite a while before I realized that PayPal has its own online shopping mall called PayPal Shops. You click the link SHOPS in the set of links at the bottom of virtually any PayPal page or go directly to https://www.pay pal.com/us/cgi-bin/webscr?cmd = _shop to visit the mall.

If you already have a PayPal account and accept PayPal, you can register to join the mall. You also have to upgrade to a premier or business account, verify your account, and sign up to earn Money Market interest on your PayPal account. Once you meet those qualifications, you can enter your website as one of the stores in PayPal Shops. You check off boxes that describe what you sell, and choose sales categories for your merchandise. Both are important; they control how shoppers will find what you have to offer when they do a search on the site. It's not clear to me how many people go to PayPal to browse through the PayPal Shops area; however, when someone pays you for an auction or other purchase, they are sent a notice that encourages them to visit your website as listed in the mall. This kind of referral is invaluable; it encourages shoppers who have already shown interest in what you have to sell and enough trust to actually buy something to return and shop for more.

Using Escrow.com

Escrow.com has been around about as long as PayPal, but it has never received the respect given to PayPal. That might be because it holds money in a way that buyers would love but sellers who are used to eBay would not:

1. The buyer agrees to purchase the item.
2. The buyer electronically transmits the agreed-upon payment amount to Escrow.com.
3. Escrow.com "verifies" the payment—a process that can take two days for credit card and PayPal payments or ten days for checks or money orders.
4. Escrow.com reports to the seller that the payment has been received and notifies the seller that the item should be shipped—but holds on to the payment while shipping occurs.
5. After the item has shipped and the buyer has had time (the exact amount of time is agreed upon by both buyer and seller when the buyer agrees to the purchase terms) to inspect the merchandise to make sure it is in acceptable condition, the buyer notifies Escrow.com.
6. Escrow.com releases payment to the seller.

This sort of system safeguards both buyer and seller. But sellers who are used to receiving "instant payment" notices from PayPal only minutes after one of their items has been purchased will probably find it difficult to put Escrow.com in charge of their hard-earned money, if only for a little while.

Becoming a Credit Card Merchant

One of the best reasons for selling on your own website is simplifying payments for your customers and avoiding the fees charged by your marketplace of choice. One of the best reasons for becoming a credit card merchant is the ability to process credit card transactions directly from your customers—you don't have to get PayPal involved in the mix, and you don't have to accept PayPal's fees. You do have to pay fees to your credit card transaction company, but if you operate both brick-and-mortar stores and online stores, you can use your credit card payment system for both venues.

Traditionally, obtaining a credit card merchant account from a bank or a savings and loan association is a time-consuming and difficult process. But a number of services are available to streamline the process. Typically, credit card services like 1st American Credit Card don't have a brick-and-mortar presence; they are dedicated solely to serving online merchants. If you don't use PayPal or another service like Western Union BidPay or Escrow.com that enables buyers to pay with credit cards, it's a good idea to obtain your own merchant account. Online shoppers are used to buying on impulse, and many of them want to be able to hand over a payment as soon as possible so that they can receive what they have purchased as quickly as possible. You do have to complete a series of steps, however, including the following:

Getting Approved

Whether you apply to a bank or online-only credit card company, you need to be approved. Any financial institution that grants credit is going to want to know that you are a real business entity. You'll probably have to submit your checking account, and you might also need to provide your tax ID number and some business references as well. A bank can take days or weeks to review and approve your application for a merchant account. Other merchant account services will take much less time.

Learning About Fees and Rates

If you apply for a merchant account from a traditional financial institution, you may be charged an application fee of $300 to $500 or more. Online companies like Merchants' Choice Card Services (http://www.merchantschoice.usa.com) do not charge an application fee.

The institution that provides you with credit and processes transactions for you has to make money somehow, of course. All merchant account companies make money on the transactions they facilitate by charging a fee called a *discount rate*. This fee usually costs from 1 to 4 percent per transaction. You'll also probably be charged a monthly fee for the service, too. Even though 1st American Credit Card Service charges no application fee, you are still charged the following if you sell through the Internet:

- A discount rate fee of 2.32 percent
- A $.25 per-transaction fee;
- A $9 monthly statement fee
- A minimum charge of $20 per month

 Note: Most merchant account companies enable transactions through the Visa and MasterCard networks. If you want to give your buyers the ability to use their American Express or Discover cards as well, you need to file an application with each of those credit card companies separately. You become an American Express merchant by going to the American Express Merchant website (http://www.americanexpress.com/home page/merchant.html). You become a Discover Card merchant at http:// www.discoverbiz.com.

Understanding Credit Card Transaction Software and Hardware

How does a transaction actually take place on the Internet? You need to have a number of elements in place, including the following:

- *A Purchase Form*. A form that buyers fill out to provide you with their name, address, and credit card number.

- *A Secure Server*. A secure server encrypts information sent to it to protect buyers' identities and financial information.

- *A Way to Connect to the Credit Card Network.* You need software or hardware that is configured to transmit the customers' purchase information to the banking network. This is what normally happens when a cashier swipes your credit card through a piece of hardware called a terminal. Both options carry their own fees. The software used by 1st American Credit Card, which is called PC Charge Express, requires merchants to either purchase it for $295 or lease it for $22 to $34 per year. The hardware used to process credit card information, which is called a terminal, costs anywhere from $17 or $26 per month or purchased for $229.

- *A Way to Verify Customer Data*. Credit card fraud frequently occurs when dishonest individuals use stolen credit card numbers to make purchases. The address associated with the card number is different from the address that the thief uses to receive the merchandise. (For example, a credit card number stolen from the owner, who lives in Illinois, might be used by a thief who lives in Bolivia and asks the seller to ship to an address in that country.) Many credit card merchants prevent such transactions by checking the credit card holder's address against the purchaser's address to make sure the two addresses match. You can pay a verification service to do the checking for you for a monthly fee, or you can do the checking yourself manually.

 Tip: ICVerify is software you can purchase from http://www.icverify .com. PCCharge by Go Software Inc. (http://www.gosoftinc.com/pro ducts/index.htm) is software that also allows you to verify credit card data yourself.

As you can see, there are many elements and fees involved with setting up a merchant account. It's quite natural to ask why you should consider going through the effort at all, when PayPal or BidPay is much simpler. One reason is that your company has many different locations, including brick-and-mortar stores. Another reason is that you want to be in charge of security, and not depend on PayPal or other services to perform the verification for you. (Fraud does occur on PayPal and, as many sellers discover, PayPal does not always provide reimbursement when it occurs.) At any rate, it's a step you should consider carefully, and only undertake when your business is well established and you have lots of credit card purchases to process.

Finding a Secure Server

Most Web servers are not secure because they don't encrypt information that is sent to and from them. Information as sensitive as credit card numbers has to be protected from thieves who would be only too happy to get their hands on legitimate credit accounts they can then use to make fraudulent purchases on other websites. To protect the information as it is sent from the buyer's Web browser to the Web server that processes the information received from filling out the form, it must be encrypted.

Most e-commerce hosting services charge an extra fee to give their clients the option of using a secure server to retrieve payment data, but there's really no other option; buyers just don't feel secure (and in truth, they shouldn't feel secure) unless they see the "closed lock" icon at the bottom of their Web browser window, which indicates that they are connected to a secure site. If you want to receive credit card payments directly from your buyers using a merchant account, you'll definitely want to find a Web host that protects your business and your customers by allowing you to use a secure server. Ask your host whether a secure server is available and, if so, what extra charges apply.

Note: The standard method of encryption used in most secure Web servers is called Secure Sockets Layer, which uses long encrypted blocks of alphanumeric characters called *keys* to protect data.

Processing the Credit Card Payments

To submit the credit card information you receive via your secure server connection to your bank or credit card company, you need to obtain point-of-sale (POS) hardware or software. The most common type of hardware is a terminal—a plastic box of the sort you see in your local retail store. The software is a program that contacts the bank through a dial-up modem or through your high-speed Internet connection. In either case, the requested purchase information is authorized and the data is transmitted to the financial institution you use. The financial institution deducts the appropriate fees from your account, and—most important—deducts the purchase price from your buyer's credit card account.

Note: You can hire a credit card processing company like VeriFone, Inc. (http://www.verifone.com) or AssureBuy (http://www.otginc.com). Both of these companies facilitate automatic credit card processing online. The buyer's shipping address is compared against the shipping address associated with the credit card and, if the addresses check out, the purchase is immediately processed. Keep in mind, though, that because automatic transactions take place so quickly, the client can make a purchase and the financial part of the transaction can be completed whether or not you have an item in stock. If the item is on back order and the buyer has already paid for it in a matter of minutes, he or she can become very dissatisfied with the delay. To prevent this type of customer dissatisfaction, some online sellers choose not to use automatic processing, and prefer to assign staff people to process each transaction themselves.

Accepting Other Forms of Payment

Because this book assumes that you are already an experienced eBay seller, you have an advantage over online merchants who are novices. You already have the answers to basic questions such as: Is it safe to accept personal checks? How long should I wait for checks to clear? How long should I wait for money orders to clear? What should I do if a customer wants to wire transfer the money? The basic rules associated with eBay sales apply to other venues as well, and they are described in the sections that follow.

Accepting Personal Checks

The good thing about accepting a personal check is that an escrow service doesn't deduct any fees for it. You get 100 percent of the payment. The bad thing is the chance that the check might bounce. How do you know that a personal check won't bounce? Conventional wisdom tells you to deposit the check in your bank account and to wait for seven to ten days. At the end of that time, if a notice of nonpayment has not been sent to you by your bank, you can release the merchandise and ship it to your customer.

Conventional wisdom falls short in several respects. Some buyers don't understand that you have the right to wait a week or more to see if the check is going to bounce. They are likely to complain to you after only a few days—or at least inquire to see where the shipment is. The truth is that a check can take up to a year to bounce. You can't tell even after a week or ten days if the check is "rubber" or not. Many sellers simply check the buyer's feedback to see if there are any complaints or evidence of nonpayment. If the buyer has good feedback, you can safely ship the item immediately after receiving the check. But many marketplaces don't have as well-developed a feedback system as eBay does; most of their members simply don't have large quantities of feedback. If you sign up with a marketplace where most users don't have feedback—or that doesn't have feedback ratings at all—you may want to eliminate personal checks from your approved payment list altogether.

Accepting Cashier's Checks

Cashier's checks seem more secure than personal checks. However, you still need to allow several days for a cashier's check to clear, just as you would a personal check. You probably won't get many cashier's checks, however, because many banks charge as much as $3 to process them.

Accepting Money Orders

My eBay advisors (PowerSellers whose opinions I value) tell me not to worry about money orders. I haven't had any problems with them myself. When a buyer obtains a money order, he or she has to pay a fee to obtain it. Because of the effort involved in going to the post office or other institution to get a money order, and the fee, you can feel reasonably secure that the buyer can be trusted.

You may also receive money orders from Western Union BidPay; this service is particularly reliable because, again, the buyer has to pay for the money order, not you. Western Union then prints a paper money order and snail mails it to you. BidPay also notifies you when the payment has been sent.

Working with Wire Transfers

Western Union wire transfers are in direct contrast to Western Union money orders. Wire transfers are notoriously insecure, and they have been the source of many Internet scams over the years. It's quite possible that the request you receive to accept a wire transfer is legitimate, but there are many other options for payment and you should encourage buyers to use one of them instead.

Accepting Cash

Conventional wisdom says no, because if the payment is lost in the mail or stolen, it's gone. You can claim to your buyer that it never arrived, but your buyer has no reason to trust you, and no way of recovering the payment (a check can be stopped or a money order cancelled). Some buyers insist that they are more comfortable sending cash and have never had a problem with this method, even if it is not one of the payment methods you specify in your auction descriptions. Use your judgment. If the buyer's feedback is good, you may want to let the person send cash if he or she insists on it. I have had buyers send me cash and haven't encountered problems—not yet, at least.

Payment methods become more critical when you leave the friendly confines of an auction site or other marketplace and start up your own website. A well-designed website can serve as the centerpiece of your online auction efforts; the must-have features and the critical choices you need to make are described in Chapter 16.

PART IV

Selling Through Your Own Website

CHAPTER **16**

Planning Your Own Website

For a growing number of businesses, eBay is only a "front door"—a way to attract customers; and eBay serves this purpose very effectively. Although it's a bit of an exaggeration to say that all 42 million of eBay's members are going to look at each of your sales, it's fair to say that the site does attract thousands, if not millions, of potential customers. Once eBay brings individuals to the doorsteps of the businesses I'm talking about, they do everything they can to point shoppers to their websites, where they can sell directly to those customers without having to pay eBay's fees.

Some sellers list only a fraction of their total sales inventory on eBay. One technique is to put a representative sample up for sale in an eBay Store so that anyone who makes a purchase can be sent a business card or information sheet containing the URL of the website. Other sellers put their excess inventory or reduced price merchandise on eBay—knowing that, in general, eBay shoppers love bargains—while putting their new or first-line stock on their own website.

I say "their own website" because an eBay Store or an About Me page is essentially a small-scale website that eBay allows you to create with eBay functioning as the host. In this chapter, you'll learn how to find your own host and create a website that you manage and control—a site where you establish your business presence just the way you want it to appear, and where you give the customers you've met on eBay or on other auction sites a place to interact with you more fully.

Choosing Your Host

It pays to shop close to home. This applies whether you are looking for new set of dining room furniture for your residence or for a website. The first place to look— especially if you are operating on a limited budget—is the company that gives you access to the Internet. That would be your own Internet Service Provider (ISP). If you want more hosting space or extra features, you'll probably need to sign up for an account with a full-time Web-hosting service—a company that focuses solely on providing clients with disk space and software for hosting websites.

> **Note:** If you have a high-speed Internet connection on a fast computer with several gigabytes of storage space and a Web server application such as Apache, you can set up your own Web server in your home or office. Nevertheless, this option is for advanced users only; along with greater control, you also gain responsibility for the problems and configuration duties that go along with running a Web server.

Hosting with Your ISP

The company that provides you with access to the Internet almost certainly gives you e-mail and Web server space as part of your account. It is to the company's advantage to do so, because it wants you to be happy with its level of service and it wants you to spend your money with it. Even if the company does not charge extra for e-mail service or Web hosting, it hopes you'll upgrade to a more robust level of service at some point.

The popular ISP Earthlink (http://www.earthlink.com), at this writing, provides customers with basic high-speed Internet access for $19.95 per month for the first six months ($39.99 per month thereafter). This package includes eight e-mail address, Web-based access to e-mail, and 80MB of Web storage space (10MB for each e-mail address you use). You also get to use the interactive Site Builder utility, a Web-based form you fill out to create and format your pages. This is everything you need for creating a commercial website. My friend Betsey Means hosts her Womanlore (http://www.womanlore.com) website shown in Figure 16-1 with Earthlink.

In the beginning, Betsey didn't pay anything extra for her site. She had a URL assigned to it by Earthlink. Such URLs look like this: http://hosting.earthlink.net/~betsey/index.html. For an extra monthly fee, she gets e-mail service and domain name support as well as Web hosting. That means she purchased her domain name "womanlore.com" from a domain name registrar (in this case, Network Solutions, http://www.networksolutions.com) and associated it with her Earthlink website. She is also able to create e-mail addresses that end in the domain name womanlore.com: Betsey@womanlore.com, info@womanlore.com, and so on.

> **Note:** You don't need to use Network Solutions to search for and purchase a domain name. It may be the oldest and best-known domain name

registrar, but it's far from the only game in town. Shop for a domain name registry that has been accredited by the Internet Consortium for Assigned Names and Numbers (ICANN) and that has authority to sell names in the domain you want (.com, .net, .biz, and so on). You'll find a list of registrars at http://www.icann.org/registrars/accredited-list.html.

Figure 16-1. You can use your ISP to host a beginning-level website that supports your auction sales.

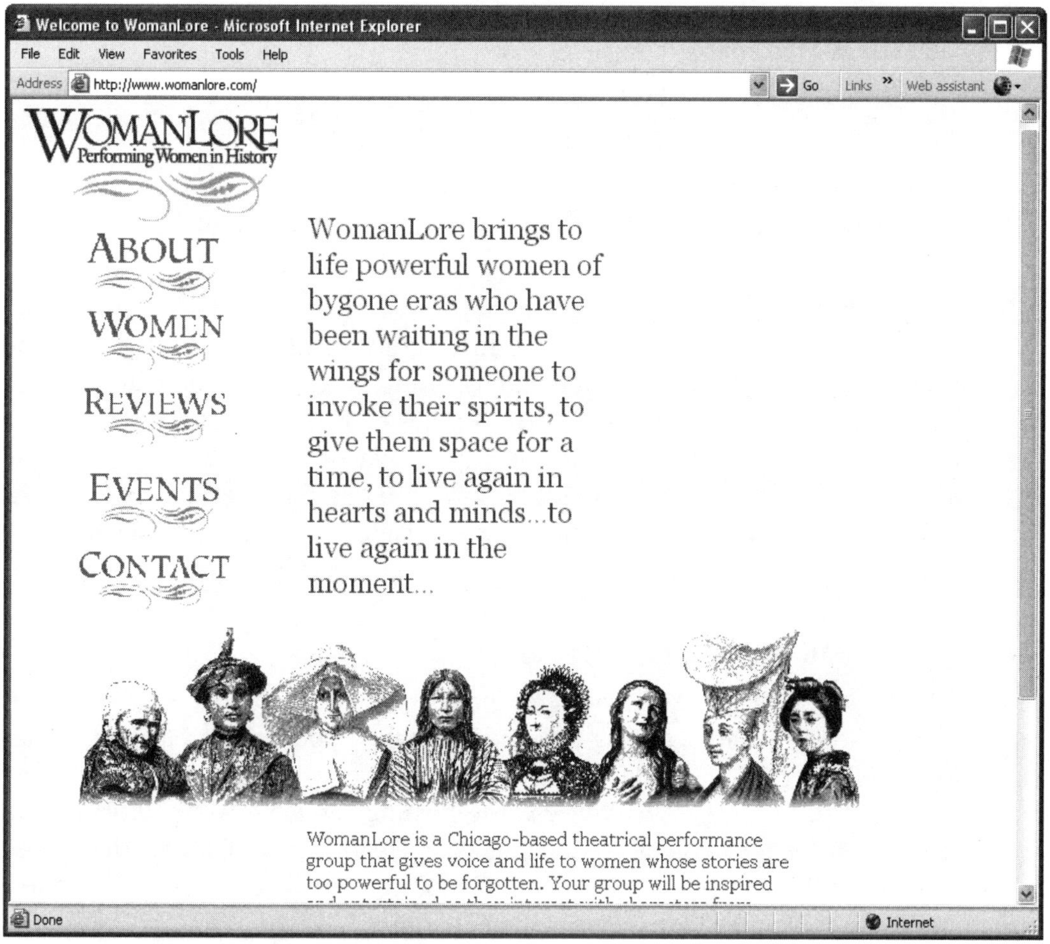

© Belsey Means Wills, owner of Womenlore, Inc.

Finding a Full-Time Web Host

If you are planning a commercial website or a site that contains a substantial level of creativity such as forms, audio, or video, you should sign up for a full-time Web-hosting solution. A full-time hosting account gives you a wide range of features needed to run a website.

You don't necessarily have to sign up with a new company (a company other than your ISP) to obtain a full-time hosting account. If you turn first to your ISP, you'll probably find that, by paying a nominal additional monthly fee, you can have the ISP give you its hosting account for full-time commercial websites. In my own case, I pay my ISP an additional $9.95 a month for a hosting account that includes:

- 500MB of Web space
- 10GB of monthly data transfers
- The ability to use my domain name of gregholden.com
- Ten e-mail addresses
- The ability to run my own Perl, PHP, and other scripts on the server
- Statistics that let me track visits to my site

Although your own ISP gives you the most convenient option for a full-time hosting account, you might find a better deal by shopping around. Where do you find Web hosts? A few directories gather detailed profiles of Web hosts and ISPs and sort them by geographic location and other qualities. Two of the best known are The List (http://www.thelist.com) and Providers of Commercial Internet Access (POCIA, http://www.celestin.com/pocia). You might also consider some of the following types of Web hosts:

Finding Free and Almost-Free Hosts

A handful of sites provide users with free hosting—at least, the account is free in terms of the amount of money being charged. In reality, you end up paying in other ways. You may have to display advertisements on the Web pages you create; you may also be required to view pages as you use the hosting service's Web editor; or you might "pay" in the sense that you have less disk space and fewer features than other types of accounts. Examples include Yahoo! Geocities (http://geocities.yhahoo.com) and Free Web Site Hosting (http://www.50megs.com).

Using Full-Time Web Hosts

It pays to plan ahead for success. Even if your business seems small now, it may grow to be big and successful before too long. You'll save yourself the time and trouble involved in moving from one Web host to another if you sign up with one that functions solely as a Web server and that gives its customers the maximum amount of resources they can expect.

A full-time Web host, like other types of hosting services, gives you space on a Web server where you can store your Web page files (and your auction photos and other documents), create a shopping cart or sales catalog if you need to, and communicate with your customers by e-mail.

Not only that, but you get a console, sometimes called a *control panel*, that helps you manage your files and your site. One example I am familiar with is Webmasters .com (http://www.webmasters.com). This site includes hosting packages that range from $9.95 to $99.00 per month.

The options for hosting a commercial website, and reasons for choosing each one, are summarized in Table 16-1.

Selecting the Right Domain Name

A domain name is an easy-to-remember alias for a computer that is connected to the Internet. Every computer on the Internet is assigned an identifier called an IP address—a series of numbers such as 145.223.76.9. If everyone who surfed the Web had to enter this series of numbers to access their favorite websites, there would be chaos and confusion.

You're already familiar with the process of choosing names if you have an eBay Store and an eBay user ID, not to mention user IDs and storefront names on other marketplace sites. When I was searching for domain names, I naturally looked to my own name first. I wasn't able to obtain the domain name Holden.com, but I was able to secure gregholden.com, which is a good alternative.

Table 16-1. Website hosting options.

If you want . . .	Choose this hosting option
To start a website for no money	Use the space your ISP already gives you.
Have an e-commerce sales site with shopping cart	Find a full-time Web host.
Your own domain name (like mysite.com)	Register your name with a domain name registrar.
A free website	Search for a free Web host that makes its customers display ads for other businesses.

Signing Up for Value-Added Services

I sometimes use the term *part-time* to describe hosting services that perform functions other than simply hosting websites. VeriSign (http://www.verisign.com), for instance, is in the security business. It sells security keys that help businesses and individuals protect the information they transmit either through e-mail or through the Web by encrypting it. But VeriSign also provides a domain name registry to registrars that deal with the public. It also provides online payment processing solutions like Payflow Link for $19.95 per month. Network Solutions (http://www.networksolutions .com) is primarily in the business of managing domain names in the .com and other domains. But Network Solutions also gives its domain name customers the option of hosting their sites.

Part-time Web hosts aren't necessarily less expensive than others. But they give you value-added services that might pay off in the long run. Consider the full-time Web host Easy CGI (http://www.easycgi.com). In the basic level of service, you get hosting for $9.95 per month that includes 3GB of disk space, support for Perl and other scripting languages that help you process forms, and support for the MySQL database environment, which can help you create a dynamic sales catalog (see Chapter 17 for more information about dynamic websites). Compare that to Network Solutions, whose basic plan costs $9.96 per month for Web hosting. You also get 3GB of disk storage, 50GB of data transfer per month, and MySQL/Microsoft Access support. In addition, you also get a free domain registration or renewal if you pay for a year in advance.

Hiring a Consultant to Help You

When you decide to create your own website, especially if it is a site designed to help you make money, it can be intimidating. When you look around at your competitors' websites, you naturally wonder how you are going to make yours of sufficient quality to compete with theirs. You should consider hiring a consultant. One of the best reasons for hiring someone is to have the person create a logo for you. Another reason is to make sure your graphics appear sharp and have the 3-D shading effects that Web surfers come to expect from professional websites.

Choosing a Web Designer

There is no shortage of individuals who are willing and eager to create websites for you or other businesses. The challenge is to find one who is affordable, has a style that is compatible to your own, and is easy to work with as well as reliable.

Where do you find such people? One of the best ways is to ask around by asking people you know or sending e-mails to people who already have websites. Look at the bottom of Web pages for a credit line such as, "Web site created by. . . ."

Look at the websites these people have created. Look at the colors and type styles. Are they compatible with your own style, with the market you are trying to reach? Are the sites complex and easy to follow? Do they seem well designed? Do the pages seem crammed with as much content as possible, or is the emphasis on clean white space? One approach is not necessarily better than another; the important thing is to find a designer whose work approaches your own aesthetic.

Sometimes, the same designers can alter their style to fit the content they are trying to illustrate visually. Debbie Levitt of the design firm As Was is a well-known Web designer who works with a staff of artists to create auction templates for eBay sellers and websites for e-commerce entrepreneurs. As Was also specializes in presentation and branding for online marketplaces. Two of the eBay-related As Was sites are shown in Figure 16-2 and Figure 16-3. Figure 16-2 is a template design for Adam Hersh Auctions. Adam is a young entrepreneur who is fast becoming one of eBay's biggest and most successful sellers.

Figure 16-2. A design like this appeals to shoppers who like printed media, particularly posters.

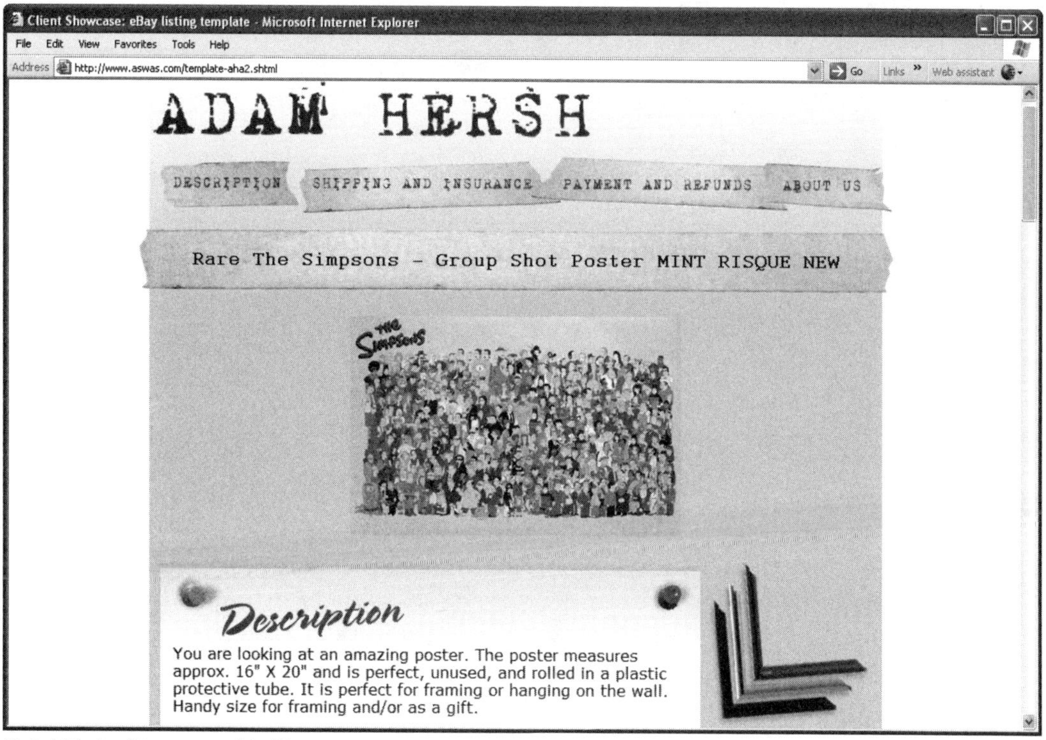

© Debbie Levitt, owner of As Was.

Figure 16-3. This design appeals to a sportier crowd, particularly those who love golf.

© Debbie Levitt, owner of As Was.

The eBay listing template for Lost Golf Balls Retail shown in Figure 16-3 was also created by Debbie. The design is more active and busy and will appeal to a younger audience more accustomed to getting visual information from many different media sources.

Levitt offers this advice to eBay sellers who are looking for a designer to create listing templates or a website, or both:

Find a designer who can capture your personality and speak to your target audience. If every design looks the same, then expect yours to look like the rest because that's what that company or individual does. Look for someone who can do a variety of styles since then they are more likely to connect with the style you want. Speak to their clients. Look at case studies and call or e-mail those people. Most importantly, sign a contract. We hear all the time comments to the effect that, "The design was never done and I can't get my money back." Or, "I don't like it and they won't make another version." Well, what does the contract say? *What contract?* Don't enter into handshake deals!

Creating a Logo

One of the best reasons for hiring a designer to help you is to create a logo for your website. Your site is an extension of your auction business. As you already know from your auction activities, professionalism is important. It's worth spending a few hundred dollars (specifically, I would guess that you can have a logo designed for anywhere from $250 to $400) to have someone create a logo for you. The one-time expense will pay off for years to come as you apply the logo to your stationery, business cards, advertisements, and any other print and marketing materials.

Solicit Bids for Your Logo and Web Design

One of the best places to find freelance designers to create a logo for you is eLance Online (http://www.elanceonline.com). This site matches professional contractors such as designers, writers, and consultants with employers who need their services.

It is also a reverse auction site, where you post a description of the project you want someone to do for you, and freelance contractors bid on it. You can review the bids they submit and choose the lowest bid, or select a contractor whose price may not be the lowest but whose other qualifications attract you.

If you're a service provider yourself, you can pay a monthly fee to bid on projects. You are also able to create a page on the site that describes your company and your experience, and that provides potential employers with references they can contact.

Plenty of businesses use logos that are simple to create; they consist of type only, with no drawings or photographic images. If you're in a hurry and you are the do-it-yourself type you, too, can create your own logo at the Cool Text website (http://www.cooltext.com).

Creating Your Website

Why would you consider paying a Web designer to create your entire website? You might do this if you are in a hurry and/or if your website is going to be an important source of income for you.

Choosing Web Page Software

If you've created an About Me page on eBay, you're already familiar with the process of creating a Web page without having to use hypertext markup language (HTML), which makes the page's contents readable by a Web browser. Like many other Web hosts, eBay provides you with a simple form to fill out so that you can enter the content and have it formatted automatically when you submit the contents to eBay.

When you create your website, you should also look for a user-friendly utility that helps you create a home page without having to work directly with HTML. If you use Yahoo! GeoCities (http://geocities.yahoo.com), for instance, you are given access to the same kind of interactive form to make a home page on that site. However, if you use Yahoo! to host your site, for instance, a sophisticated Web-editing program called SiteBuilder is available to you.

SiteBuilder, like other Web editors, gives you a wide range of menus, buttons, and other user-friendly options for creating and formatting Web pages. The nice thing about Yahoo! SiteBuilder is that you can use its built-in Site Creation Wizard, which leads you through the process of starting up a site. You also receive a selection of more than 330 templates you can use to design your pages. When you first open the program after installation, you are greeted by the Site Creation Wizard shown in Figure 16-4.

Click START, and you are led through the process of naming your site and creating

Figure 16-4. You are prompted to use the site creation wizard when you first open Yahoo! SiteBuilder.

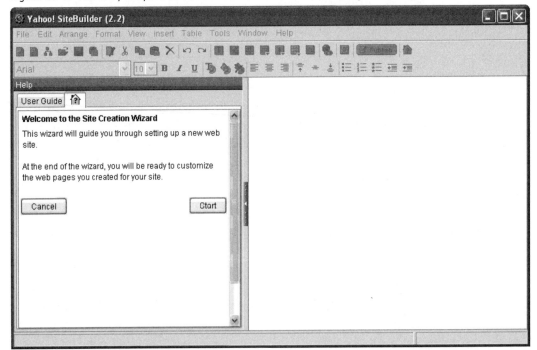

© Yahoo! SiteBuilder.

a simple set of pages for it. One of the templates, with its corresponding navigation bar, is shown in Figure 16-5.

 Note: SiteBuilder is really only useful if you have an account with Yahoo! Web Hosting or Yahoo! Merchant solutions: it's only set up to publish to these sites.

Organizing Your Website

When you create an About Me page or an eBay Store, organization is streamlined for you. Although you ultimately have to come up with something to say, the forms you fill out lead you through the process of writing the content. The classic method for brainstorming your site's look and feel is to talk it over with your friends or coworkers. You write up a list of the features you want, and you come up with a description of how you envision your home page to look. I've been known to come up with drawings as crude and crowded as the one shown in Figure 16-6.

Figure 16-5. SiteBuilder helps you get started, but you have to finish by publishing to Yahoo!

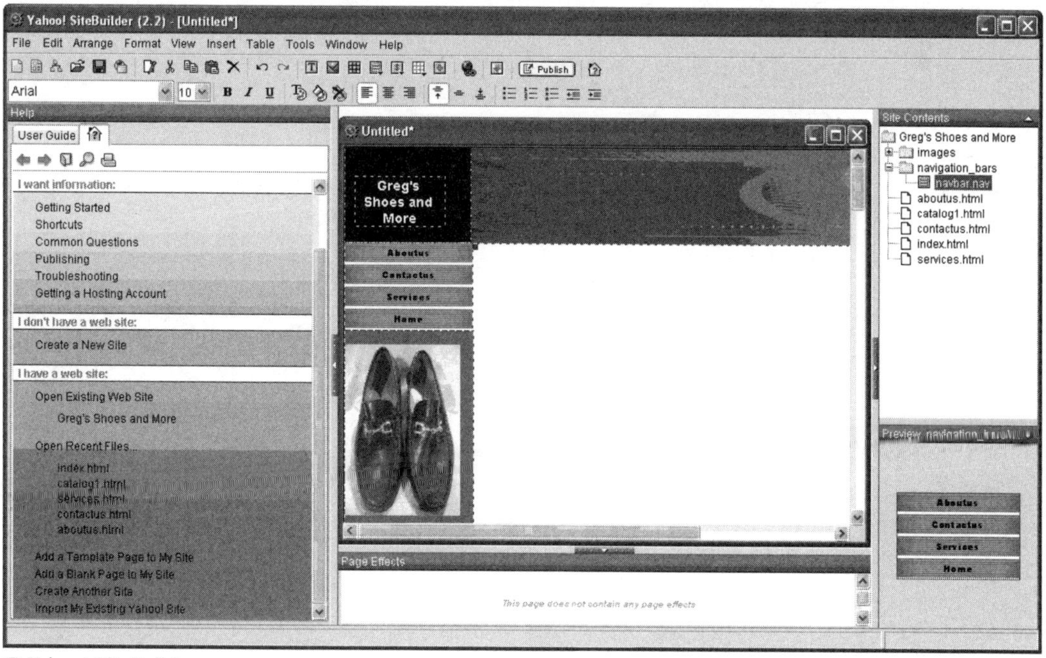

© Yahoo! SiteBuilder.

Figure 16-6. Take pencil and paper in hand and brainstorm to come up with a list of contents.

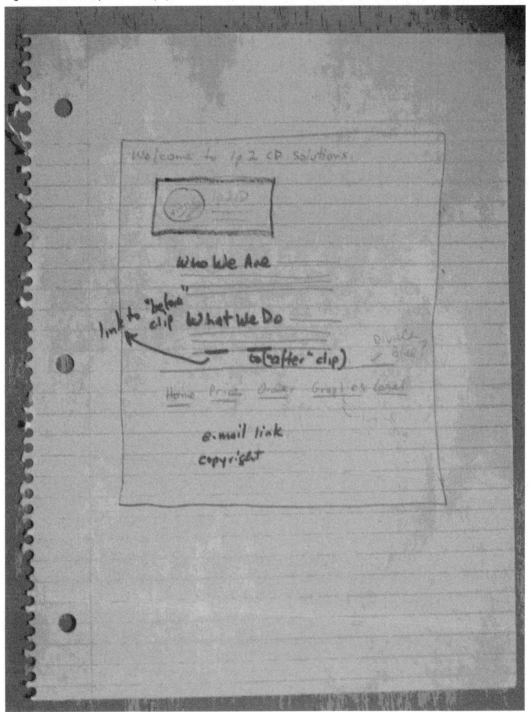

Dividing Your Content into Categories

Amazon.com has its millions of marketplace items divided into categories and subcategories through which you can search and browse. Every website needs to have its contents divided into two or more categories, too. Each category contains a single type of information, which makes that information easier to find. Categories also make website data easier to digest; rather than seeing all of a website's contents in one place (a task typically performed by a Site Map Web page), you see a short list of contents.

When you're thinking of how to design your website, make a list of all of the things you want to say and do on the site. Think of how that list can be boiled down into, say, three to five categories. Each of them can have its own home page, plus a link on your site's main home page. For example, you might come up with a rough list of tasks you want your website to perform, such as the following:

- Explain who we are and what we do
- Link to our auction sales
- Give customers contact information
- Provide links to detailed product specifications
- Sell catalog items directly to the public
- Help build our brand and increase our overall visibility
- Turn our eBay customers into repeat customers
- Let shoppers sign up for our newsletter and provide us with contact information we can use for future communications
- Give customers links to related websites and online resources we recommend
- Sell half-price items and hold special promotions

That might seem like an ambitious set of goals, but it's well within the range of most websites and their designers. How would you turn this set of objectives into categories? You group the ones that seem similar. For example, "Provide links to detailed product specifications" and "Let shoppers sign up for our newsletter" could both be described as customer service functions. "Link to our auction sales" and "Sell catalog items directly to the public" are both ways to let shoppers purchase your merchandise. They could be grouped under a heading such as Products or Sales. The next step is to group the items in your list of goals into categories; Table 16-2 gives you an example.

You should, of course, feel free to come up with your own category names, and arrange content in a way that best suits your needs. Headings like "About Us" and

Table 16-2. Website categories.

Home	About Us	Products	Customer Service	Contact
Help build our brand and increase our overall visibility.	Explain who we are and what we do.	Link to our auction sales.	Provide links to detailed product specifications.	Give customers contact information.
Let shoppers sign up for our newsletter.		Sell catalog items directly to the public.	Give customers links to related websites and online resources we recommend.	
		Sell half-price items and hold special promotions.		

"Contact Us" are widely used—perhaps even overused—and you might want to come up with something more original to make your site unique.

Including the Must-Haves

No matter what categories you come up with, make sure your website includes the following standard components:

- *A Home Page.* Shoppers and prospective clients want to know that their presence is appreciated, whether they are entering a brick-and-mortar store or an online store. A good home page can function much like a friendly receptionist, making visitors feel welcome and directing them to content they may want to investigate further.

- *Photos.* Images are essential when Web surfers go shopping online. They help prospective customers learn something about the products they're considering purchasing. The more photos you have, the more likely someone will click the BUY button.

- *Description of Who You Are.* On the Web, people can't deal with you face-to-face. They don't have the advantage of reading body language or looking in your eyes. You can, however, build trust by telling something about who you are, why you love what you do, why you're good at what you do, and why people can rely on you.

- *Description of Items for Sale/Services You Provide.* This is where you "sell" your goods or services. You have to expend some time and energy in capturing images and writing descriptions. But once you're done, you can publish the information and get it online in a matter of minutes for a fraction of the cost it would take to produce a printed sales catalog or promotional brochure.

• *Navigational Tools.* Every site should provide ways for visitors to help navigate it. Think of them as functioning like the signs and directory in a department store. You provide links, images, a site map, or a search box for your visitors so that they can locate what they want more quickly.

• *A "Customer Service" Area.* If you're conducting retail sales on your site, this area enables your customers to get questions answered and contact you if they need help. You might provide information on your returns policy, for instance. If you're creating a site for personal use or business services, this can simply be a page full of contact information or directions to your office.

It's often a good idea to draw up a quick sketch of the pages you want to have on your site. This sketch doesn't need to be complicated or beautiful. It can be as simple and crude as the hand-drawn diagram I threw together in Figure 16-7.

Linking to Your Auction Sales

When you create a website that is designed to supplement your existing sales on eBay or another auction site, one of the things you must have on your site is a link to your auction sales. Visitors to your website should have a way of finding the items you have for sale so that they can purchase the items. If you use eBay, you make use of a tool called the Editor Kit, which creates links to your current eBay sales. (See Chapter 17 for step-by-step instructions on how to use it.)

Creating Web Pages

Once you have selected a host, have a domain name lined up, and have given some thought to your website's organization, you can get to work. It's always a good idea to start small and build your site up rather than trying to create a twenty-five- to forty-page website from the outset. You might create only six to ten pages to begin with. When you start small, you don't get overwhelmed, and you have time to focus on making each one of your pages look just right.

You might consider drawing a map of your website. I usually draw these maps in the shape of a triangle. The home page is drawn at the top; the top-level category pages are beneath it; the subcategory pages are beneath them. The map helps you keep track of which pages link to each other, and how many pages you want to have.

You've probably heard the term *hypertext markup language*, which is one of the markup languages commonly used to create Web pages. Although it's a good idea to

Figure 16-7. A rough sketch of a site map can help you get started with creating individual pages.

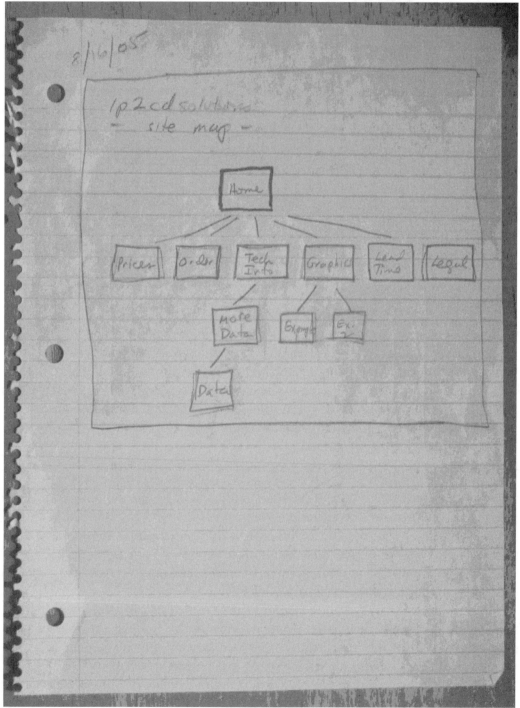

know at least something about HTML, you don't have to know how to write it. In the deep, dark ages of the World Wide Web, people had to write the HTML commands to create Web pages in the form of plain-text files. They would then save those files with the file extension .htm or .html and open them in Web browsers to test them out. It was a time-consuming process suited primarily to computer programmers. These days, you can choose from many different software programs that enable you to create Web pages without having to write HTML. These software programs go by different names; in this chapter, I'll call them Web page editors.

The Web page software that I find most convenient and easiest to use comes with the Netscape Communicator and Mozilla browser packages. It's called Composer; it's free and, while it doesn't let you do flashy things like applying Web page scripts and automatically making the same change on dozens of Web pages at once, it still performs many of the basic tasks that simple websites require. It's a great program for getting started and creating your first Web pages; if you like the process and want to perform more complex technical tricks, you can invest money in a commercial Web page editor like Microsoft FrontPage or Macromedia Dreamweaver.

 Tip: You can download Netscape Communicator, which includes Composer, at http://home.netscape.com. Mozilla is available at http:// www.mozilla.org. In both cases, you need to download the complete package rather than the standalone Web browser.

Once you have installed either Communicator or Mozilla, you launch Composer by choosing Composer from the Window menu. A new blank document appears on your computer screen with the text cursor blinking on the top line, waiting for you to type or paste something. You can paste a text file you have prepared previously in a word processing program or you can start by typing the name of your website. For this example, assume you're creating a site called The Bargain Basement:

1. Type "Welcome to the Bargain Basement." Click and hold down your mouse button and drag across the letters you just typed to highlight them.

2. From the paragraph format drop-down menu list that currently reads Body Text, choose Heading 1. This formats the highlighted words in the Heading 1 style. Six levels of headings are provided in HTML; H1 is the biggest and most important, and H6 is the least important and smallest.

Note: In the final version of your page, you might insert your company logo at the top of the page, but for now, this heading will serve as a placeholder.

3. Press ENTER to create a blank space, and then type a subheading to go with your main heading. Highlight the subheading as you did earlier, and choose Heading 3 from the paragraph format drop-down list.

4. Press ENTER and type a paragraph that describes your website and its mission, or that serves as a greeting to your customers. Your Web page editor should let you review the results as they will appear online (see Figure 16-8).

If you are graphically challenged like me, the temptation is to use type as a decoration on your Web pages. Resist this urge! Instead, stick with a tried-and-true princi-

Figure 16-8. A Web page editor lets you preview your work in "what you see is what you get" (WYSIWYG) format.

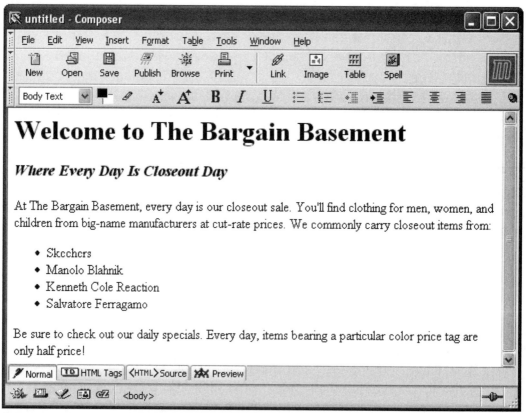

ple followed by many pros: use a serif face (such as Times or Georgia) for the text, and a sans serif typeface (such as Helvetica, Arial, or Verdana) for the headings, link buttons, and other navigational text. These are just two of the various type families shown in Figure 16-9.

You can go on adding content to your page. When you are done, save the file in a folder on your local file system. Within that folder, you should create a complete version of your website; it should serve as a backup to the version you are eventually going to publish online.

Creating Images

You already know how to take images, so it's a small step to posting images on your host's Web server rather than with eBay or your photo host. The same principles that work with eBay auction images work with Web page photos: take them at a relatively low resolution (for instance, 600 x 800), keep them as low in file size as possible

Figure 16-9. You can use sans serif, serif, or plain-text fonts in your Web design.

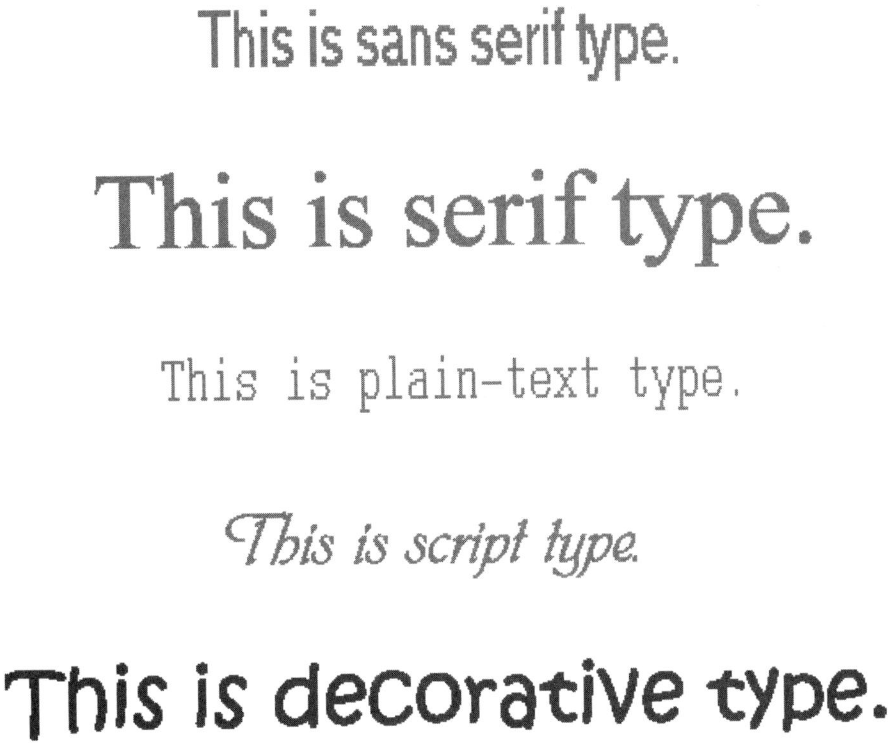

This is sans serif type.

This is serif type.

This is plain-text type.

This is script type.

This is decorative type.

(ideally, 15K to 50K), and crop them so their physical dimensions don't consume too much screen space (perhaps 2 x 3 inches, or 3 x 5 inches).

Posting Pages Online

When you fill out an auction description form and post images, you move the HTML and image files from your computer to a remote Web server. You have to do the same with your Web page files. You move them from the folder you have set up to store the local version of your site to the folder that your Web host has set up for you on one of its servers. Chances are your Web-hosting service will provide you with a user-friendly way to move the files. Otherwise, you may want to acquaint yourself with the ins and outs of using a file transfer protocol (FTP) application. FTP is simple and effective: it only has one purpose, which is to move files from one Internet-based computer to another.

FTP applications aren't flashy, so they don't require a lot of overhead in terms of bandwidth. Sometimes, you'll find that if your Web browser isn't working effectively because your wireless connection is weak, your FTP application might still be able to connect to a remote server. In order to get connected, you need to get some critical information from your Web host: the FTP address of your server, and the user name and password you should use. Typically, the information looks like this:

- Server address: web-ftp.earthlink.com
- User name: [your e-mail address]
- Password: [your password]

Once you enter the information in the appropriate boxes in your FTP application's main window, you click a button labeled CONNECT (or something similar). When you connect, you view the files on your local file system on one side of the window (usually, the left side), and the files on the Web server on the right. You select the files you want to move on the left and click a button that points toward the Web server side of the window; the file is moved from your computer to the remote machine. The WS_FTP window is shown in Figure 16-10.

One nice thing about FTP programs is that they give you the ability to create directories and move files from one directory to another. You can also use them to rename files either on your local computer or the remote server.

Checking Your Content and Your Links

Simply moving your files to the designated folder on your Web server isn't enough. It's rare that you can move a group of files online and have everything look and

Figure 16-10. FTP programs are reliable and give you control over your site's organization.

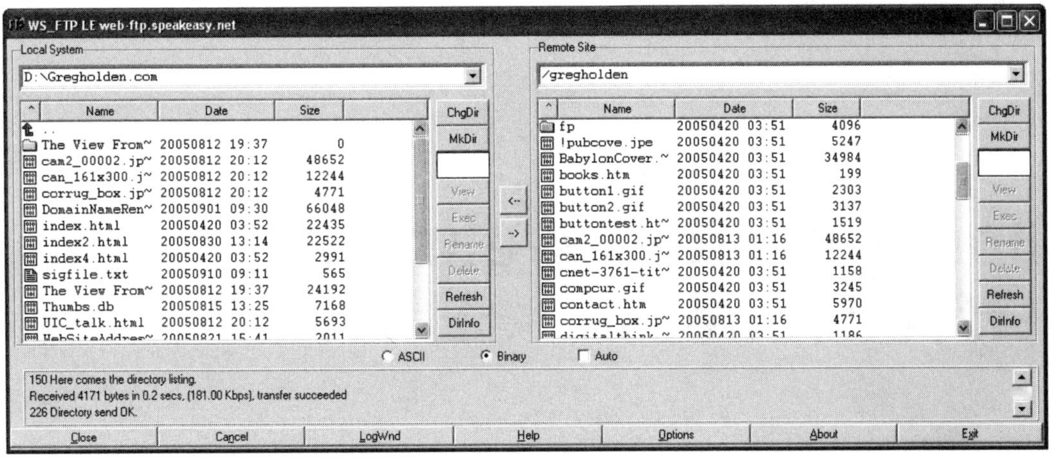

function correctly the first time. Take the time to review your pages for typos or images that don't appear quickly—or that don't appear at all. Better yet, have a friend or family member look it over closely. Because you're managing an e-commerce website rather than a personal or humorous site, you need to ensure that your site portrays you in a professional manner. It's very common to make corrections to a Web page, save the changes, move the revised file to the Web server using your FTP program, then refresh the page in the browser window to review your changes. Also make sure your prices, model numbers, colors, and other pertinent details about your products are correct as well so your customers don't get confused. Once you have your site up and running, you can gradually add features that will make it function even more effectively, as you'll learn in the Chapter 17.

Boosting Your Website's Effectiveness

What would your reaction be if you held a garage sale and nobody came? How would you feel if you opened an eBay Store and no one made any purchases from you for weeks at a time? It would probably be the same feeling you'd get if you went through the effort to create a website and nothing happened—no page views, no e-mail inquiries (except for those spammers who want to sell you the usual range of medicinal substances and other services), and no purchases. It would make even an optimistic person want to give up. But don't stay discouraged for more than a few seconds. You can take steps to boost your website by making it more effective and attractive. When you see your number of visitors and customers go up thanks to your efforts, you'll be that much more satisfied.

When my brother first put his website (http://www.lp2cdsolutions.com) online, he was afraid he had wasted his time and energy. I remember him telling me that only a few people had found his site—and after we did some calculating, we determined that most of the hits came from the two of us. A couple months later, he was very happy. He was getting more visits, and the number of business assignments he received through the website was more than enough to satisfy him and keep him busy with work he loves.

What did he do to go from sad to glad? He marketed and improved his site. He also used his first job to build more business. He made sure the work he did for his one and only client was top-notch so he could refer to the project on his site and include a glowing testimonial, which improved his credibility. This led to more business. In this chapter, you'll learn some simple and practical approaches to making your website more dynamic and effective so that it boosts your business and helps you achieve all of your goals, rather than gaining cobwebs due to lack of attention.

Making Your Site Content Rich

The best way to make your site more attractive is to make its content richer and more valuable. The Web is perhaps unique among communications media in that the amount of useful information you provide directly affects the likelihood that you'll get a response from your readers. Simply writing long Web pages full of empty words won't do the trick, of course. You have to meet the expectations you raise in the minds of your potential customers on your site as completely as possible. Since you are creating a website that will supplement your auction sales, you need to provide content that builds trust and encourages people to buy from you. Tell visitors anything that will illustrate that you have a good reputation and track record, such as:

- How long you have been in business
- How many transactions you have completed successfully
- Your feedback rating on eBay or other auction sites
- What your customers think about you, in the form of quotes or testimonials

You can also demonstrate how much you know about what you sell by providing some history of the field, or tips for selecting the right item. Having a set of links to other websites of interest for your target audience might direct visitors away from your site momentarily, but it also turns your site into a resource that will keep potential customers coming back again and again.

Managing Your Site's Links

Websites that don't perform effectively are in a sort of isolated limbo because they don't show up in enough website directories, other websites don't make links to them, and they don't contain enough links to websites that their visitors will find relevant. Simply tracking and managing your site's links—both the links to your site and from your site to other locations—can improve your overall visibility and attract more visitors.

Checking Your Links to Other Sites

If you are able to include links to other sites you know about and value, and that you think your visitors will enjoy visiting, you make your own website that much more valuable and worthy of return visits. It seems like a paradox that you should create a page full of links, or a list full of links, to websites that you think people should visit. It seems at first as though you're trying to send them away from your site to visit other locations. And in a sense you are. But chances are your visitors will find those sites on their own if you have suggested the right ones. By creating a page full of valuable links, you improve your own credibility and you turn your website into a resource that visitors will want to return to on a regular basis.

 Tip: Don't just make a link to another website. Send a message to the site's webmaster, offering to place a link on your site if that person will reciprocate by including a link to you. The more links you can make to your site from remote locations, the better placement you'll get in search engine results.

When you create links to other sites, you need to make sure the links are accurate. If you send your visitors to too many Web pages that have moved or are simply not online any more, your own reputation will begin to suffer. People will begin to wonder just how frequently you update and check the content on your own Web pages. You can do the checking manually—the time-consuming way—by following links one after another and making sure they still work. Or you can use an online utility like Link Checker (http://www.siteowner.com/badlinks.cfm), which scans the links on a Web page and makes sure they are still accurate.

Improving Links to Your Website

It's also important to check the number of sites that are linking to your site. You can do this, again, by installing a software program, or by using an online site management utility. Link Checker Pro (http://www.link-checker-pro.com) is a software program that can check thousands of links both into and out of a website. It costs $75 and up depending on the number of Web pages you want to check. The program can be downloaded as a trial version that you can try out for a thirty-day period. The nice thing about the program is that it provides you with a graphical representation of the links you make to other sites (see Figure 17-1). The map literally tells you, in a glance, how "well connected" your site is.

What happens if you find that you only have one or two sites making links to you? You have to roll up your sleeves and make sure some new links are created. The first and easiest approach is to create your own links. The owners of many websites try to improve their ranking on Google search results by simply creating dozens or

Figure 17-1. Link Checker Pro graphically maps links both to and from your website.

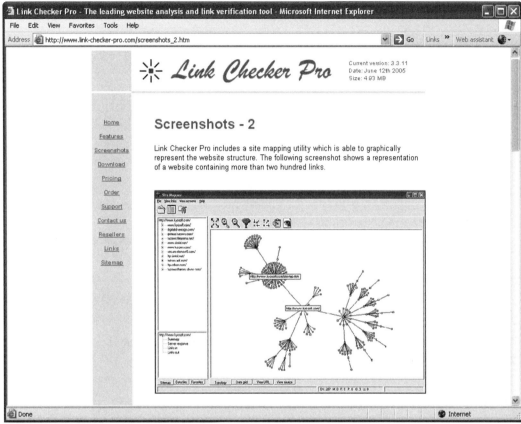

even hundreds of websites that have barely any legitimate contents. The only purpose of the sites is to show up on Google, and to create links to other websites that are owned by the same individual. Usually, the sites have absurdly long URLs, such as:

- http://127.34.222.1/this-is-a-really-long-url.com
- http://www.websitesample.net/buying-shoes-online.com
- http://www.massmarketingtips.com/a-web-page-about-a-very-specific-topic.biz

When you click through to these pages, you may or may not actually get the content you're looking for. You are likely to find a set of links to other websites—some of which may be run by the owner of the website you are currently viewing. I'm certainly not suggesting that you set up such bogus Web pages yourself. However, you can steal a trick or two from these marketers by making links to your current website from other websites you own. The obvious example is your About Me page. If you still have an account with eBay, you should set up such a page if only to make a link to your "real" website.

Suppose you have set up a website with a Web-hosting service. You have purchased a domain name that takes the form www.mysite.com. You are setting up an e-commerce catalog at that location. You still have a separate account with an Internet Service Provider that enables you to get online in the first place. Since that account almost certainly includes space for a simple website, why not create a place-holder Web page on that site—a page that contains a little information about who you are and how to contact you and that, most important, links to your primary website?

 Tip: If your ISP is America Online (AOL), take advantage of the fact that AOL allows each of its subscribers to have up to seven separate screen names. Each screen name comes with 2MB of Web server space. Many AOL users assign separate screen names to different members of their family. But there is no rule that says a single user can't create seven separate screen names, each with its own Web page. Each of the pages can link to one another—and to your primary website as well.

Once you've created as many links as you can to your primary website, you can take another step and solicit links from the websites of your family and friends. Finally, you can reach out to websites whose content is similar or complementary to your own and ask the owners or webmasters to exchange links with you. The worst they can do is say no—but in many cases, you'll get a positive response because those sites' respective owners have just as much interest as you do in maintaining well-connected, well-visited websites.

Creating an Online Sales Catalog

Shoppers on the Web are used to browsing through sales catalogs and making purchases. By creating a sales catalog on your site, you are giving them what they want and expect. As usual where the Web is concerned, you have several options when it comes to creating a catalog.

Adding Your eBay Sales to Your Website

If you still sell on eBay through either individual auctions or an eBay Store, you have an easy way to get your sales listed on your website. You can use either eBay's Editor Kit or Merchant Kit. Both are bits of software code you add to the Web page where you want links to your current eBay sales listings to appear. They differ in one significant way:

- The Editor Kit is a good tool to use if you don't sell on eBay Stores or eBay's special site for books, CDs, and entertainment items: Half.com. It gathers your auction sales listings and puts them on your site.

- The Merchant Kit gathers auction sales listings as well as your eBay Stores and Half.com listings.

To get started with the Editor Kit, go to the utility's page on eBay: http://affiliates .ebay.com/tools/editor-kit/. Then follow these steps:

1. Scroll down the page and click GET EDITOR KIT NOW.
2. Sign in with your eBay user ID and password when prompted to do so.
3. When the Create Your Editor Kit page appears, choose an option from the Dimensions drop-down list and an option from the Theme drop-down list to customize the look of the listings as they will appear on your page. You can also specify keyword searches to determine what items you wish to display, or limit your lists to Buy It Now items only or items with Gallery images only.
4. If you want to earn a little money when someone clicks on a link to a sale and then makes a purchase, choose an option from the Provider drop-down list. If you want to earn money as an affiliate, you need to choose eBay's affiliate program, Commission Junction, as the option. You'll have to apply to become an affiliate through Commission Junction and obtain a Commission Junction PID if you have not already done so. If you don't want to earn any money now but just want to see how the Editor Kit works, choose NOT AN AFFILIATE from the Provider drop-down list.
5. When you're finished, click CONTINUE.
6. A page entitled Preview Your Sniplet appears with a long and complicated-looking bit of JavaScript code displayed. For example: <scriptlanguage = "Ja vaScript"src = "http://lapi.ebay.com/ws/eBayISAPI.dll?EKServer&ai = behy1 knuhyn&bdrcol or = FFCC00&cid = 0&eksize = 2&encode = ISO-8859-1& endcolor = FF0000&endtime; eqy&fbgcolor = FFFFFF&fntcolor = 000000&

fs = 0&hdrcolor = FFFFCC&hdrimage = 1&hdrsrch = n&img = y&lnkcolor = 0000FF&logo = 3&num = 25&umbed = y&paypal = n&popup = n&prvd = 0& r0 = 4&shipcost = n&siteid = 0&sort = MetaEndSort&sortby = endtime&sort dir = asc&srchdesc = n&tbgcolor = FFFFFF&tlecolor = FFCE63&tlefs = 0& tlfcolor = 000000&track = &width = 570"></script>

7. Click just before the first less-than (<) sign at the beginning of the script. Then press and hold down the SHIFT key and click just after the last greater-than (>) symbol to highlight the entire code. Press CTRL + C to copy the code into your computer's clipboard.

Once you have copied the code, you need to paste it into your Web page. This requires you to open up the page where you want to add the listings in a Web editor—not your Web browser, but a program like Mozilla/Netscape Composer, Microsoft FrontPage, Macromedia Dreamweaver, or Allaire HomeSite. Alternately, if you don't have any of those applications, you can open up your home page file with the built-in text editor that comes with Windows, called Notepad.

Making Your Site Dynamic

Websites that offer a catalog worth of merchandise for sale put a burden on the site's owner or webmaster. Every time something is sold, it is taken from the company's inventory. It needs to be removed from the catalog or reordered when no other examples of the item remain in the catalog. Not only that, but shoppers also need to know how many items are currently in stock and what their current price is. You can update the information manually, just as you would a typo or other bit of text, by making the change and republishing the Web page to your site.

This kind of website is *static*—the contents don't change until the site's Webmaster changes them manually. In an environment in which thousands of catalog items are offered and perhaps dozens of them are being purchased in a single day, the burden of updating the site manually quickly becomes excessive.

Most high-volume e-commerce websites are *dynamic*—in other words, the contents change every time someone visits the site. There are several ways to do this. Here are just two options:

- Assemble the data in a database program, then connect the database's contents to the website using a program like Macromedia Cold Fusion.

- Write the pages using a scripting language like PHP, and have the contents drawn from a MySQL database.

In either case, the contents that the visitor actually sees are assembled dynamically from the database when the user requests the page. It's beyond the scope of this book to set up such a site for you, so you should consult with a Web designer.

Streamlining the Payment Process

Chapter 14 goes into detail about different options available to you for accepting electronic payments from your customers. Along with a sales catalog that is either frequently updated manually or dynamically updated, you need some technological features that make shopping easier.

Shopping cart software enables your customers to keep track of items that they select while they continue to shop through your inventory. When your customer is ready to check out, the shopping cart displays the items they've selected and totals up the purchase price as well as any sales tax that might be applicable. The customer can delete any items that he or she doesn't want, and then move on to make a secure credit card payment (as described in Chapter 14). GoECart (http://www.goecart.com/shopping_cart_software.asp) is a Web-based shopping cart service. It is available for a free thirty-day trial period; after that, the software carries a setup fee of $124.95 to $499.95 and a $79.95 to $199.95 monthly fee. ShopFactory Light (http://www.shopfactory.com/) is software you download and install on your own computer; it supports a sales inventory of fifty products and is available for $149.

 Tip: When you sell through your own website as well as on eBay, you need to find an ongoing source of merchandise. See Chapter 20 for tips on how to do this.

Marketing and Advertising Your Website

If you have an eBay Store, you know how important marketing is. You include a link to the store in your auction descriptions, and you may also purchase eBay keywords to direct potential buyers there. When you create a website, you need to do the same kind of marketing. How do buyers find your site? You have an advantage if you sell on eBay or other marketplaces, because you can create personal Web pages that include links to your site. And as you develop a clientele of customers, you should send them periodic mailings that include news about new products or special promotions you're offering on your website.

Other than your own links, the best kind of marketing you can do these days is search engine keyword advertising. Search engines represent the most popular way in which consumers locate products on the Internet. A website that tracks Internet statistics, called StatMarket (http://www.websidestory.com/products/web-analytics/ datainsights/statmarket/overview.html.), reported in late 2004 that a full 41 percent of all search referrals were being done by Google (http://www.google.com). The service that came in second place, Yahoo! (http://www.yahoo.com), had about 27 percent of the search market business. These two services are the ones on which any business needs to concentrate its efforts.

Listing Yourself on Yahoo! and Google

Everyone who has surfed the Web knows how search services work: A consumer enters a keyword or phrase in a search box on Google or Yahoo!. A *keyword* is a word describing a subject that you enter in a search box to find information on a website or on the wider Internet. Suppose you're trying to find a source for iPod accessories. You'd naturally enter the term "iPod accessories" in the search box on your search service of choice, click a button called SEARCH, SEARCH NOW, GO, or something similar.

When you send a keyword to a search service, you set a number of possible actions in motion. One thing that will happen is that the keyword will be processed by a script on a Web server that is operated by the search service. The script will make a request called a *query* to a database file. The database contains contents culled from millions (even billions, depending on the service) of Web pages.

The database contents are gathered from two sources. In some cases, search services employ human editors who record selected contents of Web pages and write descriptions for those pages. But Web pages are so ubiquitous and changeable that most of the work is actually done by computer programs that automatically scour the Web. These programs don't record every word on every Web page. Some take words from the headings; others index the first fifty or a hundred words on a website. Accordingly, when I did a search for "iPod accessories" on Google, the sites that were listed at the top of the first page of search results had two attributes:

1. Some sites that had the word *iPod* in the URL, such as http://www.apple.com/ ipod/color/accessories.html.

2. Other sites had the phrase *iPod accessories* mentioned either in the title or at the top of the home page.

This is only one kind of search result, however. When you submit a keyword or phrase to a Yahoo! or Google, the search results you get back actually fall into two categories.

The ones in the center of the page are results that indicate how closely the consumer's keywords matched the keywords on a particular Web page, combined with complex and secret formulas that indicate how "popular" the Web page is to begin with (in other words, how many links are made to it).

The results in the right-hand column are paid advertisements. Businesses bid a certain amount to Google or Yahoo! to have the results displayed. When someone enters a keyword and that keyword is one that businesses have bid on, the highest bidders are displayed in the paid ad area of the search results. Google calls its keyword ad program Google AdWords. It's one of the most popular and cost-effective ways to advertise a website because you only pay if someone responds to your ad by clicking it. It's called *pay-per-click advertising*; the innovative thing is that you determine how much you're going to pay for each click.

Purchasing AdWords

The AdWords program lets you place an ad that appears on Google only when someone searches for your chosen keywords. You only pay Google when someone clicks on the ad. Here's a real-world example: I was asked to provide some suggestions on how a major automobile company could advertise a new tire service. I pointed the company toward AdWords. I explained that suppose someone is searching for the keyword *tire* on either Google or Yahoo! Four companies have placed bids on those keywords: Toyota ($.50 per click), Just Tires ($.40 per click), Firestone ($.35 per click), and Bridgestone ($.30 per click). Toyota's ad will appear at the top of the paid ad area because it has the highest bid. It will also have to pay $.50 to Google every time someone clicks on the ad—which should be linked to one of Toyota's Web pages related to tires.

You can either write your own ad or have Google do it for you. You also have control over where your ads appear—you can choose specific countries or cities. You can also set a daily budget for your program so your spending doesn't go over a certain amount.

Google has a Keyword Tool that you can access for free and that suggests additional keywords you might pay for. For instance, people who searched for *tire* or *tires* on Google also searched for:

- Rims
- Goodyear
- Radial
- Tread
- Yokohama

- Pirelli
- Ply
- Treads
- Studded

The tool also suggested more specific keywords or keyword phrases such as *tire ratings, Goodyear tires, wheels and tires, tire chains*, and *tire dealers*. It's worth spending a few more dollars per month to add these related terms to your keyword advertising campaign.

Putting Key Keywords in Your Web Pages

Businesses can and should also take steps to improve their placement in the "regular" (nonpaid) search results on Google and Yahoo! One way to do this is to add critical keywords to the HTML of their Web pages. There are three places where key terms should be added:

1. *Headings.* Most services index the main headings on a Web page.
2. *The Opening Text.* The first fifty words of text on a Web page, some search services index only the first fifty words and no more.
3. *The META Tag Section of the HTML for the Page.* This is a part of the HTML that doesn't show up on the Web page that visitors see when they connect to your site. The person who creates your Web pages knows what META tags are.

Tip: A service called Wordtracker (http://www.wordtracker.com) does daily surveys of the keyword queries made to various search engines. It creates lists of what it finds to be the most popular search terms. You might be able to look at this site and determine what the most popular tire-related keywords are.

Taking out a Sponsored Ad on Yahoo! or Google

You can improve your listing on Yahoo! search results by paying anywhere from $25 to $300 or more per year to become a sponsored website. Your site is listed in the Sponsored Sites box at the top of a Yahoo! category. The exact cost depends on the popularity of the category. Sponsored Sites appear in a blue shaded area at the top of a page of Yahoo! search results; these listings are separate from the paid keyword ads in the right-hand column. When I searched for sponsored ads on Yahoo!, the companies at the top of the page were Yokohama, eBay, and The Tire Rack.

A sponsored ad is only one type of advertisement you can take out on the Web, of course. You can also pay to have an old-fashioned banner ad displayed on someone else's Web page. However, targeted keyword ads are efficient and cost-effective, and they enable you to reach potential shoppers who are actually interested in what you have to sell rather than everyone who happens to visit the page where your ad is displayed. Making yourself visible is important whether you are marketing yourself online or offline. In many cases, it can help you to develop an offline presence such as a brick-and-mortar store so that you can reach buyers in your local area. Chapter 18 and Chapter 19 examine the move from online to offline sales.

PART V

Moving from Online to Offline Sales

Opening a Brick-and-Mortar Store

It seems like a paradox to go online to start a business without having to incur the expense and trouble of opening a real storefront in a mall, shopping strip, or other real-world location. But the fact is that a small number of highly successful sellers on eBay and other sites have gone on to open a brick-and-mortar location. It's a valid option for generating more business close to home.

Opening a physical storefront, even if it's only a booth in an antique mall or consignment shop, gives you a new way to sell. It can help you find new sources of supply, too. Many suppliers won't deal with eBay sellers or sellers who only operate "virtually" out of their homes. They want to sell to businesses that have a physical location. Not only that, but having a physical store encourages residents in your local area to bring you inventory to resell on eBay.

And I've found, from the sellers I've interviewed, that having a physical location that is separate from your home office brings other advantages. It helps you to be more organized and to separate your eBay or other sales activities from your home life. Your family doesn't have to deal with merchandise piling up all over your home, and they get to see you when you're not working. Opening a physical location can be a major undertaking, of course; you have to comply with many local regulations and go through the work of decorating and furnishing your shop. This chapter will examine the pros and cons of this option for moving beyond eBay and becoming a part of your local business community.

Choosing the Simple Option: A Space in a Mall

I once asked a husband-and-wife team of eBay PowerSellers how they found a supplier. They sell accessories for model railroad collectors. The wife (who didn't want her name publicized) told me that they had a booth in an antique mall. For a nominal monthly fee, they could use the antique mall's address as their own business address.

An antique mall is a physical store that is broken into dozens or even hundreds of separate display spaces. A display space might be a small room, a single display case, or a shelf within a display case. Individual sellers within the mall rent space so they can let prospective buyers see and inspect their merchandise. The bigger the space they rent, the higher the monthly fee they pay to the mall. Malls sometimes charge a flat rate for a square foot of space: you might pay, for instance, $2.50 per square foot. If you get a booth that is 6 feet by 6 feet, you pay a sizeable $90 per month in rent—which makes your eBay Store monthly rent look cheap by comparison. And it's up to you to arrange your merchandise, put up signs advertising your business, and price each one of your items.

Note: You don't need to put up signs advertising your business in someone else's antique mall. Many sellers simply put their items on the shelves and never identify their own name or that of their company.

The idea is that, by gathering many sellers into a single location, an antique mall or consignment shop can attract many more shoppers than each of those sellers would on their own. There are variations within the mall idea: antique malls specialize in antiques, while consignment shops sell items that are collectible and valuable, and household goods that are more affordable. However, the idea is the same: many sellers gathered under one roof so buyers can conveniently shop in one location.

Tip: If you're an eBay seller thinking of moving to an antique mall or other brick-and-mortar location, consult with fellow sellers on the OTWA message boards. You'll also find an informative article "How to Start and Maintain an Antiques Booth" at http://www.finetuning .com/articles/p0-2110-how-to-start-and-maintain-an-antiques -booth.html.

How do you choose the right mall? Visit some malls in your area and see if you like how they look. Also search for malls that have merchandise compatible to your own. You don't want to sell costume jewelry in a mall that specializes primarily in furniture, for instance. Also look for a mall that is not only affordable but that is in a well-trafficked location and that markets itself. If you're lucky, the booth you rent will be in a mall that advertises itself widely, perhaps even on the Internet itself. That way you can go full circle—from online seller to brick-and-mortar merchant and back to the Web again. Those antique dealers and other merchants who have booths in the Crown Point antique mall have each one of their booths photographed and described online.

Also, choose a mall that is in a convenient location. You'll need to go there at least once a week, if not more often, to collect money, restock inventory, and get any mail or shipments you have received. It's a good idea to change your merchandise—or at least move things around so they are displayed differently—on a regular basis. Antique malls attract repeat customers who are always on the lookout for new items. If you move a doll from the bottom of a trunk where it's been sitting for weeks to the top shelf of a display case, for instance, you might suddenly find buyers for it.

You may also be asked to work in the mall by greeting customers and opening display cases for them, perhaps one day a month. Be sure to read over the contract the mall owner gives you. Make sure you know how much notice you have to give if you want to leave the mall. Finally, choose a mall that is open to accepting mail and deliveries from you. You might have to pay an extra charge for this service, but if it is the only way you can get merchandise from wholesale suppliers, it is worth the monthly fee.

 Caution: Evidence from my own experience, from talking to other sellers, and from scanning message boards suggests that antique malls are a dying breed. They're being pushed out of business by changes in the economy (less disposable income among much of the population) and by eBay itself. Don't expect to make a huge amount in sales from them. Instead, rent a small space in a booth and work out an agreement with the owner so you can use the address for deliveries from your suppliers.

Starting a Drop-Off Store

An eBay drop-off store is a brick-and-mortar location that is dedicated to helping individuals sell on eBay. Typically, these stores are started by sellers who are especially competent in their fields, have achieved success, and are looking for more merchandise to sell on consignment. There are, after all, millions of people around the world who have items around their households that would sell well on eBay, but who are intimidated by the prospect of selling on the site.

There are lots of challenges with starting a drop-off store. First and foremost is the competition. There are already a number of big operations like the Auction Drop chain (http://www.auctiondrop.com) that have franchises around the country. It's still possible to compete with this big chain if you are willing to provide better customer service than it does, more personalized attention, and more effective marketing in your local area. Just a few blocks from my home, an independently owned drop-off store called Express Drop is doing just that. Owned by two women in their twenties, the store is thriving and attracting visitors from throughout the state and neighboring Indiana and Wisconsin.

A second possible obstacle is that, unless you are discriminating about what you sell, selling on consignment can be a lot of work for very little profit. You might make 30 or 40 percent of each sale, but the time required to talk to customers, prepare sales, and pack and ship can quickly whittle your potential profit down to a few dollars per sale. A third challenge is that you're opening a brick-and-mortar store, so you have to comply with local regulations, apply for licenses and permits, and furnish your store with signs and fixtures that make it seem to the public that walks through the door like you know what you're doing. (See the section that follows, "Opening a Retail Location," for more information.)

Despite all these hurdles, it may still be worthwhile to operate a drop-off store. Why? When you have a physical location, you can sell big-ticket items you might never handle otherwise. You don't have to spend much (or any) time looking for items to sell; instead, a steady stream of merchandise comes through the door. Auctions by David, a drop-off store located in Algonquin, Illinois, until recently sold boats, RVs, motorcycles, and other big, bulky items. Owners could literally drive their bulky merchandise into the Auctions by David parking lot. Owner David Portugal and his staff could photograph them and sell them online. In the case of a $10,000 boat, a 30 percent seller's fee looks pretty good.

 Tip: David Portugal's top tips for would-be drop-off store operators include finding enough space, and making sure you have room to grow. Also, take the time to locate your store in a well-trafficked location such as a major intersection. You can then put up street signs that will catch the attention of anyone who walks or drives by.

When you have a drop-off store, you can't always control what people want you to sell. They might bring you items that you know won't fetch a high price or possibly any bids at all. You know you might make only a profit of a few dollars on the deal. Because of this, most drop-off stores limit consignment customers to handling only items that will sell for a minimum price—for example, $50. When someone comes to the counter with an item to sell, the proprietor turns to a computer and checks eBay's Completed Auctions to get an idea of how much it might fetch if put up for sale. And if a buyer is dissatisfied with a consignment item you sell and asks for a return, you have to tell the customer that the item needs to be relisted and that the profit they thought they were going to make isn't forthcoming after all—at least not right away.

Opening a Retail Location

Whether you open a drop-off store, an antique store, or another shop, going "public" with your business is a dramatic change. You're no longer working out of the quiet of your home, appearing only to carry boxes to the post office on a regular basis. Now, everyone—including the city and state—knows that you're selling on eBay for a living. You've got to be brave, forward-thinking, and have a clearly defined business plan because you're going to be confronted with lots of new challenges on the way to hopefully expanding your income. Some of those challenges are described next.

Complying with Local Regulations

A reader of my eBay books approached me at a seminar I was giving. "I wanted to start up my own eBay business and sell out of my home. I wanted to do everything aboveboard, so I called the city of Chicago. They told me I could sell online but that I couldn't store any of my inventory in my home." If she couldn't store any inventory, she didn't understand how she could operate her business. The city of Chicago requires a $125 Home Occupation License to operate a business from a residence. There's also a Second-Hand Dealer's License ($550) required of anyone who sells jewelry made of precious metals or gems, hardware, or coins. But whether you can legally sell what you store apparently depends on whom you ask. The women who run the drop off store I mentioned earlier, Express Drop, were not told about such a regulation when they met with city inspectors and obtained their necessary licenses. They certainly store what they sell and ship out of the same premises.

The point is that there are probably similar regulations in your own city, and you should be aware of them so you don't break the law in the course of trying to buy and sell on eBay.

Obtaining a Tax ID Number

If your state charges sales tax (and at this writing, all but six U.S. states do), you'll need to obtain a tax ID number. This number, also sometimes called a resale certificate, enables you to buy or sell anything in your state legally. It doesn't matter whether you sell online or in a brick-and-mortar store; you need to be registered with your state and obtain this vital piece of information. The reason for obtaining a sales tax ID number is simple: it enables you to collect sales tax from buyers who are located in the state in which you have a physical business presence (in other words, the state in which you live) so you can report this to your state's income tax department.

> **Note:** At this writing, Alaska, Colorado, Delaware, Montana, New Hampshire, and Oregon do not charge sales tax. See Chapter 20 for more information on what a sales tax ID number is and how to get one.

Becoming a Licensed Auctioneer

You've probably seen traditional auctions in which a professional auctioneer—someone who is able to talk at lightning speed—goes through one item after another and sells them to bidders who are either physically present at the sale, calling in to representatives on the phone, or bidding via the Internet. This kind of traditional auctioneering isn't going away any time soon. However, there is no doubt that eBay has cut into the business that goes to the traditional auction houses.

In an effort to protect traditional auction businesses and regulate eBay sellers, several states have enacted laws that require eBay sellers who sell on consignment to obtain a state auctioneer's license. I live in a state that has just such a law in place: Illinois. Tennessee is another. Typically, you have to take a course in auctioneering that lasts several weeks, pass an exam, and pay a fee of several hundred dollars to obtain such a license. Not only that, but you probably have to renew the license on a periodic basis.

Before you do anything with your consignment business, check with your state Department of Commerce to see if these laws apply.

Getting Your Store Stocked

By now, it should be clear that opening a brick-and-mortar facility is a major undertaking that requires planning and organization. You should only consider expanding to a brick-and-mortar store if the following two conditions apply:

1. You are making a reliable, steady income on eBay or other auction sites.
2. You have a steady source of merchandise to sell.

The first requirement is hard enough. But the second is the critical one, because without a steady supply of merchandise that people want, you won't achieve the goal of a reliable, steady income in the first place. Most auction sellers begin close to home, by emptying out their attics and garages. They move on to emptying out the storage areas of their friends and family members. Then, they make the leap of purchasing low-cost items that they can resell at a profit. There isn't any single secret for finding a steady supply of saleable items. You either have to shop your local flea markets, garage sales, estate sales, and wholesale shops to find not-quite-new merchandise, or you have to strike an agreement with a wholesale supplier to sell you new items that you can resell. There isn't any rule of thumb, but common sense suggests that you should be selling on eBay and other auction sites through a full year at the very least before you think about expanding. That way you have a sense of how online auction sales proceed through various seasons of the year; with this knowledge, you can plan ahead for "fat times" and "lean times" that crop up in any business.

 Tip: The section "Find an Ongoing Source of Merchandise" in Chapter 17 examines in greater detail the topic of finding a steady source of wholesale merchandise.

Not only do you have to find merchandise to sell in your store but you also need store fixtures as well. Fixtures are things like lights, shelves, doors, windows, a cash register, display cases, carpeting or flooring, and anything else that makes your facility look welcoming. If you have especially valuable items such as antique jewelry, like many sellers you'll want to have a locked display case that an employee has to open so potential buyers can inspect the goods.

Advertising the Brick-and-Mortar Way

When you open a physical location, you need to advertise it. This isn't just an additional burden that is placed on you, however. Having a brick-and-mortar store *allows* you to advertise locally, which opens up new possibilities for finding business. When you have a physical location, you can take out a classified ad in your local phone book or your newspaper. Announce that you want to buy entire estates, or that you buy antiques. When you have a store that people can visit, you gain credibility. You also have a convenient location where buyers can drop off large-scale items like furniture—items that don't sell easily on eBay, but that you can best sell through your own storefront.

Choosing a Location, Location, Location

One of the keys to getting your name before the public that is just as important as advertising is choosing a good location for your store. Pick a well-traveled area, and one where parking is available. If you can locate yourself on a busy street in a town or city—and one with bus stops where people are likely to congregate—so much the better.

When it comes to locating your store, give some thought to a loading area: a place where customers can easily drive up and drop off bulky and heavy merchandise like motorcycles, riding lawn mowers, jet skis, and so forth. One of the advantages of having a drop-off store is the ability to accept such merchandise on consignment. Amy Mayer and Ellen Navarro (shown in Figure 18-1), who operate the Express Drop store near my home in Chicago, located their store at an intersection with four-way stop signs on a main street that heads to one of the main expressways in the area. They also have a garage where they can accept and store bulky items from customers.

Placing Judicious Advertisements

If you are on eBay, are already an experienced seller (perhaps a PowerSeller), and have your own website, you are way ahead of the other brick-and-mortar businesses on your street. You don't need to suddenly start dumping large amounts of money in newspaper and magazine advertisements, billboards, or flyers distributed door-to-door around your neighborhood. Be conservative and judicious about how you want to advertise your store. Be sure to print up a set of postcards with your business's name and contact information and set them out on the counter of your store. You can hand them out to your customers, who can pass them along to others in your local neighborhood.

 Tip: If you can contact your local news media to tell them that you're open for business, you might just be able to gain some valuable (not to mention free) publicity. Because eBay drop-off stores are still relatively new, their very existence is considered newsworthy.

Figure 18-1. Choose a location where you get lots of traffic and your customers can easily drop off big merchandise.

© Amy Meyer and Ellen Navarro, Express Drop.

Even if you rent a booth in an antique mall, you don't necessarily have to depend on the mall's advertising. You can place an ad on your local version of Craigslist (see Chapter 10) or in your local newspaper. If you have a booth or a space in a mall, be sure to place a card with the URL of your eBay Store or website on it so that shoppers can look through a wider selection of your merchandise.

Keeping Good Records

Whether you rent part of a display case in a mall or have a 3,000-square-foot warehouse that you periodically open to the public, you've got a whole new set of information to track carefully. Maintaining good records of your inventory, what's been sold, and what you spent along the way can prevent you from losing or misplacing items and help reduce your taxes, too.

All of the expenses associated with your physical facility are items you or your tax professional can count at tax time, including the following:

- The rent you pay
- Your utilities
- Property taxes you are charged
- Mileage you incur when you drive to purchase merchandise or perform other business-related tasks
- Supplies such as price tags, lightbulbs, paint, signs, silver polish, and much more

Make sure you keep your receipts, and that you write down in a record book not only the amount you paid but also the date the expense occurred and a brief description of what the expense was for. (Rent, mileage, and supplies are all counted in different places by your tax preparer.)

Keeping track of each item in your inventory by assigning it a number and recording how much you paid for it helps you determine pricing. It also lets you track merchandise so you don't lose anything. Having expense and inventory information can help you in yet another way, because you can review the information periodically (say once a month, or four times per year) so that you can purchase more wisely in the future and determine where to spend your income. If you bought a group of saltshakers and napkins and only the napkins have sold, for instance, you need to rethink how many saltshakers or other kitchen utensils you purchase in future. You need to purchase items that you're sure you can sell, either online or in your brick-and-mortar facility.

Dealing with the Public

If you're the shy, retiring type like me, you might have a hard time adjusting to dealing in person with the public. According to the women who run the drop-off store in my neighborhood, you need to have a thick skin. Almost every day, you get complaints, questions about shipments, or demands from customers who aren't pleased with the speed of a sale or who don't understand why something didn't sell for the same price it was said to be worth in that collector's price guide.

You need to have a positive attitude, and you need to be as patient as possible, or you'll get complaints from your customers, which can lead to bad word-of-mouth comments or bad feedback on eBay itself. You also have to exercise as much care as possible when going through merchandise your customers bring you to sell; you never know if some rusty old cast iron truck or wooden fishing lure that seems unattractive when you first glance at it will turn out to sell to thousands on eBay.

Be prepared to answer a lot of questions from clients who seem to want to know everything about how the process works. People who shop online, or who are interested in selling online, are researchers. They want to know everything about how everything works. They aren't afraid of technical facts and figures, either. It's important to train your employees so that they don't appear less knowledgeable than those who call in. Provide your staff with a list of frequently asked questions, either printed on a sheet of paper or on your computer network, so they have a set of talking points ready when they consult with your potential clients.

Dealing with Employees

You might be able to start up your drop-off store all by yourself. But sooner or later, you're going to need to hire employees to help you. Hiring employees who will work in your store and possibly interact with the public is far different from hiring a high school student to help with your packing after school. You need to advertise for employees, conduct interviews, check references, provide insurance and other benefits, and handle payroll tax requirements.

It's also important to train your employees to be patient with your customers, who will be likely to ask "obvious" or simple questions about how eBay works. A number of customers might want to watch sales being prepared so they can learn how to sell on eBay themselves, or at least to understand how the process this works. Anything that can build trust among your customers will benefit you in the long run. By instructing your customers you might be showing a small number of them how to sell on eBay on their own, but for most, you'll be showing them how much work they *don't* have to do, and only providing them with more of a reason to purchase from you in the future.

 Tip: Teaching is another way in which you can share your experience and expertise with others while supplementing your income, too. Many experienced eBay sellers make a few extra dollars by teaching classes on eBay at their local community college or at seminars they organize themselves.

Dealing with Technical Requirements

When you are working on your auction sales at home, you really only need a single computer. Some sellers use more than one machine so that they can research auctions on one monitor, while keeping track of their current sales and any e-mail inquiries on the other. When you run a brick-and-mortar store, you definitely need two or more computers, and perhaps more monitors. My local eBay drop-off store has a clever two-monitor system: there are two computers at the front desk (one for each of the proprietors) and each of the computers has two flat-screen monitors. One monitor points out toward the customer, and the other is visible to the proprietor. This enables the customer to see exactly what the employee sees when he or she researches eBay; by following the search results, they can be sure the employee isn't giving them false information about the probable value of an item.

It goes without saying that you'll need to have a high-speed Internet connection at your brick-and-mortar facility, and you'll need to network your computers together. You'll need firewall hardware or software to protect your network. You might need a separate machine to process photos and to handle accounting and inventory information. In short, you need a small-scale computer network at your store; if you can set up and maintain it, so much the better, but if you can't or don't have the time, it's worth the extra expense to hire a consultant to provide the technical expertise you need.

Opening a Warehouse

Storage space—or rather, the lack of it—is the bane of many successful eBay sellers. When your merchandise starts to overrun your living space and boxes are piled up in the hallways, it's time to find a storage facility. For many of the biggest and most successful eBay sellers, that means building or renting a warehouse—a place with a loading dock, lots of room for storage and packing, and possibly even office space where you can do your eBay-related computer work.

For some eBay businesses, a warehouse is a necessity. Businesses like Ready Medical (http://stores.ebay.com/READY-MEDICAL) use a 40,000-square-foot warehouse in California to store lots of medical equipment, much of it bulky and heavy. Their showroom is displayed in Figure 18-2.

The Gold and Titanium level PowerSellers on eBay need warehouses simply because they move thousands of items each month. Kevin Harmon, a PowerSeller who sells DVDs and other entertainment-related merchandise through the eBay Store Inflatable Madness, uses a warehouse for office as well as storage and shipping space.

If you're looking for a warehouse, try to find one that has:

- A loading dock
- A location near an airport or major post office hub, so shipping can be expedited

Figure 18-2. A warehouse makes it easy to move large items.

© Lisa Vanesco. Ready Medical.

- An office area
- Plenty of parking space for you and your employees

Once you move your staff, your merchandise, and your equipment into your warehouse, you don't want to be moving into a new facility any time soon. So make sure you find a facility that is bigger than you need initially and that gives you room to grow. Once you have a physical base of operations, you are able to continue your business's expansion toward new venues. And it makes sense to start close to home; some local venues for reaching customers—trade shows, flea markets, and traditional auctions—are described in Chapter 19.

Trade Shows, Flea Markets, and Other Offline Sales Venues

Even the most dedicated and obsessed computer wonk needs to get out and breathe some fresh air once in a while. It might seem incongruous to discuss such old-fashioned sales venues as flea markets and real-world auctions. But I've been surprised by hearing from some eBay sellers that, for certain types of merchandise, they go to a traditional auction house, or they attend the local flea market.

Expanding your business beyond eBay is all about matching your merchandise to the proper venue. When you have bulky items like bookcases and chairs that will fit in your car but would be hard to ship through eBay, the flea market might be the quickest way to get rid of them. Flea markets can be a good place to find merchandise, too; you can use the knowledge you've gained online to pick up items at flea markets that will be most likely to sell. And you just might realize higher prices for what you have to sell in the real world than you would online, where there is a wealth of sales information and many other items for sale. My mother, an experienced flea market seller for many years, knew she could sell a set of "Flow Blue" plates by W.H. Grindley for $50 to $75 each at the flea market. However, when she gave them to me to sell on eBay, we couldn't sell any for more than $40 or $45.

For many sellers, trade shows provide a good source of merchandise to sell on eBay and online auctions. But trade shows can be difficult to find. And when you go there, it can be bewildering to find merchants with items that might sell online. In this chapter, you'll learn some tricks of the trade that will help you utilize trade shows and other offline venues to your best advantage.

Working the Trade Show Scene

No matter what kind of merchandise you buy and sell, you need to know about any trade shows that are held in your area of business. A trade show is a big gathering that brings together businesspeople who sell similar products. The show lets the businesspeople compare notes, display their wares, and hopefully find new customers for what they have to sell. Trade shows are, in fact, specifically set up to attract buyers who are looking for wholesale suppliers. For the most part, the buyers are representatives of retail stores. But eBay sellers can attend as well, either to display what they have or to find additional supplies of merchandise to sell.

 Note: You might have to demonstrate (by providing your business name, contact information, and a tax ID number) that you are a legitimate businessperson who is in the trade to attend a trade show. Most trade shows are intended for wholesale, business-to-business transactions only rather than retail sales.

Many of the biggest trade shows, such as the Consumer Electronics Show, are held in popular convention centers like Las Vegas and Chicago. If you live in one of those areas, you're lucky; otherwise, you'll have to do some traveling and planning ahead. First, you need to find trade shows. This isn't always easy. Trade shows don't always advertise in the local paper. You might check with the convention bureau in your area, or trade journals in your field of business, to find them. You can also look on the Web for sites like TSNN.com (http://www.tsnn.com), which collect names and dates of a variety of trade shows. However, websites aren't always comprehensive, so you need to do some searching on your own, too.

Once you find a trade show you're interested in, take a two-person approach. Team up with someone at home who is on a computer that is connected to the Internet. Go to the trade show and have your cell phone handy. Write down the names and model numbers of items you are interested in, and report back to your partner. Ask your partner to look up the items on eBay and see if there is much demand for them. When you find a particular model or color that people like, talk to the vendor.

You don't necessarily have to visit a trade show expecting to make purchases, either. Trade shows are also terrific locations for doing research on products you might want to sell online. You learn who the hottest manufacturers are and discover new products you never knew existed. If you are looking for merchandise, however, make sure you get off the beaten path. Keep in mind that the biggest manufacturers already have individual sellers who carry their products on eBay. If you're just starting out, it's also a good idea to visit the booths of small, little-known businesses that aren't yet on eBay. You might discover a product that isn't being sold on the auction site, and you might become the first distributor for it.

If you are primarily interested in selling rather than buying, you've need to employ some tried-and-true, one-on-one sales techniques. Meeting people at a trade show is like selling to them on the Web because you need to answer questions, invite them to learn more about you, or otherwise interact with them in a minute or less, or they'll move on to the next display. You have to do a hard sell: greet visitors and ask questions that are specific: "What kinds of power tools are you looking for?" or "Have you seen the latest in curtain rods?" Listen to what they have to say, and ask open-ended questions. Try to gather as many business cards as possible so you can follow up at a later date.

If you like to sell to the public and miss the person-to-person interactions you don't get on the Internet, you'll love trade shows. You'll also love the fact that buyers who attend trade shows are serious about what they want. They tend to buy in quantity and, when they find a supplier they like, they stick with that supplier. Keep the following guidelines in mind when you encounter someone who expresses serious interest in your products:

- Be sure to establish a minimum order amount, such as $50 or $200, and stick with it.
- Make sure the wholesale price you set for your work is going to give you an adequate profit.
- Have an order form printed up before the trade show and hand it out to prospective buyers. The form should list your models and prices as well as your contact information and payment terms.
- With new buyers, don't be reluctant to ask for 100 percent payment up front, or at least 50 percent down with the balance to come cash on delivery (COD).
- If you are lucky enough to receive a large order that you know you cannot fulfill immediately, offer a delivery schedule that matches your ability to produce the product—for instance, one-third up front, one-third in a month, and the final third in two months.

Another benefit of selling at trade shows is that it is customary for the buyer to pay for shipping, although some wholesalers offer free shipping as a perk to attract more business.

 Tip: American Express Business Resources has a Web page entitled How to Sell at Trade Shows. The page (http://www10.american

express.com/sif/cda/page/0,1641,15836,00.asp) contains useful pointers for getting the attention and retaining the interest of those who stop by your booth and show interest in your products.

Getting Local Sales at Flea Markets

Selling at flea markets is easier than you think. Yes, you have to pack your items in boxes and haul them to the sale. Yes, you have to get up very early in the morning—often, before the sun—to get to the market on time and set up by the time customers begin to flow in. But all of your work is over in a single day. And rent is inexpensive—some markets charge $15 or $25 for a space. And if you're a social animal who likes meeting your fellow sellers and talking to shoppers in person, you'll find flea markets a much less lonely place than eBay, where it often seems like you are working in isolation.

They're Not Just for Collectibles Anymore

The Internet has transformed flea markets. Both buyers and sellers know that you can find treasures more easily, and often at a better price, on eBay than you can at the flea market. You see fewer and fewer quirky one-of-a-kind household collectibles. More and more shoppers go there to buy new or almost-new household items. They're also more knowledgeable than they used to be because, in many cases, they've already done research on the Internet and know what something is worth.

The bottom line is that you're no longer out of place if you have large quantities of wholesale clothing, perfume, or other items for sale at the flea market. You can sell wholesale household merchandise in the real-world market just as you can on eBay, and although you have to get there early and rent a space (in some cases, for as little as $15), you don't have to deal with insertion or Final Value Fees at the end of the sale, either.

Tip: Some flea markets let you sell things you would never dream of selling online. The flea market held by New Holland Sales Stables, Inc. every Monday lets the public bid on horses and other livestock, for instance. You can find out more about this and other Pennsylvania flea markets at http://www.fleamarketguide.com/pa.htm.

Researching Flea Markets Online

It might seem illogical to find flea markets and plan out flea market sales strategies using your computer. But the flea markets that are closest to you might not be the best choices. Looking online gives you some initial information without having to drive hundreds of miles to check out a bigger market. The following sites serve as good starting points:

Flea Market Guide

Your first online resource for flea markets should be the Flea Market Guide (http://www.fleamarketguide.com), a comprehensive listing of flea markets throughout the United States. This site holds the details of thousands of flea markets, with contact information, hours, fees, and other necessary information. A simple search of your town or neighborhood should help you select the best place to sell your merchandise, if you take the time to contact all the possible markets and find the best deal. Most states or cities also have listings for flea markets, if you want to make sure you're not missing anything.

Tip: Sometimes a specific category of merchandise will have a site where you can search for sales, such as Booksalefinder.com, a useful site that sends you biweekly information about all the book sales in your area, up to 30 miles away. This lets you keep tab of library sales, book auctions, and dealer liquidations more effectively than doing an hour of research a day.

Openair-Market Net

This superb site (http://www.openair.org) is a global listing of open air markets of all kinds, like farmer's markets, flea markets, and street vendors. The resources here are changing all the time, and include an active discussion forum about running a street market business, which can allow you to follow trends and establish connections. Other sources of information on the site include listings of market associations, archives of past discussions about the problems of running a business, and tips on how to create a web presence for your flea market business. This site is motivated by a desire to help vendors succeed in their business, so you can trust that their information is reliable.

Tip: AuctionBytes editor Ina Steiner wrote an informative column about a huge flea market in her own area—Brimfield, Massachusetts. Big regional markets like this one are open virtually every day and attract tons of shoppers. Find out more about the ins and outs of selling at this market at http://www.auctionbytes.com/pages/abu/ y200/m04/abu0011/s03.

An Online Flea Market: SwapThing.com

SwapThing.com (http://www.swapthing.com) is a relatively new site devoted exclusively to swapping merchandise, trading goods, and services online. There is no fee to post an item here, and only a $1 charge on completion of a deal. The major advantage of this site for someone running an auction business is that it provides a great place to divest unsuccessful merchandise, or even to improve your inventory by swapping something that has sat on your shelf for years for an item in the specialty you've established for yourself. The free listing and the low completion fee mean that you will reach many potential customers who either cannot or do not want to use eBay or another traditional site.

SwapThing.com currently boasts more than 3 million listings, with many professionals using the site to advertise their services as well. A recent addition to the site is a forum for discussion among users, and coming soon are profile pages to help tailor your presence on the site. SwapThing.com also offers a program called Share-Thing where nonprofits can list their needs on the site, and donors can match those needs, receiving a tax-deductible receipt for their donations. This sort of site, based on the trading of goods and services rather than conventional buying or selling, seems to be growing online, especially among small communities like universities and planned communities. By becoming familiar with the use of a site like SwapThing, you might be placing your business in an advantageous position for the next few years of Web-based commerce.

Going Back in Time: Real-World Auctions

Sometimes, eBay and the other marketplaces described in preceding chapters aren't always the best places to sell items. On more than one occasion, I've looked up the prices of antique plates or Coca-Cola memorabilia so that I could sell them on eBay on my mother's behalf. When I reported exactly how many competing products were up for sale and how they were being offered for, say, $10 on eBay, she said, "I could get $25 or $50 for it at the flea market."

You might be better off selling things like furniture or desirable antiques at traditional auctions where live auctioneers wield gavels and call out the high bids. Traditional auctions still take place in many parts of the United States, especially rural areas where farm equipment is frequently sold off at auction. Traditional auctioneers are often experienced at selling motor vehicles and industrial equipment, and many have appraisal services as well. And even if you feel reluctant to leave the familiar confines of the Internet and hand over your precious merchandise to someone else to sell, keep in mind that many traditional auctions now offer some form of online bidding in addition to the bidding that goes on at the place where the sale is actually being held.

Learn How Real-World Auctions Work

In true old-fashioned auctions you have no reserve prices, no printed catalogs, and no computerized bidding process. You have an auctioneer, who conducts the bidding and keeps track of who the highest bidder is, often with the help of assistants who track bids and take down the names of bidders. You have the auction house, the organization that provides the physical location for the sale. You have to consign the items you want to sell well before the sale, so the auction house can include it in the list of items for sale.

One of the nice things about real-world auctions is the fact that buyers who take the time to travel to the auction house and wait several hours for an item to come up for bids are likely to be serious about bidding. You have the option of setting a reserve price for an item if you want to. And there is the fact that the event itself can be exciting, especially when attendance is good and bidders are actively participating.

One of the not-quite-so-nice things about traditional live auctions is the buyer's premium: in addition to their high bid, winning bidders pay an additional fee to the auction house itself. A reasonable fee is 10 percent, although many auction houses charge 15 percent.

Research Real-World Auctions Online

The best online site to research local and specialty auctions is http://www.auction guide.com. You can use this site to search for auctions by location or category of merchandise, to list your own auctions free of charge, or to post free want ads for equipment. One of the convenient features of the site is that you can search two ways—either sort by location through its auctions and auctioneers directory or search by time through the calendar of auctions the site maintain for each region on the map. Auctionguide offers an excellent introduction to the types and terminology of auctions, and also has a page devoted to the different kinds of auction software available, for both online and offline auctions. This site will help you find the best auctions for your business, and if you need to hold an auction, it is a great way to reach thousands of buyers in your area.

There are many similar sites that allow you to search auctions by specific location, like http://www.midwestauctions.com, or by category of merchandise, like http://www.farmauctionguide.com. If your business is focused on a specialty market or region, see if there is a devoted site online. It will save you time and energy, and you're more likely to reach truly interested customers with your ads or by attending the auctions listed there.

Another online guide to offline auctions is the Internet Auction List, at http://www.internetauctionlist.com. This site has a large number of listings and you can search for auctions by date, category, or keywords. However, compared with Auction-Guide, this site is cluttered with advertising and less friendly to use. Listing your auction with the Auction List is fast and free, so you might want to check in with this site every now and then. Be sure to check your information on an auction offline, however, before you drive 30 miles on a Saturday morning only to find that the benefit auction was cancelled a week ago and no one thought to remove the Internet posting.

PART **VI**

Supplying Your New Storefronts

CHAPTER 20

Finding New Sources of Merchandise

As you have learned in preceding chapters, you could conceivably expand your exiting eBay sales presence to include book and CD sales on Amazon.com, your excess inventory to Overstock.com, your electronics components on uBid, and live auction jewelry sales on Bidz.com, to name just a few options. Having multiple sales will boost your income, but only if one important requirement is met: you need to have a sufficient amount of merchandise to sell.

Ramping up your sales means ramping up your inventory and stepping up your sourcing activities. For many businesses, it means making a step up from finding merchandise on your own, one piece at a time, to ordering in bulk. To those who already order in bulk, it may mean ordering even more, or becoming an official dealer for a particular brand of items—for example, you might become an authorized seller of a line of cosmetics.

The challenge is finding new sources of sales inventory at a time when millions are already selling on eBay and other venues. Luckily, you are hardly the first seller to be in this situation. This chapter will discuss some tried-and-true techniques that other sellers have used before you. These include gathering inventory from wholesale distributors, from people in your own neighborhood, and from other Internet sellers so that you can keep your storefronts supplied with a steady stream of stock to sell.

Improving the Quality—and Quantity—of Your Inventory

I gave this chapter the title "Finding New Sources of Merchandise" rather than "Finding More Merchandise" for a reason. *More* isn't necessarily better when it comes to sales inventory on eBay. Most sellers would agree that it is preferable to sell one hundred items for $500 each, netting you a $250 profit for each one, than it is to sell five hundred items for $100 each, with only a $50 profit per sale. Fewer sales mean fewer items to list, pack, and ship. For a one- or two-person eBay business, high-priced items are ideal—as long as you can find a steady stream of regular customers for them, that is. To ensure sales all year 'round, it's best to not only expand the range of items you offer but also to sell more high-priced items in addition to your less expensive offerings. Some suggestions for what to look for are explored in the sections that follow.

Don't Be Afraid to Think Big

The most obvious way to expand your inventory to accommodate new sales is to boost the number of items you already purchase and resell online. One thing that separates small auction businesses from bigger and more successful operations is volume. I can vouch for this on a small scale. In my first few weeks as a seller, I experienced the results in Table 20-1.

Table 20-1. Sales volume versus gross income.

End of Sale	Items Offered	Items Sold	Gross Income
7/10 (Sunday)	6	1	$62
7/16 (Saturday)	12	3	$61
7/17 (Sunday)	15	10	$324
7/23 (Saturday)	12	6	$96
7/24 (Sunday)	20	9	$218
7/31 (Sunday)	28	14	$330
8/7 (Sunday)	31	14	$467

These results impressed two important principles upon me: First, if you have identified a source of items that people want to buy, your income will generally go up the more you have to sell. Second, rather than having all your sales end on a Sunday, it's just as effective to spread out your sales so they end on both Saturday and Sunday. I've since learned that scheduling sales so they end on weeknights is even more effective.

Big-time sellers aren't afraid to think really big. Instead of thinking in terms of dozens of transactions like I do, they think about hundreds or even thousands. They know that, if they can increase the number of items they have for sale by a factor of two, three, or more, their profits are likely to increase by the same amount. The big obstacle for many sellers is doubt—you don't know if you'll make back the additional amount you spend on your purchases, and you are afraid you are spending profits you won't get back. You have to take a leap of faith and avoid holding back when it comes to purchasing new sales inventory. Buy as much as you can, even if it seems like more than you can handle to begin with.

Also make an effort, if you can, to buy many variations on a single line of product. This doesn't work if everything you sell is a one-of-a-kind collectible gathered from estate sales. But if you sell new consumer goods, for example, look for variations in the product line that you don't carry already. If you buy five hundred pairs of shirts in the same color and from the same manufacturer, in sizes ranging from small to extra-large, it becomes easy to list them because you take one set of photos and create one sales listing. You can easily duplicate subsequent sales listings because only the prices differ from one item to the next.

You can sell these sorts of variations on a theme even if you don't deal in new merchandise. For example, I don't sell new items myself, but I try to stick with certain brands that have demonstrated high demand. In Figure 20-1, you can see that I'm

Figure 20-1. If possible, sell merchandise with different sizes, colors, or models to streamline the listing process.

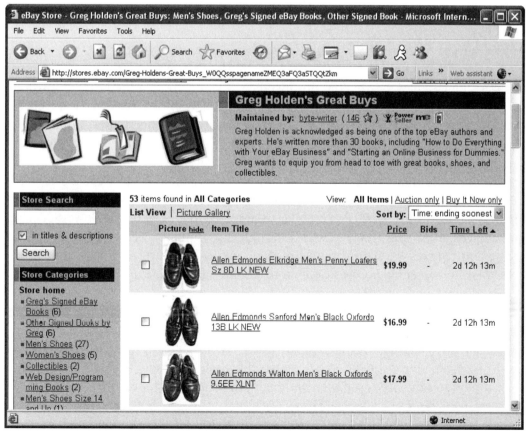

offering three pairs of shoes by Allen Edmonds. Creating the descriptions was easier than usual because I could reuse standard information about the quality of the manufacturer; I only had to change a few sentences describing the individual shoe. It's even easier for sellers who put identical items up for sale; they only have to take one set of photos and reuse them for each item.

 Tip: One way to turn around a higher volume of merchandise is to become a wholesale supplier for other businesses that sell at online auctions. By selling large quantities of merchandise at cut-rate prices to other auction sellers, you not only increase your volume but your profits go up as well. You can still sell individual items for larger products. However, many successful sellers build up their inventory and are able to turn around a higher number of transactions by selling in bulk at wholesale in addition to selling one item at a time.

Expand Your Price Range

High-priced items that are also in high demand are ideal products for eBay and other auction venues. On Amazon.com, for instance, if you can sell a hard-to-find textbook or technical manual for $75, it is far better than selling fifteen paperback novels for $5 each. When I think about merchandise that yields big profits, I always think about Drew Friedman, who sells on eBay under the eBay Store name White Mountain Trading Company (http://stores.ebay.com/White-Mountain-Trading-Company). Drew sells premium fountain pens that command prices as high as $7,000 each. The profit on these pens is so great that, if Drew sells only one pen per month, he has made enough money to make his PowerSeller quota. He's the envy of his PowerSeller acquaintances. He spent many weeks searching for suppliers before he was able to locate and contact the manufacturer of the pens in Missouri. And only after a personal visit to the company was he able to obtain an agreement to be an authorized dealer of those pens on eBay.

However, high-priced items don't sell consistently at all times of the year. They tend to sell well during the busy holiday season, for example, but during the summer, you often discover that the high-ticket items are languishing unsold in your eBay Store. To make up for the difference between high-demand and low-demand times of year, it pays to sell both low-priced and high-priced merchandise and to offer a range of items for sale. For instance, Drew Friedman also sells $79 watches, collectible medals for $12.50, and $69 golf shoes in addition to his high-end pens.

Expand Your Sales Options

Frequently, eBay members who participate in the PowerSellers discussion boards express one of their greatest fears, which is that they can be suspended by eBay at any time if one of their buyers makes a complaint against them—whether that complaint has merit or not. If they depend on eBay for all of their income, a few days of being offline can be a disaster.

Although some sellers stick with a single proven marketplace to conduct their business, many others diversify to achieve a greater level of security. They sell in the venues described in previous chapters—their websites, brick-and-mortar stores, or other auction venues.

> **Tip:** eBay recently created a new area called Reseller Marketplace (http://reseller.ebay.com/odcs/custom.html?template = start), which is intended for suppliers and manufacturers who want to liquidate extra inventory quickly. In theory, the merchandise listed in this area is offered in large quantity and low cost. It is a good place to look for bargains in your area of business.

Obtain a Resale Certificate

No matter where you sell or where you obtain your merchandise, you'll find it helpful to obtain a legal document that identifies you as a certified reseller in the state in which you reside. The document in question goes by different names depending on where you live. Some states call it a resale certificate; in others, it is called a reseller certificate, certificate of resale, or something similar.

In any case, a resale certificate is easy to obtain, yet remarkably significant to wholesale suppliers and manufacturers you might want to deal with. In order to find the document for my own state, Illinois, I did a search on Google for "obtain resale certificate Illinois." At the top of the search results I found an Adobe Acrobat version of the form CRT-61, which I need to fill out to obtain a certificate from the Illinois Department of Revenue. (You can find this form yourself at http://www.revenue.state.il.us/taxforms/Sales/Crt61.pdf.) Your state's department of revenue (the office that handles your state income taxes) can also tell you where to mail the form and whether a fee is required; typically the fee is $20 or less.

For a small amount of labor, you obtain a certificate and a sales tax ID number you can submit to wholesalers. Many wholesalers require a sales tax ID number so they have an indication that you are a legitimate businessperson. Even more important, you are complying with the law when you do so.

Make Sales Contacts at Trade Shows

Trade shows may be time consuming and traveling to attend them can be expensive, but they are invaluable for making the sorts of personal contacts that can lead to profitable relationships with wholesale suppliers. Wholesalers, many of whom have been in business far longer than you have, are more comfortable with handshakes and discussion over drinks than with orders placed over the Internet. By attending trade shows, you are meeting them on their territory and helping to give them more of an incentive to do business with you.

 Note: As described in Chapter 19, trade shows are one of your best options when it comes to finding wholesale suppliers. I refer you to that chapter for tips about how to "work" trade shows when you are researching new products to sell and when you have wholesale merchandise you want to sell to other businesses.

Develop a Winning Business Attitude

Sometimes, the attitude you take toward buying and reselling on eBay makes a huge difference in the volume of merchandise you are able to turn around. If you have a negative, anxious attitude, you aren't going to find new products to sell or expand your business the way you want to.

Finding more merchandise to sell depends in large measure on your expectation that you *will* find more to sell. Simply anticipating a higher volume of sales often will cause you to produce them. And don't wait for conditions to be perfect to start buying more merchandise and putting it up for sale in new locations. Expect that you're going to be busy, and act as though you have already expanded; adopting a successful approach will ensure that you will do what you need to do to increase your volume.

 Tip: If you are dissatisfied with your sell-through rates or the number of bids you are getting, ask someone to evaluate your auction descriptions. Contact by e-mail successful sellers whose listing templates you admire, and ask if they would mentor you. The worst they can do is say no; at best, they'll give you useful tips on how to upgrade your sales.

Locate the Holy Grail: A Reputable Drop-Shipper

For many sellers on eBay, Overstock.com, and other venues, the ultimate resource is a drop-shipper: a supplier that provides you with merchandise to sell, but that stores the merchandise you purchase in its facility and ships it out for you when you make a sale. It might sound too good to be true, and often, it is: many drop-shippers respond slowly and provide you either with poor service, poor quality merchandise, or both. But because there *are* some good drop-shippers around, many sellers eagerly hunt for them.

For those who (like me) want to be able to control every part of the sales process, drop-shippers can be frustrating. If they say there is a power outage, flood, or other problem at their facility, you have to take their word for it. But it's still up to you to explain to your customers what the problem is. You are also called on to deal with any packing or shipping deficiencies that are the drop-shipper's fault. But in truth, this doesn't happen very often—and the same outages can slow you down just as much if they occur to you personally.

The disconnect between you and the merchandise you sell has other implications. You have to inspect samples of the items carefully before you put them up for sale, and you need to either take your own photos or depend on the drop-shipper to provide you with accurate images. Because drop-shippers generally want to hold on to your business, it is not to their advantage to misrepresent what they sell and have you cancel future orders. Once you find a drop-shipper that seems reputable, the company is likely to want to ship promptly and pack carefully to hold on to your account.

One of the great advantages of working with drop-shippers is the ability to order in bulk. As I've already said, the more you can sell, the more you are likely to make in terms of gross sales. If you don't have room to store, for instance, one thousand espresso machines, a drop-shipper gives you a practical alternative to renting your own warehouse space. Drop-shippers also save you a considerable amount of time because they enable you to focus on e-mails and sales descriptions, not to mention the act of successfully receiving payment for what you sell, so you don't have to spend hours photographing, packing, or running to the shipping office. The drop-shipper handles all of those time-consuming steps for you.

Drop-shipping is such an attractive prospect that you have to be careful when you shop for a supplier. The moment you start looking for them online, you'll encounter e-books, CDs, and websites that invite you to purchase lists of drop-shippers. The lists might contain contact information for some drop-shippers, but they also contain lots of useless data as well. Do your own research. Attend trade shows and look for manufacturers and wholesalers in your area of business. You can also the websites of drop-shippers and sign up so that you can sell their merchandise. When you find a candidate, follow these steps:

1. Talk to the drop-shipper personally. Ask how far removed the supplier is from the actual manufacturer of the items it offers for sale. If the drop-shipper is at the end of a long chain of middlemen, its supply chain may not be strong; you might run into a bad situation—someone places an order, and you discover that your drop-shipper is out of stock. You then have to immediately offer a full refund and hope you don't get negative feedback.

2. Get the contact information for one or two sellers who use the drop-shipper, and check out the references.

3. Pay for a few samples you can inspect and put up for sale.

4. Create your own descriptions and take your own photos so they are better from those of any other sellers who carry the same merchandise from the same supplier.

5. If you are happy with the results, put in a bigger bulk order.

 Tip: Troy Breitmeyer, a seller who has worked extensively with drop-shippers, published an informative article about the pros and cons of working with them at http://ezinearticles.com/?Drop-Shipping-Can-It-Work-for-Your-Small-Business?&id = 79155. In addition, eBay Radio also has regular features on product sourcing. You can listen to archives of past shows and read transcripts at http://www.ebay radio.info.

Finding Help with Sourcing

If you already have a student, a relative, or other employee to help you, you know how much having an extra pair of hands can help with completing transactions. Having other eyes and hands at your disposal can help you to find merchandise to sell, too. You don't have to rely solely on your own initiative. Look around your list of acquaintances and make a list of the people you already have on hand who can help you do your searching. Some suggestions for assembling a sourcing "team" are mentioned in the sections that follow.

> **Tip:** Plenty of Web-based businesses are happy to help you find suppliers. One of them, World Wide Brands, is run by the person who contributes product sourcing information to eBay Radio. Check it out at http://www.worldwidebrands.com/wwb/default.asp.

Hire Neighborhood "Pickers"

It's difficult to keep on top of all the garage sales in your area as well as the new stock that comes in to the local secondhand store on a daily basis. I've heard of at least one eBay seller who hired a network of people in her neighborhood to gather merchandise for her to resell online. You can do this too, on a small scale, by enlisting the help of friends, relatives, and neighbors. Offer to pay them a bounty on each item they bring in, which will give them an incentive to find as many items as they can.

> **Caution:** Never pay someone to send you leads for wholesalers. You have no way of knowing how recent the data is.

Make Friends with Your Wholesalers

I've discovered that, over the years, when I visit the same secondhand stores or antique shops, the proprietors get to know me. If I ask, they'll put me on a list to call me when a particular type of item comes in. I've heard that some buyers are able to make friends with the managers of the local Goodwill store or other secondhand store; at the very least, the managers will let them know when the next shipment of merchandise is coming in. In fact, on the Goodwill website (http://www.goodwill.org/page/guest/about/howweoperate/Shopping/bargainhuntingtips) you read the following suggestion from the company itself:

> **Introduce yourself to the staff, and ask them about items you're looking for or what they would suggest as a good buy. Establish yourself as**

a regular customer and the staff may even call you to let you know when certain items arrive in the store.

At the most, you might be allowed the first chance at some choice merchandise because you are a repeat customer. The point is that you have to ask: find out when your local consignment shop or secondhand store puts out the items you want, and be as friendly as you can to the people who work there.

One of the best ways to get on a wholesaler's good side is to buy a large amount of merchandise on a regular basis. Many of the resale store chains allow companies and individuals to buy in bulk. You have to buy a huge amount of stuff, and you have to make the purchase from the chain's distribution center rather than an individual store. You might have to pay several hundred or even a few thousand dollars, but you get as much as 40,000 pounds of merchandise—enough to fill a tractor trailer truck. That sort of inventory can last you for months and bring you big profits.

The author of the Seller Sourcebook Blog writes (at http://blog.sellersourcebook .com/blog/_archives/2005/4/1/541454.html) about striking up an agreement with the St. Vincent de Paul distribution center and being able to sort through inventory on days when the center is closed to the public. He came out with eight full shopping carts of clothing for $165. The same author suggests contacting your local dry cleaners and offering to purchase unclaimed clothing. In most cases, the cleaners are happy to make some money from the items they've already worked on.

 Caution: The obvious place to look for wholesale merchandise, eBay's own Wholesale Lots section, requires you to do a lot of searching if you are to find a diamond in the rough—in other words, a bulk supply of desirable merchandise you can resell for a profit. Ask yourself: if a merchant can go through the effort to list the bulk lot on eBay, why couldn't that person have simply sold the merchandise himself or herself? It's likely to be second-rate merchandise that wouldn't sell otherwise. You might have to browse through dozens of pages' worth of listings to find one that fits your needs.

One of the best resources for wholesalers is China, but it's a difficult market to break into because of language and cultural barriers. In Chapter 21, you'll find resources for finding both suppliers and buyers by taking advantage of international marketplaces.

Reaching Overseas Buyers

The reason that eBay and other online marketplaces work is because they enable you to find buyers for what you have to sell from around the world. It's a thrill when someone located thousands of miles away buys what you are offering and leaves you positive feedback for it, too. Often, you discover that there is a special market for special products. I've been amazed to find that brightly colored Nike TN cross-training shoes sell especially well in France. I know that if I could find a steady supply of Nike TNs in the right colors and match them up consistently with French buyers, I could sell lots of them.

Sourcing the merchandise is a challenge all by itself, and it's one that was examined in Chapter 20. This chapter suggests more efficient and effective ways of reaching overseas buyers for what you have to sell. The strategy is easily overlooked, given the fact that iOffer, Amazon.com, and other marketplaces already attract potential buyers from other countries.

I'm talking about accessing websites located in other countries, the contents of which are often presented in languages other than English. Although a large part of the world visits the U.S. version of eBay, eBay itself has locations in many other countries. If you speak a foreign language, you can find an audience of potential customers for your specialized products. There are also many auction sites other than eBay that are located in other countries. By listing your products there you can stand out from the crowd and find the customers you want.

Looking at Chinese Marketplaces

When speaking at a conference in May 2005, eBay's CEO Meg Whitman commented that China could be eBay's largest local marketplace in the next five to ten years (http://auctionbytes.com/cab/abn/y05/m05/i16/s03). When you look at the numbers and consider China's rapidly growing economy, you have to wonder at how great

China's influence will be on e-commerce in general and online auction sites in particular. For sellers who are hungry for new customers, China is rich with promise. But China is also important as a source of wholesale suppliers. The primary marketplaces available to sellers in China (some of which are limited to those who have some fluency in Chinese or can have their listings translated into Chinese) are listed next.

Alibaba

Alibaba was founded in 1999 by an entrepreneur named Jack Ma. In August 2005, it partnered with Yahoo!. Under the agreement, the two companies will work cooperatively to build Yahoo!'s brand in China. Alibaba consists of several separate marketplaces:

- *Alibaba International (http://www.alibaba.com).* This is the Alibaba business-to-business (B2B) market for global trade, which has 1.5 million registered users. Nearly half of its business is reported to be from North America and Europe. The home page is in English; this site is meant for a worldwide audience.
- *Alibaba China (http://www.alibaba.cn).* This is Alibaba's Chinese marketplace for online B2B transactions within China itself. The site is completely in Chinese.
- *TaoBao (http://www.taobao.com).* This is a consumer marketplace and person-to-person marketplace much like eBay.
- *AliPay (http://www.alipay.com).* This is Alibaba's payment system, which is supported by China's four largest banks.

If you speak Chinese and have items to sell to individual buyers, turn to TaoBao. Otherwise, turn to Alibaba—but it's primarily a resource for finding wholesale suppliers.

TaoBao

TaoBao (the name means "digging for treasure" in Mandarin) is Alibaba's consumer auctions site and a direct competitor to eBay in China. It has grown to 9 million registered users since being founded in 2003. The site is in Chinese, however; this is the place to turn if you speak Chinese and you want to reach individual buyers in China. Taobao.com has become the most successful challenger to eBay in the Chinese marketplace, taking in more than 40 percent of the Chinese online auction business in 2004.

TaoBao's main advantage over eBay is the absence of service fees for basic usage.

Listings are free, and no Final Value Fees are charged. The site draws its revenue from large businesses that purchase extra services such as accreditation. Taobao has placed itself as the true "Chinese" auction site, emphasizing its all-China staff and only presenting a Chinese language version of this site. Keep a close eye on TaoBao: China is widely considered to be the fastest-expanding region for online business, soon to have over 100 million online users, second only to the Unites States—and growing at a faster rate than the United States.

Alibaba's B2B Marketplace

As stated earlier, Taobao.com's parent site, Alibaba.com, is the largest online Chinese marketplace with more than 1 million registered users, most of them small- and medium-size businesses. As with Taobao, there are no fees for basic services, but there is a wide array of extra products to purchase to help increase your business's credibility and visibility through the site. You can also purchase a Trustpass, a system of accreditation to increase buyer confidence, which allows you to post your inventory on Alibaba's Hot Products channels. These products are the first seen by visitors to the site and act as in-site advertising for your sales.

Suppose you want to sell supplies in bulk to another business. Begin by registering to use the site; select your country from the list at http://us.my.alibaba.com/user/join.biz and click CONTINUE. On the next page, you are asked to specify whether you want to sign up to buy or sell on the site—or both. In either case, you are signing up for a basic level of services that include the following:

- For buyers, the ability to search for products and send inquiries directly to suppliers
- Rather than searching for products, the ability to post Trade Leads that tell sellers what you are looking for, and receive quotations from them
- For sellers, the chance to submit quotes on Trade Leads that buyers have posted
- The ability to post twenty Sell Trade Leads, which are essentially sales listings
- The ability to display a total of five photos of each product
- Space for publishing a profile of your business

Each sales lead you post (as well as each Trade Lead) is reviewed by Alibaba. It's possible you might be asked to submit more information about what you want to sell. Alibaba also offers an innovative software program called TradeManager that you download and install on your computer. The software keeps track of Alibaba members with whom you have had contact so that you can get in touch with them more easily. You can use the software to have a conference call with your contacts; you can even send e-mails to a group of your contacts at the same time—for instance, when you want to announce that you have a new line of products for sale.

 Note: Alibaba.com is a well-developed business-to-business site with a large community of buyers and sellers. Anecdotal comments left on eBay's discussion boards by PowerSellers indicate that Alibaba can be a good source for suppliers, but emphasize the importance of making sure the seller has the Alibaba TrustPass. The TrustPass program authenticates the identity of the seller with a third-party credit agency.

eBay's EachNet

EachNet (http://www.ebay.com.cn) is eBay's person-to-person sales marketplace in China. The site is completely in Chinese. The site was purchased by eBay in 2003 at a time when there was virtually no competition in the auction market in China; since then Taobao has become a serious competitor. One reason is that Taobao does not charge for listings, while EachNet does. However, EachNet has cut its listing fees; an article in China Daily (http://www.chinadaily.com.cn/english/doc/2005-05/09/con tent_440384.htm) reported that listing fees were the equivalent of 7.5 cents or less per sale. In summer 2005, eBay launched a Chinese version of its payment service PayPal to help streamline transactions.

EachNet claims that, by charging fees for listings, it avoids the flood of low-quality items that (it claims) populates Taobao. For sellers who are fluent in Chinese and want to break into the market, it is important to pay attention to both marketplaces. See which venue sells the type of merchandise you already carry, and place your energies there. You might also consider selling the same quantity of similar items in both locations, as an experiment, and then evaluating which site yields better results.

eBay's Reseller Marketplace

Global Sources Ltd. is a partner with eBay that enables its clients to post merchandise on eBay's EachNet. The service is provided outside of eBay through Reseller Marketplace, a site specifically intended to enable eBay PowerSellers to locate merchandise they can resell online.

Selling on eBay's Global Sites

If you are fluent enough in a language other than English to be able to write auction descriptions in that language, you have a big advantage over other sellers. You have the opportunity to reach the millions of potential buyers who live in non-English-speaking countries and who shop on one of the twenty-six international sites listed at the bottom of eBay's home page. A representative selection of the sites, and some suggestions of what you might sell there, appear in Table 21-1.

Table 21-1. eBay's international sites.

Country	Name	URL	Merchandise of Local Interest
Argentina	MercadoLibre	http://www.mercadolibre.com.ar/home_visitor.html	Champagne and cigars
Australia	eBay Australia	http://www.ebay.com.au/	Australian Football League caps and jackets
Canada	eBay.ca	http://www.ebay.ca	Canadian beer coasters, bottles, promotional items
Hong Kong	eBay.hk	http://www.ebay.com.hk	Dolls and accessories related to the Blythe Barbie doll
Philippines	eBay.ph	http://www.ebay.ph/home	Philippine coin sets
United Kingdom	eBay UK	http://www.ebay.co.uk	Wedgwood, Royal Doulton porcelain

An overseas marketplace enables individuals to trade items of local interest in languages other than English and currencies other than the U.S. dollar. Overseas sites are of particular interest if you have items that are in demand in other countries. If you are able to purchase a group of the Nike TN shoes I mentioned at the beginning of this chapter, for instance, you'll find some shoppers who speak English well enough to shop on the main U.S. website. But you are likely to reach more buyers if you can write the descriptions in French and offer the shoes on the eBay France website. An antique copy of Don Quixote, in Spanish, will sell in eBay Spain. You can quickly perform currency conversion, so that you can offer the item in the currency used on the marketplace (such as Euros) by using the Universal Currency Converter at http://pages.ebay.com/services/buyandsell/currencyconverter.html.

Tip: Timeshares and vacation properties are among the most popular items to buy and sell internationally. If you have a property that might appeal to someone overseas, don't hesitate to offer it in an international marketplace.

Language Considerations

As a seller, you've probably received e-mail messages from individuals whose grasp of English is weak. As long as they get the essential message across, everything is OK. When you are creating an auction description, a mistake in a size or brand name or model number can be a disaster. If you write a description in English and you hope to reach overseas bidders, you need to use language that is as clear and simple as possible in your descriptions. The same applies if you attempt to write a description in a language that is not your mother tongue.

You can use free translation services like BabelFish (http://babelfish.altavista .com) to write a description in English and translate it to any of eleven different languages, including Chinese (either simple or traditional), Dutch, French, German, Spanish, Portuguese, Greek, and Japanese. But stay clear of slang phrases like "this pair of sunglasses is eye-catching" or "this jacket is all that." You're more likely to end up with gibberish than with a translation that makes sense.

Note: BabelFish isn't the only online translation service around. You might compare the translation you get from BabelFish to the one produced by WorldLingo's Free Online Language Translator (http://www .worldlingo.com/en/products_services/worldlingo_translator.html). However, don't expect an online utility to do as well as a human being; if you can find a friend or a student to translate your listings, you'll be much better off.

International Payment Services

Anyone who has had to ship to other countries and deal with customs forms knows that things are more complicated when you deal with international buyers. In many countries, PayPal is accepted, and if it is, your payment system is no different than from domestic buyers. Western Union BidPay also gives you a good alternative; buyers can use it as long as they have an American Express or Visa card for debiting purposes.

If PayPal isn't accepted and BidPay isn't available, you can choose from one of several escrow services that facilitate online payments. As described in Chapter 15, an escrow service acts as an intermediary between buyer and seller. The escrow service receives payment from the buyer and holds on to the money until the buyer has had an opportunity to inspect and approve of the item that has been shipped. Only then is payment released to you, the seller. The best-known escrow service is Escrow .com (http://www.escrow.com). However, you might also make use of the following other payment services:

- *Moneybookers.com (http://www.moneybookers.com).* This isn't an escrow service as such, but a PayPal-style online payment service that is especially set up for European users.
- *Escrow! (http://www.escrow-europa.com).* This service accepts payments in U.S. dollars, Euros, or British Pounds.
- *Iloxx Safe Trade (http://www.iloxx.de/ebay).* Use this service only if you speak German; the site is not available in English.
- *Triple Deal (http://www.tripledeal.com).* A European payment service that requires a one-time setup fee of 2,000 Euros or a monthly subscription fee of 85 Euros.

Escrow services aren't without their faults, of course. Dishonest users send fraudulent e-mails pretending to be from escrow services, and these sometimes trick users into giving up their money. The same precautions you take with spoof e-mails that purport to be from eBay apply to other payment services: don't click on links embedded in e-mails; carefully inspect the URL at the top of a Web page that purports to an escrow service; enter the escrow service with which you have an account by typing in the URL of its home page. And don't respond to any requests from a payment service for your credit card numbers, social security numbers, bank account numbers, or other personal information; they already have the information they need and won't be asking you to confirm it by e-mail.

 Tip: Be sure to keep time zone considerations in mind when you schedule your auction. If you start a seven-day sale at 9 P.M. in your local time zone and you don't do any extra scheduling, the sale will end at 9 P.M. the following week, which is around 3 A.M. in Europe. Remember that what is a good time for you isn't necessarily a good time for your overseas customers.

Countries to Avoid

There are good and bad people in every country. However, the bad people who prey on online auction sellers frequently come from a handful of countries. Yahoo!, in the Help section of its Classfieds service (http://help.yahoo.com/help/us/class/class -45.html), suggests that sellers be wary of buyers who come from Romania, Macedonia, Belarus, Pakistan, Russia, Lithuania, Egypt, Nigeria, Colombia, Malaysia, and Indonesia. (The Philippines is sometimes cited as a country frequented by fraud artists.)

Does this mean you should turn away anyone who makes a purchase from you simply because of where they come from? That would be sure to attract negative feedback. Instead, be extra careful with buyers from those countries. But remember that most people are basically good. If someone buys something inexpensive from you, chances are you'll have no problem with them. But if you sell computers or high-end electronics equipment, you've need to be careful. Make sure the buyer has an obvious e-mail address that is easily traceable. If someone asks you if they can pay by wire transfer or cashier's check, consider these to be warning flags.

Even then, you might find that the person is basically honest. I had a customer from Belarus make a relatively inexpensive ($40 or so) purchase from me. He said he could not obtain a PayPal account and could not use BidPay because he had a problem with his credit card. He asked to pay by wire transfer. I tried to stay patient and polite, and gently said I preferred PayPal or a money order. After several weeks, he was able to get a PayPal account after all. The deal went through, and he turned out to be a very nice person.

Exploring Other International Marketplaces

If you're the adventurous type and you have a love of travel, you'll enjoy exploring some of the many international auction and sales marketplaces around the world. Often, these sites feature exotic or unusual items you wouldn't find anywhere else. If you have an item you think the local customers might want, you can put it up for sale. Here are a few examples:

Bidorbuy (South Africa)

This site (http://www.bidorbuy.co.za) welcomes members from Afghanistan to nearby Zimbabwe. As a shopper, you might be able to find exotic items like Tanzanian blue opal jewels. In fact, the Diamonds and Fine Gemstones categories are among the most popular on the site. One interesting feature for sellers is the option to restrict bids to only those individuals who have a credit card on file with Bidorbuy. Starting prices have to be in South African Rands. The site automatically relists your item for you if it doesn't sell. It's free to list items for sale. If they are sold, you are charged a "Success Fee" of 3.5 to 5 percent depending on the amount of the winning bid.

DeRemate.com

This trading community operates in the following ten countries: Argentina, Brazil, Chile, Colombia, Mexico, Peru, Puerto Rico, Uruguay, Venezuela, and the United States. Go to the site's home page (http://www.deremate.com), where you are presented with a list of the countries covered. Click on the name of a country, and you go to a site specifically devoted to merchandise from that country. All listings are in Spanish, but if you are located in the United States, your listings can appear in the U.S. version of the site (http://usa.deremate.com).

Eurobid.com

Eurobid.com, an auction marketplace based in Paris, France, is ideally suited for sellers in the United States and other countries. The obvious reason is that the site is in English (though, as described in the bulleted list that follows, you can use multiple languages for a single description). Another good reason is that it is free to sell on Eurobid.com. The site charges no listing fees, no "Success Fees," and no Final Value Fees. Here are some other notable features that overseas sellers will find attractive:

- Sales can last anywhere from seven to thirty days.
- The site has its own escrow service for payments.
- You can specify that sales are automatically renewed after the original sales period ends.
- You can have your auction title description presented in as many as four of five possible languages: English, French, German, Italian, and Spanish.
- Eurobid.com will scan your photos and e-mail them back to you if you are willing to go through the time and effort of mailing the images to their office in France.
- You specify your own bid increment of between 10 and 40 percent.

Another nice feature is that the Sell an Item form includes a button labeled TRANSLATOR. You can write your description in your native language and have it translated instantly by the auction site.

Kijiji.com

This network of classified ad sites isn't well known to U.S. sellers. That is because Kijiji—the name means "village" in Swahili—posts classified ads in Germany, China, Spain, Canada, England, France, Scotland, Ireland, Wales, Poland, Turkey, Taiwan, Japan, and a few other countries, but not in the United States. Kijiji, which is affiliated with eBay, is not a single site but a group of networked classified ad sites. In New Zealand, Australia, and other English-speaking countries, the individual sites go by the name of Gumtree. In Switzerland, the name Kijiji is used and listings are in German. In the Netherlands, the local site is in Dutch and called Marketplaats.

If you speak the language and have a connection to a city or region somewhere else in the world, Kijiji gives sellers a way to market items that are *very* local in interest. Keep in mind that the classified ads are primarily of houses for sale and apartments for rent. And the site is oriented toward local buyers and sellers who want to connect to one another across town rather than around the world. Nevertheless, in virtually all the cities included in the Kijiji network of sites, there are categories such as "Stuff for Sale," "Miscellaneous," and "Business Services" that might be relevant to overseas sellers.

It's free to post ads, but be selective: read the current contents of the Stuff for Sale section and see if there is anything remotely like what you have for sale. You don't want to be accused of submitting ads that are considered spam. Most of the ads are for dishwashers, couches, and other heavy furniture that wouldn't ship well. Click the button labeled POST A FREE AD and scan the form that is provided to see if there are restrictions as to where the item that is being offered is actually located. You may well find that the form only works if the item is located, for instance, in the suburbs of Liverpool, England, or Edinburgh, Scotland. You might also find that buyers don't want to pay for shipping because the site is primarily oriented toward individuals who expect to drive and pick up the merchandise from other individuals. When does it make sense to post an overseas ad on one of the Kijiji network sites? If you have business equipment to sell overseas and you are willing to post in the Business Services section; if you already live in an area covered by one of the classified ad network sites; or if you are planning to visit one of the areas covered by the ads for an extended period and you are willing to have someone come to you to pick up your merchandise—and pay you in the local currency.

No matter which sales venue you choose, and whether it is of local interest or oriented toward overseas sellers, the key is making personal connections. You need to not only match your merchandise to the types of items buyers want but also find the right hosts for your sale listings. You can also benefit by striking up partnerships with auction service providers, trading assistants, and even with your competitors. These connections can make you a smarter seller, and you can find out more about how to make those connections in Chapter 22.

CHAPTER **22**

Partnering with Other Sellers

You might start out selling on eBay all by yourself. However, when you expand your sales operations and move to other venues besides eBay, you will probably need help. Everyone needs a partner to call on for support. For some, it might be a family member or coworker who helps to complete sales listings or shop for merchandise to sell. For others, a partner might be a person or group of people they meet on eBay's discussion boards and to whom they turn when they have a question or simply want to complain about something and blow off steam.

I've been surprised by the number of prominent PowerSellers who are friends with other PowerSellers, many of whom are their direct competitors. At first glance, you might think eBay is a place for lone-wolf sellers—people who want to keep their suppliers to themselves and not share information with others. Although it is true that sources of supply are usually a closely guarded secret, it also seems to be true that the more open you are with your knowledge and your experience, the more you get back in the form of contacts, information, and acquaintances who can make your work more enjoyable.

I'm not suggesting you collude with other sellers to drive up prices. I'm only suggesting that you don't work in a vacuum—and that networking refers to more than connections between computers. If you work the discussion boards, join user groups, go to eBay Live and other events, you will learn just as much as you give. And you'll be a better seller for it, whether on eBay or not.

Making Friends with Your Competition

One of the things that makes eBay special is the extent to which buyers and sellers communicate. I'm not saying they collaborate, because that would poison the market-place and seriously damage the level of trust. But on the discussion boards, chat rooms, and eBay Groups, and at gatherings like eBay Live, they help and support one another.

Participating in Discussion Groups

Your first resource for striking up collaborative relationships with other sellers should be eBay's community area, which includes discussion forums, chat rooms, eBay Groups, and the Answer Center. The community area is a place you can always turn to when you encounter problems or questions or just want to learn to do business better.

For example, suppose you buy and sell women's vintage handbags. You are doing well, and you want to expand to complementary items. You need to ask experienced sellers for advice. Where can you turn? You can participate in any (or all) of the following discussion forums:

- *The Antiques Discussion Board.* This is one of eBay's category-specific discussion areas, and it might provide you with tips on finding other vintage apparel and accessories.
- *The Clothing, Shoes, and Accessories Board.* This board is specific to individuals who sell clothing and accessories; you're sure to find tips and ideas here.
- *The Vintage Clothing and Accessories Board.* This forum is even more specifically focused on vintage apparel.
- *The Clothing Chat Room.* This is an informal forum for socializing, exchanging tips, and sharing common interests.
- *Mentoring Groups.* These are user-created forums within eBay groups that are specifically devoted to helping other members. Many of the groups cover topics related to selling.
- *Seller Center.* You could post a question on this discussion board to cast a wide net and hopefully attract answers from many different sellers.
- *Workshops.* Some of eBay's user workshops cover topics related to selling antiques and clothing. One workshop entitled "Outlet Malls-Catalog Returns and Overstock" might help with sourcing, for instance.

You should visit several of these venues to find the one that best fits your needs. Workshops are held periodically as "live" events in which participants can exchange messages with a moderator. But you can read archived transcripts of the proceedings long after the event is over. Just be aware that the type of discussion held in a discussion board is more focused and task-oriented than in a chat room, where things are more informal. The place to start with shopping for a forum to fit your needs is at the Community Overview page (http://hub.ebay.com/community).

> **Note:** The eBay website isn't the only auction marketplace that operates its own discussion forums. I'm just citing eBay because it's the best-known example of a marketplace that has an active user community. Venues such as Alibaba.com (http://www.alibaba.com) and Trade Me (http://www.trademe.co.nz) also have their own discussion boards, while iOffer calls its discussion area "clubs" (you'll find them at http://www.ioffer.com/club/browse.do). The general ideas expressed in this section apply to participation on those forums, too.

Joining a User Group

When eBay members meet in person, they end up having fun and learning from one another. One of the best things about eBay, in fact, is the culture of openness and cooperation—of community spirit—that members exhibit and that reigns supreme when members meet in person. I saw this myself when I attended a conference of PowerSellers. "She helped me get into the business," one seller said of Angie Cash, who runs Cashco1000. "That guy is a really great seller," many said of Jonathan Garriss, one of the cofounders of the successful eBay business Gotham City Online. The sellers who attended enjoyed comparing notes about sales software, problems that occurred while dealing with buyers, and complaints about eBay itself. No one would talk about who their suppliers are, of course; this is the trade secret that no one on eBay gives away openly. But aside from that, the people I talked to loved the opportunity to feel that they were not working on their own but were part of a larger group.

The group that sponsors the gathering, the Professional eBay Sellers Alliance (http://www.gopesa.org), is only for the top-level PowerSellers. But when it comes to finding other eBay sellers who are willing to provide help and advice, your best resource is perhaps eBay Groups at http://groups.ebay.com/index.jspa?ssPageName = comm;f;f;US&categoryID − 1&redirccted − 1. The eBay Groups area was set up by eBay within its user community for users themselves to create and moderate groups. You might find groups based in particular U.S. states or metropolitan regions. Other groups focus on a particular activity (being a trading assistant or using a seller tool, for instance). Others bring together members with common interests that have nothing to do with eBay, such as gardening, recipes, history, and book clubs.

When it comes to finding fellow sellers who can help you further expand your business, I strongly recommend joining one of the user groups that are included under the heading Seller Groups. That's an obvious choice. But you'll also benefit from the regional groups. You'll find that there is an eBay user group located in practically every state in the United States, as well as in Canada, Malaysia, Russia, Portugal, and many other countries.

To find and join a group in your local area, follow these steps:

1. Go to the eBay Groups main page (http://groups.ebay.com/index.jspa?ssPage Name = omm.:f:f:US&categoryID = 1&red irected = 1).

2. Under the heading Regional, click your state name, or click VIEW ALL if you don't see your area listed.

3. Find a group that interests you. If you live in a big area like me, you may well have multiple groups to choose from. I found one called ChicagoArea PowerSellers that seemed just right.

4. Because this is a public group, anyone can join. I only had to click the JOIN GROUP button that appears on the group's home page to join up. (For private groups, you need to approach the group's leader and ask to join.)

Once you join, you can view existing discussion topics and contribute to them, or you can start your own discussion. You might even get the chance to create a personal profile and post photos that other members of the group can view, if your group's leader has provided this option.

If you're lucky, the group you join will hold face-to-face meetings periodically. User groups are great for socializing and sharing experiences with other sellers in person, in a focused and intimate way that a huge gathering like eBay Live doesn't provide. But you can also use these meetings to gather suggestions about how to sell better, whether on eBay or other auction sites. Don't be reluctant to ask questions such as:

- What kinds of things do you sell?
- How do you find new items to sell?
- How do you research what is in demand?
- How do you research a wholesale supplier to make sure the company is reputable?

The question on everyone's mind—where do you find suppliers?—is not going to get you very far. You can, however, ask in general where other sellers find their items—whether they receive merchandise on consignment, whether they go to estate sales, or whether they shop through warehouse stores and "dollar stores" in your area.

Finding Complementary Merchandise

When you know people in the trade, you are a smarter buyer and seller and a more informed appraiser of merchandise. You see this sort of cooperation all the time on the PBS television series *Antiques Roadshow*. When in doubt, an appraiser will consult with a trusted colleague to get a second opinion. Smart businesspeople learn from one another and cooperate rather than jealously guarding all their trade secrets.

When you have trusted colleagues with whom you can consult, you can gather suggestions for items that complement your primary line of sales merchandise. If you sell pens, for instance, it's natural to offer other items that the owners might need, such as carrying cases, ink, or display cases. For shoe sellers, polish is a natural add-on. If you sell sunglasses, look for a supplier of eyeglass cases. The point is to use your imagination—think like your customers, and anticipate what they might need after they make a purchase from you. Table 22-1 gives you some examples to help stimulate your imagination. It presents merchandise offered by PowerSellers I have

Table 22-1. Primary and complementary lines of auction merchandise.

Business Name or User ID	Primary Merchandise	Complementary Products
GlobalMedia	DVDs, VHS tapes of TV shows	CDs
Blueberry Boutique	Luxury ties, shorts, suits	Sunglasses, jewelry
Bootywear	Sexy lingerie and other clothing	Telephone calling cards
Aleegold's Wholesale Shoppe	Italian, Disney, and other charms	Charm bracelets
Dallas Golf	Golf clubs	Golf balls, bags, club-making equipment
Abovethemall	Women's purses, wallets, checkbooks	Pill boxes, card cases, cosmetic cases

met or interviewed, and shows concrete examples of what constitutes complementary products.

Hiring a Trading Assistant

Even if you already sell on eBay—and this book assumes you already have some selling experience—there are times when you need the help of an experienced person to move beyond eBay's conventional auctions and fixed-price sales. One of those occasions arises when you try to sell on eBay Live Auctions: when you attempt to register, you discover that you either need to be a dealer in antiques, art, or collectibles or you need to consign your merchandise to a certified dealer who has already registered with the site. If you consign with a one of the licensed auctioneers who sells on eBay Live Auctions, you pay a relatively low consignment fee—typically, only 5 percent if the item sells. Another situation occurs when you attempt to sell on a foreign auction site; rather than having to convert currency and deal with language differences, you might be better off turning over a portion of your profits to a trading assistant who is accustomed to dealing with local buyers.

Joining GoAntiques

A wide variety of dealers in art, antiques, jewelry, and other collectibles regularly sell on eBay Live Auctions. But GoAntiques (http://www.goantiques.com) is one of the site's most frequent sellers, typically holding several auctions each week. There is another reason for singling out GoAntiques: they also give auction sellers a place to set up their own storefronts.

Because GoAntiques holds live auctions so frequently on eBay Live Auctions, you can be certain that they know the ins and outs of this auction format. Live auction sales tend to be more complex than conventional auctions. First, buyers need to register online beforehand; this gives you a greater level of control over who can bid, but it also places the burden on the seller of having to review and verify all the registrations as well. Second, bids can come in three ways: on the auction floor, on an absentee basis before the sale starts, and during the sale itself. The staff of the auction house needs to call out Internet bids during the sale (which, in eBay Live Auctions, can begin and end in less than a minute) and compare them with absentee bids already received and auctions placed in the auction house itself.

Typically, catalogs describing all the items for sale in an auction are placed online (or published in book form) weeks or even months before the sale. On eBay Live

Auctions, sellers not only need to be certified auction houses or professional dealers in antiques, art, or collectibles but they are required to pay a $1,500 insertion fee to list their catalog of items. And there is a Final Value Fee of 5 percent charged to winning Internet bidders, plus a Buyer's Premium that goes to the auction house (frequently, as much as 20 percent of the purchase price). With all those factors and requirements, it's just not practical for casual auction sellers to list a catalog full of lots on eBay Live Auctions. You have to partner with GoAntiques or another licensed auction house, but the advantage is that, because of the buyer's premium, you only have to pay a consignment fee of about 5 percent if you sell the item. You will also be able to list a reserve fee on the items you sell in order to protect your advantage.

If you are an antiques dealer and join GoAntiques—in other words, if you register to sell through the GoAntiques website—you gain space in which you can create your own Web page; you get access to a merchant account that lets you process credit card purchases made through your website; and you get advertising and marketing exposure. A subscription costs $39 per month, plus a 10 percent commission for each item sold on your GoAntiques-hosted website.

Tip: If you're looking for options for researching items you have for sale, and you want to go beyond eBay's Completed Auctions feature, look at the PriceMiner service offered by GoAntiques (http://www .priceminer.com/login/home.jsp). This pricing tool costs $9.95 per month, and contains data from eBay, GoAntiques, and the well-known online antique network TIAS. The searches aren't always very focused—I did a search for the terms "Chinese Foo Dog" and had to look through several pages of listings until I actually found a Foo Dog—but when you do find what you want, you get a substantial amount of background information that can help you write good descriptions.

Using Specialized Trading Assistants

A specialized trading assistant is someone who is well versed in using a particular auction site or in selling a certain type of merchandise. For instance, the South African auction site listed in Chapter 21, bidorbuy.com, lists a small number of trade brokers who can help owners of merchandise by conducting sales for them (http://www.bidorbuy.co.za/customjsp/tradebroker/tradeBroker.jsp).

Joining an Online Mall

One kind of partner you can add to your team is a business that operates an online shopping mall. The conventional reason for joining a mall has always been added attention: by setting up shop in a place where other popular sellers exist, you stand a good chance of having the customers of those other stores pay attention to you and look into what you have to sell. But some malls are so well known that joining them can add credibility to your own business operation. There are dozens if not hundreds of online malls around the Web, so this is hardly a representative summary. The following three sites are well known, highly regarded, and specialize in antiques and collectibles of the sort regularly sold on eBay and other auction sites:

Joining TIAS.com

TIAS (http://www.tias.com) is one of oldest online antiques dealers; the site boasts that it originally went on the Web in 1995. TIAS is an online antiques mall; if you're familiar with the concept of a brick-and-mortar antiques mall, you'll understand how TIAS works. You pay a monthly fee to rent a storefront on TIAS. In return, when a shopper looks for something by either browsing or performing a search through TIAS's catalog of items for sale, your items will potentially be included in the search results. The search results tend to be extensive and the search utility is well focused, so shoppers tend to have a good experience on this site.

In addition to gaining customers who search the TIAS website, storefront owners each have their own website within the site. Your site can have its own look and feel, and you can set your own sales policies. Be aware, though, that both TIAS and Ruby Lane (described below) are discriminating about the businesses they host. They will review your site for its look and for the quality of your merchandise so they maintain their desired standards of professionalism. Detailed plans and prices for setting up an antique mall are included in Appendix B, but a month-to-month plan of $39.95 per month is available, which enables you to try out the site to see how well it works for you.

 Note: If you don't want to set up a full-fledged storefront on TIAS and just have one or two items to sell, you can place classified ads for them. Ads can contain sixty to ninety words and up to four photos. Each ad costs $10; for additional exposure in TIAS's Collectors Newsletter you pay $25.

Joining Ruby Lane

Ruby Lane (http://www.rubylane.com) is another long-standing online antiques mall that, like TIAS, contains a well-developed search system and an extensive sales inventory. The site operates an e-commerce mall for dealers in crafts, collectibles, and antiques that is very popular with those who deal in antiques and collectibles. My rough count indicates that Ruby Lane has more than 1,500 member shops. The shop directory enables visitors to sort through shops to find the ones that have the most expensive or least expensive items, the ones that are closest to where they live, and the ones that have been online the longest.

Like TIAS, Ruby Lane helps its store owners advertise and bring in customers. The site also encourages you to do what you can to promote your store yourself, and to provide a high level of service to your customers. The staff is there to advise you on the technical aspects of setting up or managing your shop.

One good thing about setting up shop on Ruby Lane (or on TIAS) is the ability to sell on eBay. Both sites allow store owners to list their merchandise on the auction site as well as in the mall. You pay a $50 setup fee to set up shop, $12 a month as an advertising fee; and a minimum of $15 per month to list items in the Ruby Lane "mall." See Appendix B for more details.

Exploring Just Glass

Just Glass (http://www.justglass.com) opened in 1998 and is regarded as the most popular online portal for glass enthusiasts. The site offers auction and classified listings that are open to dealers in carnival glass, crackle glass, crystal, Depression glass, lamps and lighting, and many more categories. Visitors will also find a show calendar, an online magazine, book reviews, and a price guide. Just Glass has a UK-based site (http://www.justglass.co.uk) and a mall for dealers who sell glass (http://www.just glassmall.com). Three hosting plans are available, ranging from $35 to $80 per month; for more information, see Appendix B.

APPENDIX **A**

Online Auction Marketplaces

The good news is that you have numerous options for moving beyond eBay to sell in new ways and in new venues. The bad news is that you have *numerous* options to choose from when you move beyond eBay. Not only that, but the "cast of characters" is frequently changing in the field of online auctions and e-commerce.

Your time and resources are limited. If you already sell on eBay, and particularly, if you have a so-called day job, you can't spend lots of time experimenting with four, five, six or more auction sites. You need to make the right choices for your business as quickly as you can. In this appendix, I've attempted to gather together the various auction marketplaces covered in this book, along with cost comparisons for each. Some brief comments on each marketplace follow. Finally, you'll find a list of auction service providers and other resources that will help you find new sales venues.

Resources for Auction Sellers

- *AuctionBytes (http://www.auctionbytes.com).* An excellent resource for news and articles on online auction sites, including tips and reviews for sellers.

- *Froogle (http://froogle.google.com).* This is the Google comparison shopper, for researching prices and details about merchandise.

- *Kovel's (http://www.kovels.com).* The best-known antique and collectible price guide around, Kovels lets you research items online too obscure or specialized for Froogle.

- *Bluebook (http://www.kbb.com).* The most convenient site for assessing the value of used vehicles, Bluebook values are standard for all types of cars. Including their price for your vehicle in your listing will help gain your buyer's confidence.

Table A-1. Auction and other marketplaces.

Site	Auction?	Fixed-Price Sales?	Listing Fee	Final Value Fee (FSF = Final Sale Price)
Amazon.com Auctions (http://auctions.amazon.com)	Yes	No	$.10	5% for FSP of $.01–$.25, $1.25 plus 2.5% of amount over $25 for FSP of $25.01–$1,000; $25.63 plus 1.25% of amount over than $1,000 for FSP of $1,000.01 or above
Bid4Assets (http://www.bid4assets.com)	Yes	Yes	$5 for basic, $25 for deluxe	10% for FSP of $0 to $25,000; 9% for FSP of $25,000–$100,000; 8% for FSP of $100,001–$200,000
Bidville (http://www.bidville.com)	Yes	Yes	Free	5% for $0.01–$25; 1.25% plus 2.5% of amount over $25 for FSP of $25.01–$1,000 $25.63% plus 1% of amount over $1,000 for FSP of $1,000.01 or above
Bidz.com (http://www.bidz.com)	Yes (incl. three-minute auctions)	Yes ("Close Now" prices allow sales before auction closes)	$1 per listing	10% of final sale price

eBay (http://www.ebay.com)	Yes	Yes	$.25 ($.01–$.99); $.35 ($1–$9.99); $.60 ($10–$24.99); $1.20 ($25–$49.99)	5.25% (FSP of $.01–$25); $1.31 plus 2.75% of amount over $25 (FSP $25.01–$1,000); $28.12 plus 1.5% of amount over $1,000 (FSP of $1,000.01 and above)
eBid (http://www.ebid.net)	Yes	Yes	Free	Free
ePier (http://www.epier.com)	Yes	No	Free	2.5% (FSP of $0 to $25); $.63 plus 1.5% of amount over $25 (FSP of $25–$1,000); $15.25 plus .5% of amount over $1,000 (FSP over $1,000)
FaithBid (http://www.faithbid.com)	Yes	Yes	Free	2% of FSP
iOffer (http://www.ioffer.com)	Yes	Yes	Free	Free for iOffer Lite (starting price $4.99 or less). On iOffer, FVF is $.50 for final sale price of $.99 or less, $.75 for $5 to $9.99, $1.25 for $10 to $24.99, 5% of items with final price of $25 to $99.99
IronPlanet (http://www.ironplanet.com)	Yes	No	$500 for inspected equipment, $75 for uninspected equipment	6.4 to 12.5% of final sales price

(continues)

Table A-1. Continued.

Site	Auction?	Fixed-Price Sales?	Listing Fee	Final Value Fee (FSF = Final Sale Price)
Just Beads! (http://www.justbeads.com)	Yes	Yes	$.30 ($0–9.99); $.55 ($10–24.99); $1.05 ($25–$49.99)	
LabX (http://www.labx.com)			$3 (less than $50); $6 (less than $200); $18 ($200-$500)	Free
Liquidation.com (http://www.liquidation.com)	Yes	No	N/A	15% of final sale price, with minimum of $150 (Auction Bytes.com)
LiveDeal.com (http://www.livedeal.com)	No	Yes	Free for local classifieds	10% of FSP or $100, whichever is less.
MightyBids.com (http://www.mightybids.com)	Yes	Yes	Free	4.5% (FSP of $.01-$25); 2.5% (FSP of $25.01-$1,000); 1.5% (FSP of $1,000.01 and above)
Overstock.com Auctions (http://auctions.overstock.com)	Yes	Yes	$.20 ($.01–$.99); $.23 ($1–$9.99); $.40 ($10–$24.99); $.79 ($25–$49.99)	3.25% (FSP of $0–$25); 2% (FSP of $25–$1,000); 1% (FSP of $1,000 and above)

PenBid.com (http://www.penbid.com)	Yes	Yes	Free	5% (FSP of $0–$500); 4% of amount between $500 and $1,000 for FSP of $500–$1,000; 2% of amount over $500 for FSP over $1,000
uBid (http://www.ubid.com)	Yes	Yes	Free for Certified Merchants	12.5% for final sale price of $1 to $25; 10% for $26 to $250; 7.5% for $251 to $500
Yahoo! Auctions (http://auctions.yahoo.com)	Yes	Free	Free	

- *BizRate (http://www.bizrate.com).* A free comparison-shopping site like Froogle, but BizRate gives you more information. Consider using both sites to price high-value merchandise.

- *Andale (http://www.andale.com).* Andale is a company that sells online business software, and you can purchase image enhancers, site counters, and other handy research aids at the site.

- *Infopia (http://www.infopia.com).* A service provider that helps business set up storefronts and do advanced selling on auction sites, including eBay.

- *Marketworks (http://www.marketworks.com).* One of the oldest and most respected auction service providers, with several hosting plans and many tools to streamline the selling process.

- *Zoovy (http://www.zoovy.com).* An increasingly popular auction service provider, with tools to automate e-mail, feedback, relisting, and other common and repetitive tasks.

Online Storefront Solutions

The one strategy that nearly all successful eBay PowerSellers pursue is to move from having eBay being the intermediary to dealing with the public directly. These sellers move to direct sales by starting up their own e-commerce websites. However, starting up your own website, marketing it, and receiving credit card payments from the public is not without costs. You have to find a host for your electronic storefront, and you are likely to incur other fees for posting photos, processing credit card transactions, and so forth.

Your choice of storefront host is important, because if you don't have experience creating Web pages and need support, a host can be much more than a company that gives you space on a Web server. Your host can help you gain attention for your site, assist with marketing, provide you with software for formatting Web pages, space for uploading photos, and transaction processing services as well. The Web is replete with businesses that seek to perform this sort of role—for a fee, of course. Your goal is to find a host that will make your business proceed more smoothly and not break your budget in the process. Here are some suggestions for storefront solutions and the packages they offer:

Amazon.com zShops

Amazon.com's own online mall isn't as popular as its marketplace, but it gives sellers another option that enables them to sell on one of the Internet's most popular sites.

- Setup Fee: None.
- Monthly Fee: To open a zShop, you must take out a Pro Merchant Subscription of $39.99 per month.

- Sales Commission: 5 percent of sales from $.01 to $25; for sales of $25.01 to $1,000, 1.25 percent plus 2.5 percent of amount greater than $25; for sales over $1,001, 1.25 percent of any amount greater than $1,000.
- URL for More Info: http://zshops.amazon.com.

Bidville

Bidville (http://www.bidville.com) is an online auction site that also lets sellers put merchandise up for sale through their own storefronts. Prospective buyers can search through storefronts at http://stores.bidville.com/storefront.

- Setup Fee: Free
- Monthly Fee: $5 for Basic Store; $10 for Featured Store
- Sales Commission: 5 percent of final sale price up to $25; see URL for more details
- URL for More Info: http://stores.bidville.com/storefront/fees.html

BuyItSellIt

This service (http://www.buyitsellit.com) specializes in providing Web hosting for e-commerce sites. A hosting package includes credit card processing through PayPal and counters to track the number of visits to your site.

- Setup Fee: Free thirty-day trial offered with space for ten products
- Monthly Fee: $9.95 for Small Business Online Store; $19.95 for Platinum Online Store
- Sales Commission: None
- URL for More Info: http://store.buyitsellit.com

ChannelAdvisor

ChannelAdvisor is a popular solution for auction sellers who need sales software to boost their productivity. ChannelAdvisor Stores allow customers to feature items for sale, combine auction and store sales, and keep all of their products in one place.

- Setup Fee: Free for ChannelAdvisor merchant users
- Monthly Fee: N/A
- Sales Commission: Call 1-866-264-8594
- URL for More Info: http://www.channeladvisor.com/solutions/merch_soft_stores.asp

eBay Stores

The easiest and most obvious storefront option for eBay auction sellers. Listing in a store is far more economical than listing an auction sale. However, store items generally don't get as much attention and marketing is essential.

- Setup Fee: Free thirty-day trial offered
- Monthly Fee: $15.95 for Basic Store; $49.95 for Featured Store; $499.95 for AnchorStore
- Sales Commission: Insertion Fees and Final Value Fees apply, Final Value Fees are the same as for eBay auction transactions; however, if you list using the Store Inventory Format, listing fees are only $.02 per item
- URL for More Info: http://pages.ebay.com/storefronts/Subscriptions.html

eBay ProStores

If you don't already have an e-commerce website, consider this hosting option from eBay. You get a shopping cart, credit card payment processing, and your own domain name.

- Setup Fee: Free thirty-day trial offered
- Monthly Fee: $6.95 for Express Store; $29.95 for Business Solution; $74.95 for Advanced Solution; $249.95 for Enterprise Solution
- Sales Commission: 1.5 percent for Express Store; .50 percent for other store options
- URL for More Info: http://www.prostores.com

ePier Advanced Stores

If you use ePier for auctions, consider using its hosting option, which gives you free phone support and an unlimited amount of image hosting.

- Setup Fee: N/A
- Monthly Fee: $12.95 per month; $65 for six months; $99 per year
- Sales Commission: N/A
- URL for More Info: http://www.epier.com/AdvancedStores/default.asp

GoAntiques

If you are an antiques dealer, you may want to sign up with this company, which specializes in online auctions of antiques and collectibles.

- Setup Fee: None.
- Monthly Fee and Sales Commission: If you pay $39 per month, you also pay a 10 percent commission on each sale. If you pay $79 per month, you pay a sliding sales commission of 6 percent on sales up to $1,000, 4 percent of the next $4,000 (up to $5,000) and 2 percent for anything over $5,000.
- URL for More Info: http://www.goantiques.com/join.

iOffer Stores

iOffer (http://www.ioffer.com) is a good alternative for sellers moving beyond eBay. If you start to sell on iOffer in quantity, you may want to consider setting up to an iOffer Store.

- Setup Fee: None
- Monthly Fee: None
- Sales Commission: $.50 on sales up to $4.99; $.75 for sales from $5 to $9.99; $1.25 on sales from $10-$24.99; 5 percent on sales from $25-$99; for sales over $1500, $40 plus 1.5 percent of amount over $1500
- URL for More Info: http://www.ioffer.com/stores/index.jsp

Just Glass Mall

If you specialize in selling glass items, you can rent space in this online mall. Your items are also shown on the partner site Trocadero.com.

- Setup Fee: None
- Monthly Fee: $35 for a Business store, $55 for an E-Commerce store, $80 for an Enterprise store
- Sales Commission: None
- URL for More Info: http://www.trocadero.com/join/justglassregistration.html

Loudfrog

Loudfrog (http://www.loudfrog.com) charges no listing fees, and charges a flat 1 percent sales fee for items that sell, which makes the site particularly easy to use.

- Setup Fee: None
- Monthly Fee: $5 for Basic Plan (up to 20 items); $10 for Bronze Plan (up to 50 items); $20 for Silver Plan (up to 150 items); $30 for Gold Plan (up to 500 items); $50 for Platinum Plan (up to 2,500 items)
- Sales Commission: 1 percent of final sales price
- URL for More Info: http://www.loudfrong.com/help_service_plans.aspx

Marketworks

A popular auction service provider designed primarily for full-time businesses rather than casual sellers.

- Setup Fee: None
- Monthly Fee: You pay a minimum $29.95 or total monthly transaction fees—whichever is higher.
- Sales Commission: Transaction fees for e-commerce storefronts are 3 percent of sales price with a $6 maximum and a $.20 minimum.
- URL for More Info: http://www.marketworks.com/mwsite/whatwedo_faqs.asp

TIAS.com

One of the oldest online antique malls around, this site is a proven resource for anyone who wants to sell antiques and collectibles on the Web.

- Setup Fee: Two-month trial period offered
- Monthly Fee: Packages start at $34.95 per month; fixed-price sites cost $99 per month
- Sales Commission: 2 percent Final Value Fee on auction sales; 10 percent Final Value Fee on fixed-price sales
- URL for More Info: http://www.tias.com/makeashop/

Vendio

This popular auction service provider is used by many top eBay sellers.

- Setup Fee: Two-month trial period offered
- Monthly Fee and Sales Commission: Bronze Plan: $4.95 per month plus 1 percent Final Value Fee up to $4.95; Silver Plan: $9.95 per month plus $.20 per item fee; Gold Plan: $14.95 per month plus $.10 fee
- URL for More Info: shop.vendio.com/my/shop/overview.html

Yahoo! Merchant Solutions

Formerly known as Yahoo! Stores, this popular website is well-known among e-commerce merchants.

- Setup Fee: $50
- Monthly Fee: Packages $39.95 for Merchant Starter; $99.95 for Merchant Standard; $299.95 for Merchant Professional
- Sales Commission: 21.5 percent for Starter; 1 percent for Standard; .75 percent for Professional
- URL for More Info: http://smallbusiness.yahoo.com/merchant

Zoovy

Like other auction providers, Zoovy specializes in helping eBay sellers but can provide e-commerce solutions for all online businesses.

- Setup Fee: Two-month trial period offered
- Monthly Fee: $74.95 per month or 2 percent of your sales, whichever is greater
- Sales Commission: The 2 percent fee mentioned is capped at $5 per transaction
- URL for More Info: http://www.zoovy.com/pkg-store/

Top Ten Tips for Moving Beyond eBay

You probably remember what it was like to sell your first item on eBay. Selling your first pieces of merchandise outside of the world's largest online auction site will bring back that memory. A leap of faith is involved. In order to provide a smooth landing for your leap (instead of a big *thud*), you need to follow some tried-and-true principles that other sellers have explored before you. They have been explored throughout this book, and are summarized in this appendix.

Develop the Right Attitude

Before you make any dramatic change in the way you do business, you need to make a change in your attitude. When it comes to expanding your activities beyond eBay, you need confidence. You need confidence in the merchandise you sell. You need the kind of confidence that says, "I'm going to double my sales volume and start selling on my website and two other auction venues this year. By the end of the year, I want to boost my gross income by 40 percent." Keeping your goal in sight at all times and having the confidence that you'll get there will help you take the steps necessary to do it, whether you need to work even longer hours, hire assistants, find a brick-and-mortar space, or overcome other challenges.

Build on What You Know Already

Whether you decide to stop selling on eBay altogether and move to other venues is up to you. Personally, I recommend throughout this book that you don't cut your ties to an auction marketplace that has more than 40 million members around the world. Maintain a presence on eBay, and branch out when you have achieved success on the site. Don't move away from eBay out of desperation or exasperation. Rather, expand your sales gradually when you are in a position of strength. Build on what you do well currently. Take your most successful products, and put more of them up for sale on other sites. Use Mr. Grabber (see Chapter 5) to take products that didn't sell immediately and list them on iOffer. Use your existing shipping, listing, and packing methods and expand them. In other words, don't reinvent the wheel.

Be Flexible and Try New Approaches

The off-off-eBay marketplaces you've read about in preceding chapters follow eBay's example only up to a point. Some of them operate quite differently than eBay's system of auctions, fixed-price sales, stores, best offers, and so on. Amazon.com, for instance, gives you an easy way to add your used books, CDs, DVDs, and other household goods. Live auctions let you sell items in a matter of minutes and watch the bids come in at the same time. Selling on your website puts the burden of shipping, payment, and other aspects of completing a transaction completely up to you. The point is to be flexible and try out new ways of selling so that you can find more customers and boost your bottom line.

Match Your Merchandise to the Venue

The fact that you have so many choices when it comes to selling online means that you can actually tailor your marketplace of choice to the inventory you have to sell. In many cases, items sell better on the Web when you target them to a dedicated group of knowledgeable users or collectors. If you sell fountain pens, you might have better results on a small niche auction site like PenBid.com than on a large catch-all marketplace. If you have medical equipment to sell, look to one of the venues that allows individuals to offer expensive and highly technical equipment for sale. Finding the right place to put your items before the eyes of just the right customers often means shopping around for niche or specialty auction sites of the sort described in Chapter 8 and Chapter 9.

Find the Right Operational Partner

Going it alone and trying to do everything by yourself only gets you so far. I know from personal experience that when you are the only one shopping for merchandise, creating listings, and packing and shipping, you have ultimate control. You also have limitations in the amount of merchandise you can put up for sale. Many PowerSellers I know have signed up with auction service providers like ChannelAdvisor, Market-Works, Zoovy, or Vendio to help automate repetitive and time-consuming processes such as e-mails, feedback, and relistings. An operational partner adds to your monthly expenses, but many sellers find that they are worth the expense because they boost productivity and streamline processes that are often tedious and time consuming.

Sell on Your Own Website

For many PowerSellers, expanding sales from eBay to their own website is the first and most effective type of business expansion to make. For these sellers, eBay is an unmatched way to gain new customers. Once they sell to those customers, these sellers do everything they can to direct the customers to their website for subsequent sales. By selling directly through a website, they aren't subject to any service outages eBay might experience, and they don't have to pay fees for listing or completing a sale. They can make links to other websites in their auction descriptions and sell merchandise that isn't subject to eBay's list of prohibited goods. They make more money per sale, plus they gain even more control over their business activities.

Expand Your Sourcing Efforts

Finding enough good merchandise to sell is perhaps the biggest challenge facing anyone who wants to expand an eBay business to other marketplaces. Before you start signing up for accounts with Web-hosting services or other auction venues, make sure you have the inventory to support it. Perhaps the best solution for finding more inventory is to have consignment sellers come to you on a steady basis with items to sell on eBay. You can do this by opening your own drop-off store or brick-and-mortar store, or by advertising your services as a trading assistant. But be prepared to spend more time looking for suppliers, either at trade shows or through wholesale supply sites like Alibaba.com.

Move from B2C to B2B E-Commerce

Although eBay is primarily oriented toward person-to-person sales, many successful sellers use eBay to sell in quantity to other businesspeople as well. They group their merchandise into large groups called *lots*, which they sell for a reduced price. Although the profit margin per item goes down, they still make money because the quantity sold is so much larger than usual. Start thinking about ways in which you can reach other businesses—even other eBay and auction sellers. You are sure to find members by listing on B2B websites like Alibaba.com, or by traveling to display your wares at trade shows, where you can take orders.

Ask for Help/Consult with Your Colleagues

Don't go it alone. Remember that you are part of a larger group of sellers. Work the discussion boards on eBay and on your marketplace of choice and ask for advice on how to proceed with any of the strategies listed in this appendix. You'll be surprised at how open some sellers are with their time and experience. Often, the most successful sellers are also the ones who are most open with the media and with other businesspeople. Also look for partners who can help you with marketing and advertising. For example, by signing up with an antiques mall like TIAS or Ruby Lane, you can gain more attention for your business and even gain a certain amount of prestige, because these are popular and highly regarded online venues.

Buy Globally, Sell Locally

Many of the options for moving beyond eBay that are described in this book are ones that focus narrowly on buyers in your local area. These include flea markets, a brick-and-mortar store, and classified ads. When you take the approach of limiting your audience to people in your own part of the country, you actually increase the range of items you can sell. You can think about heavy appliances, motor vehicles, and furniture that are difficult if not impossible to sell on eBay. Classified ads are simple and inexpensive, and they can include photos, too. Sites like Yahoo! Classifieds and the many versions of Gumtree and Kijiji found around the world give sellers new ways to reach customers in their own geographic vicinity.

Index